HOMERIC RHYTHM

$\blacklozenge$

A Philosophical Study

Paolo Vivante

Contributions to the Study of World Literature,
Number 82

GREENWOOD PRESS
Westport, Connecticut • London

Library of Congress Cataloging-in-Publication Data

Vivante, Paolo.
    Homeric rhythm : a philosophical study / Paolo Vivante.
      p. cm.—(Contributions to the study of world literature,
  ISSN 0738-9345 ; no. 82)
    Includes bibliographical references (p.) and index.
    ISBN 0-313-30363-0 (alk. paper)
    1. Homer—Versification. 2. Greek language—Metrics and
  rhythmics. 3. Epic poetry, Greek—History and criticism.
  4. Philosophy, Ancient. I. Title. II. Series.
  PA4205.V58 1997
  883'.01—dc21   96-50293

British Library Cataloguing in Publication Data is available.

Library of Congress Catalog Card Number: 96-50293
ISBN: 0-313-30363-0
ISSN: 0738-9345

First published in 1997

Greenwood Press, 88 Post Road West, Westport, CT 06881
An imprint of Greenwood Publishing Group, Inc.

Printed in the United States of America

The paper used in this book complies with the
Permanent Paper Standard issued by the National
Information Standards Organization (Z39.48–1984).

10 9 8 7 6 5 4 3 2 1

To Vera

Contents

Preface

This book is much concerned with the concepts of time and existence, perception and expression. I interpret Homeric verse on these basic grounds. It is my object to find an inherent poetic reason or *causa sui*, without necessarily invoking tradition or epic convention.

With this intention, I show how the Homeric narrative breaks into single acts and states of being that pass before us in the field of vision while the upward and downward movement of the verse-rhythm renders them as rising and vanishing moments. There is always a sense of coming to be and passing away. Descriptive variety thus yields ground to the feeling of a perpetual time-beat, occurrence becomes recurrence, and the very tempo of the verse ensures the domain of form and typifies the momentary. Hence come the repeated phrases—the "formulas". They are indispensable in bringing out this aspect of time; they are ultimately due to a mode of perception and not to compositional technique.

Part of what I say in these pages (especially in chapter 4) I have already said in previous work; but now everything takes on a fresh significance in relation to rhythm. Thus I have often dwelt on Homer's sense of time; but now this sense is made palpable through its intimate connection with the inner timing of the verse. Similarly I have often explained how Homer focalizes the action; but now this focus is sharply evinced by the high-point of the central caesura. Or, again, I have written elsewhere about Homer's sympathetic insight into nature; but now this quality appears intrinsic to a verse that highlights kindred rhythms in all animate and natural movements.

Rhythm so conceived deeply affects the contents. Far from being a mere medium of composition, the verse becomes a form of thought that penetrates the material and conditions the subject-matter. The same nimble style that singled out moments of focus also fashioned their cumulative impact and created a sense of real duration, thus detaching the story from its mythical background. The consequences in the treatment of character and action were enormous.

It will be objected that I rely too much upon my own aesthetic sense. Such an objection is irrelevant. For the aesthetic sense is here an object of inquiry, hardly a matter of taste. It is part and parcel of the phenomenon in question. It is, in fact, an element in nature; and I test it on the basis of abundant evidence. We have, in other words, the undisputed appeal of the Homeric poetry through the ages; and what I do is to seek the source of this appeal in the actual forms of expression—a task that has hardly been attempted so far.

Acknowledgments

Thanks are due to many friends and colleagues for their interest and support. I am especially grateful to Professor Norman Austin for reading my manuscript and giving me encouragement. The help of my wife Vera was indispensable in the many perplexities surrounding my work. I am also thankful to John James, a master in print technology, for generously coming to my aid in moments of need.

Chapter 1

Introduction

HOW THIS BOOK CAME ABOUT

Homer, I always believed, marks the triumph of expression. He gives "a local habitation and a name" to anything under the sun. Gods, people, animals, man-made objects as well as natural elements are highlighted in their identities; acts and states of being are assigned their moment of fullness. Image and form reign supreme. Quite apart from any moralistic or didactic purpose, things are celebrated through the simple fact of being mentioned in their natural contours. Could such a language be the mere result of an oral compositional technique evolved through previous ages? Is it not to be identified with a mode of perception and expression? You may assume that everything in Homer is traditional, but you may also wonder on what poetic value did the tradition rest. For, surely, there can be no question of a mere *vis inertiae*. Parry only saw a traditional style of composition here, but even his system of formulas could be seen in a different light by bearing in mind a principle of perception.[1]

I approached the question in an earlier work,[2] pointing out the sense of form in Homer's noun-epithet phrases—those formulas that constituted the cornerstone of Parry's system. We find, for instance, "so spoke swift-footed Achilles" but "they feared because Achilles had appeared." The epithet tends to be dropped where a syntactic complication or a pointed intention is in the way; it tends to appear in the simple and straightforward presentation of an act. We thus have, through the epithet, a materializing touch. A concrete presence is unobtrusively summoned up before us. Image and action thus merge in unison: the act vivifies the image, the image confers solidity to the act. Here, in these open spots, the sense of form finds its occasion and emerges in its own right. We are brought back to the pure existence of things, away from narrative complications. Even so, in ordinary life, we dwell upon the imagery of things when we are not pressed by an ulterior purpose.

Such a principle of expression holds true in these pages; but what now stands out uppermost is a process within the verse and not the use of a certain phraseology. In other words, the question is: how does one explain the verse itself—its vital fluency and consistency? Here Parry left us with a sore dilemma: one must consider, on the one hand, the metrical scheme and, on the other, the formulas that fit into it and fill it up. These are two abstractions, by themselves incapable of producing the integrating movement of the verse. Which one precedes which, and what agency blends them together to produce so enthralling an effect? We lack here any notion of motivating force, and Parry's metrical point of view can give us no answer. Hence, all at once, the idea of rhythmic impulse appeared to me more fundamental than that of metre. The rhythmic impulse surely comes first, drawing the language into its movement and precipitating the use of the hexameter.

Rhythm makes us realize the inner unity of the verse and avoid what is most strident in the theory of oral composition: the emphasis on construction and manipulation rather than natural self-coherence, and the insistence on compositional skill rather than poetic touch. Just as things inextricably blend in a moment of sense-perception, so do the parts coalesce in the encompassing movement of the verse.

But how can we do justice to so delicate and elusive a matter? How can we explain a mystery? We can only ascertain its presence. Analysis must go hand in hand with synthesis, we must get attuned to the music of the verse as a whole even while we distinguish the varying degrees of tension in the expanding modulations. I debated these ideas and problems in lectures from coast to coast, there were sympathetic audiences, and there were fruitful questions and answers. Most appreciative were the students: a girl wrote to me that whereas she had previously read Homer as prose, she now read him as poetry. Even the followers of Parry sympathized with my concerns.

Through the 1980s and early 1990s, it was a period of scattered notes, impressions, insights, false starts, and resumptions, but there was always a sense of discovery as though in pursuit of some elusive truth. The present book is the result of such research and speculation. Its validity lies in the degree to which the reasoning makes sense.

WHAT IS VERSE?

This book is, therefore, about verse. It is my aim to get as close as possible to that point in which thought, diction, and metre inextricably combine. Herein lies the essence of rhythm. Although it is hardly possible to account for such a point in theoretical terms, a sense of this ideal goal will help us set aside secondary concerns that would obstruct us in this attempt.

What is verse? There should be a philosophy of verse. I do not mean an aesthetic analysis of any given verse, but a principle applicable to all verse. The problem is of an ontological nature. We may postulate it in simple but radical terms: Why does verse exist at all? Why is it that all poetry in any age or country is uttered or written in verse? The very etymology and meaning of the word "verse" tells us that we stop at a certain point; we *turn* before reaching the margin of the page, and we start another line. Why is it so?

There is obviously a question of length. A verse cannot be too long: a statement of, say, more than twelve words would dilute into prose and lack its center. Such length, however, is not a mechanical or arbitrary measure. It is native to a full-blown utterance. It takes the time of breathing in and out. We might argue that such is the maximum length consistent with apprehending a verse all at once and repeating it word by word. The power of verse relies on this concentration in time. A moment is filled with meaning, and meaning is transfused into the moment. It is as if our very breath or our heartbeat that counts the time acquired an intellectual transparency. This concurrence of a physical and a mental impulse cannot fail to produce a forcible effect.

A verse is thus a point of focus: there is an indispensable reference-point, but also radiation. A mere point would be no more than the bare mention of a thing or an act, but here we are made to feel its impact, its actuality, its taking place—and yet never so discursively or descriptively as to weaken the focus. We have, in other words, both expansion and contraction: form clinging to its self-identity through the very occasion that brings it out.

Homer in particular gives voice to this effect. He always renders meaning through the way it is made manifest. The verse-rhythm is not so much a flow of pleasing sounds as an articulation of what happens: fact becomes occurrence, an act becomes movement, a quality or state becomes a mode of being, a thought is inner realization rather than any given notion or idea. Rhythm is here at home. It finds in meaning a way of being bodied forth; and verse is not so much a medium of composition as, rather, a form that appropriates the process of composition to its ends.

We are thus made aware of rhythmical values over and above the topical interests of a passage: degrees of movement and rest, fullness and vacancy, abatement and resilience. Homer's concrete treatment makes these degrees palpable. The noun-epithet phrases reveal their rhythmical role here. Take, in Il.3.423, Helen joining Paris in his chamber: ἡ δ' εἰς ὑψόροφον θάλαμον κίε δῖα γυναικῶν [and she, to the high-roofed chamber, she went, the divine among women]. We have a simple act of going, but notice how it is expressed. From the initial "she" to the final noun, Helen's presence spreads through the verse, quickened by the nimble verb near the center. The effect is one of lightness and solemnity at once. The epithets give fullness to the moment by simply touching off what is there. We linger upon steadfast shapes even while the passing act removes them from our view. Transience finds solidity, and solidity is in turn dissolved. We have rest in movement and movement in rest—at once, tranquillity and motion. A translation such as "Helen, divine among women, went to the high-roofed chamber" would only give us embellished description. The force of Homer's verse lies in its rhythm—in the way the words take position, in the way each pause hints suspense, and in the way the parts integrate to realize a growing presence. It would be inadequate merely to point out a combination and adaptation of metrical formulas: the verse has an intrinsic unity, and it came on one wave of rhythm.

I hope that this book serves as an incentive to study verse as a fundamental form of expression, no less fundamental than the word or the sentence. My concern is verse *qua* verse: its direct appeal to the senses and not any narrow aesthetic point, its inner movement and not any external metrical scheme. Here is an experience of verse that is common to us all, but it is dimly apprehended and seldom accounted for. Studies in metre give us rules for which there is no apparent poetic reason; aesthetics and literary criticism treat the matter at a distance or ignore it altogether. We miss attempts to make us appreciate a verse more keenly by explaining why it is composed as it is.

HERMANN FRÄNKEL AND MILMAN PARRY

Parry posed a formidable challenge. His exhaustive classifications of the ways in which formulas fit into the hexameter leave little room for exceptions, and we are left to admire how the system works; a necessitated economy of diction proves adequate to the needs of expression. Here is a perfected technique, an end-result massively shown as an established fact. But for what end? For what poetic reason? The aim of this book is to set the phenomenon in a different light. Parry was at each step a tacit, implicit counterpoint. Indeed, the book could hardly have been conceived the way it is without Parry. More and more I was led away from the static acknowledgment of stolid facts towards the sense of a fluid poetic process within the verse form.

If Parry was a decisive factor through his very challenge, I found positive food for thought in Fränkel's essay on the hexameter,[3] an essay whose implicit and perhaps unintended value has not been fully realized. First hailed as opening a new era in the study of verse and rhythm,[4] it did not enjoy the success that might have been expected. It is interesting that it was first published in 1926, two years before Parry's first exposition of his formulaic theory,[5] and yet Parry does not mention Fränkel. We need not attribute Parry's silence to ignorance, for his approach was essentially a different one: he focused on the formulas insofar as they facilitated the work of oral composition; he did not seek the intrinsic qualities of the verse itself.

A philosophical spirit runs through Fränkel's essay. Old rules are placed in a new light by the intent to see through them. It is as if the hexameter were freed of its crust, made into a form of thought rather than a means of versification.

Thus Fränkel berates scholars for not giving any enlightening reasons or not doing justice to the spirit of the art-form when they laid down laws prohibiting a word-end at certain points of the hexameter: the outcome was passive acceptance and discouragement of any further research. "Such resignation is unnecessary" he writes:

As soon as we look at how the extant verses are articulated and stop asking what verse-structures were avoided, we shall realize how simple and transparent were the rules followed by the poets and how these rules contributed to an original and creative system whose significance by far transcends any metrical technique. . . .What so far has been regarded as the fruit of an obscure and compartmentalized skill thus becomes a luminous verse-style that half-identifies with the language, lends itself to any nuance. A positive articulation of the verse through the words of the text is tantamount to harmonizing the unfolding contents with the metrical process of the hexameter. . . .If we appreciate this nimble art, each verse will appear to take a new force of expression up to the point at which we can really hear and see all at once its sound and movement.

Metre by itself is inadequate here. It must come to terms with meaning. It cannot crudely and arbitrarily cut out any contents into feet. We need rhythm and modulation. Fränkel's presentation of the hexameter is based on rhythmic units of meaning (cola) and the pauses (caesuras) that necessarily separate them from one another. This intermittent fluency also applies to our voice in ordinary conversation, but in the Homeric hexameter any casualness gives way to an organic sense of form. The verse is naturally divided into two parts by the main central caesura, and these parts are again subdivided into two by minor caesuras: as a result we normally have four cola marked off by three caesuras. But where exactly do cola and caesuras occur in the verse? It

is a question of sense, sound, and harmony between the parts. In this
connection, look at the verse as consisting (like any given development)
of three phases: beginning, middle, and end. The structure is so
conceived that the first phase offers four favorite positions for the
caesura, the middle and end two positions respectively. At these points
the articulation of the verse appears to be most sensitive, favoring
punctuation or word-end and phrase-end.

Even these bare indications show an organic formative principle.
The initial phase is likely to be more tentative or eager in that the caesura
is one out of other possible ones, the middle is more incisive because the
caesura is like a watershed in the verse; and the final phase is steadier in
that the caesuras rarefy in proportion to its length. As a result,
punctuations or intervals decrease as the verse moves to its end. The
emerging picture appeals to the senses and the mind. The effect is one of
rise and fall, climax and anticlimax, a restless start and a subsiding
cadence. Thus a tense beginning anticipates a calm conclusion in Il.1.43:

ὣς ἔφατ'/ εὐχόμενος· ‖ τοῦ δ' ἔκλυε / Φοῖβος Ἀπόλλων.

so did he speak / in prayer, ‖ and him heard / Phoebus Apollo.
The priest's anxious appeal comes to rest in the listening god. Fränkel
writes:

Through its internal organization each verse becomes a miniature stanza, and
each of its cola can present a life of its own within the encompassing form. The
first colon, for instance, can be lively and energetic, the second more objective
and composed, the third colon is often emotional . . . emphatic . . . while the last
one, again, is graver and solemn. The long fourth colon, rounding off the verse,
tends to mention eternal things and permanent institutions of our world. The
great names of gods and heroes often give the verse a final resonance.

These remarks only give us an inkling of the matter. There are
countless ways in which meaning may be distributed through the verse.
It is an object of this book to explore these ways in further detail.
Fränkel himself half-invites us to do so when he writes:

Each colon can take specific functions of many kinds; and we might account for
these variations. It would be an attractive task to try and establish the most
significant arrangements, analyzing each type according to its grammar,
meaning, style, rhythm. But it is not necessary. All we need is to take any
passage and pronounce, hear, understand the hexameter in the supple structure
of its cola. A hitherto unsuspected life will start throbbing in the verse: the
rhythm of the syllables is joined by the expressive rhythm of the cola wherein
swing into motion the things which the poet tells us about.

The path thus laid open is full of promise. Its very tentativeness is challenging. We do not tread on the secure ground of hard and fast categories, but touch on delicate points of balance that cannot be pinned down—points where spontaneous modulations find their place within the accepted mold. Our purpose is to establish tendencies, not rules. We need not be dismayed if the three caesuras and the resulting four cola are not necessarily realized, or if the relation between the parts is continually altered by the dynamics of the verse. The hexameter is never quite crystallized. Form is fed and made vital by the very irregularities and exceptions it can master and contain.

We can therefore see how rhythmical tendencies emerge, gather momentum, prevail, and finally impose themselves. To this end, statistics play an important role in the works of O'Neill[6] and Porter.[7] Though they are unsatisfactory, statistics throw some light on what they are intended to prove; and it is the aim of these scholars to bring out features that are commonly ignored by metricians.

O'Neill's "inner metrics" deal with the metrical length of words insofar as they fit into certain positions. Quite apart from their meaning, words are the "masonry" of the verse, "blocks of various sizes and shapes" that make the verse what it is. O'Neill finds fixity of word-length and positions here—a fixity that suffers relatively few exceptions and testifies to the poet's striving for form. Can any further significance be elicited from this sense of form? A glance at O'Neill's statistical tables shows a convergence of longer words towards the middle and end, an alternate thinning and thickening of the vocal material—a modulation, a movement such as is suggested in Fränkel's essay.

This connection between Fränkel and O'Neill is brought out by Porter: "The foot may be described as a small cycle or wave superimposed on the large rhythmic wave of the line", Porter writes. And, the metrical quantities of words or word-groups, identified with succeeding cola, produce balancing proportions. A refining analysis thus tells us that the final "dying fall" of the verse is foreshadowed in the second colon, or that avoidances of word-end offset one another in the first and second half. Correspondences and echoes within the verse come to our notice: a sense of rise and fall, lightly intimated at the beginning, comes to full fruition at the end, like a note that is rehearsed before it is fully realized. But what stands out is the total effect—the way in which the overarching rhythm is reflected in the constituent parts. Details thus prefigure the whole and the whole gathers in itself what, in the details, contributes most to the sense of form. The idea of what lies ahead pierces through the interplay of the parts. Porter mentions in this respect "a pattern of expectancy"; but he immediately adds that the word "pattern" might be too static to describe "the dynamically formative and ever-changing structure of the line."

Porter is, to my knowledge, the only scholar that sympathetically pursued Fränkel's line of thought. Traditional students of metre could hardly applaud. On the other hand, criticism in our age took quite a different direction: the interest shifted more and more from expression itself to its role in a given environment. Thus, what stands out in Homeric studies is the cultural oral milieu, and the verse is weakened into a matter of technique subserving an ulterior purpose. Fränkel, though unawares, points in the opposite direction: verse as a principle of realization, conditioning the material and refining the sense of poetry.

SENSE OF TIME AND THE RELATION BETWEEN THE VERSE AND THE POEMS

Fränkel concludes his essay with a tribute to the hexameter's perfection of form, remarking how simple, palpable, and meaningful is the way in which each verse brings it out; but he does not elaborate on any further cognitive significance. Porter, on his part, disclaims any critical or aesthetic intention right at the outset. And yet the work of these scholars is full of philosophical implications. We are driven to wonder beyond the basic coherence of form and meaning: what unacknowledged or implicit sense of truth prompted the conception of the verse?

My interpretation of Homeric verse belongs here, as highlighting an unfolding moment and the subsequent extension of the idea of time to the poems as a whole. The notion of verse-moments spontaneously arises from considering the way Homeric verse so often sets off a self-contained act or state of being, while the concentrated time-span of the general action naturally suggests the effect of these cumulative verse-moments. Or, in other terms, the tempo of the verse inevitably conveys a pulse of time; but so concrete is Homer's mode of representation that this elusive tempo is reflected in the process of what is actually happening, and so persistent is this practice that the action itself seems to create its own time and duration. We have a self-developing action: no summing up, no empty intervals, and no historical or mythical periods to be filled with events.

I take an empirical view of time: time at one with rhythm and at one with action. My chapters entitled "Rhythm and Metre," "Order of Words," and "Enjambment" treat the time-rhythm in connection with single verses or combinations of verses. "Time and Verse" surveys the ways in which Homer's sense of time conditions the style, influences the composition of the poems, vivifies the sense of values, and characterizes

Homeric poetry in distinction from other epics; while "Apollonius Rhodius" clarifies these principles by way of contrast. Finally, my "Conclusion" shows how the various quandaries of the Homeric Question may be lightened by considering the way Homer's treatment of time signals an incisive advance in the portrayal of action. My "Bibliographical Essay" reviews other schools of thought in relation to my own; it is not intended to be a real bibliography on the subject.

Time, rhythm, and meaning are made manifest through one another in Homeric verse; and, from verse to verse, this subtle interplay gathers momentum, reaching beyond any single verse and extending to the poems as a whole. This book should encourage the student to read Homer creatively—identifying with an unfolding rhythmical meaning, not merely gathering information within the confines of a predetermined subject-matter. Rather than looking at the finished product, we explore it from within; rather than making static facts consistent with one another, we have an opening perspective. Attention to the verse is essential here, for the verse filters the elements of narrative and discourse into a quickening form and further movement. The imposition of a narrative thread becomes secondary. It is the verse that creates the story step by step; and things only appear to exist insofar as they are brought to the fore by the moment which the verse-form encloses. Rhythm has thus a liberating, or purifying, influence on the narrative itself, barring the way to anything superfluous, adventitious, incongruous, unnatural, or false. It is surely not extravagant so to magnify the force of rhythm. It works implicitly, subtly, and unobtrusively, refining rather than revolutionizing all at once; but in the long run it is no less effective than the proclamation of new ideas.

There is, at any rate, a common quality that transpires through the details and the whole. The simplest way to reach it is through the verse itself, for verse is not just a medium of composition. It is poetry already, in embryo, a key-note to the poem. Circumscribed as it is, in one point of focus it offers opportunity for the closest scrutiny, even while intimating the sense of a larger strain—much as a twig rehearses the whole tree or a chromatic touch leads us through a whole painting. In our ignorance of Homer's times, the verse stands out most clearly as firsthand evidence; and on its strength we may refashion a Homeric present.

ON READING HOMER ALOUD

If nothing else, this book is an invitation to read Homer aloud, recite, memorize—a practice that has become obsolete, in spite of today's emphasis on "oral poetry."

To read verse aloud (or to let it ring in the mind's ear) is a way of making it palpably real. It spaces out, it takes its place and time. It seems to become self-existent. Within its compass the words take position and dimension. Repeat them at length; and their order or mutual relations will appear to be inevitable. Introduce any change; and it will violate the flow of both voice and sense. Interpretation or translation, grammatical and metrical analysis were preparatory stages: now the verse is an object of contemplation rather than study. The utterance itself , the delivery do it justice. Language here rises to its full value: we are drawn to this sensuousness of meaning as to a fundamental link between existence and expression.

While these considerations are more or less true of all verse, they apply most clearly to Homer. Words and word-groups in Homer tend to regular and recurring collocations that attune us to a basic mode of perception; a hero rises up and speaks, a wave crests up and splashes on the shore, a wind gusts up and presses on a cornfield, an emotion emerges and seizes the midriff. The central caesura is often a watershed, and the verse traces upon events a design that is embedded in the nature of things.

Our voice modulates accordingly. Just as interpretations of Homer should not wander off into symbolism , even so in reciting we should not strain the pitch and, for instance, turn undertones into arbitrary asides. Avoid, therefore, any deliberate effect of grandiloquence or irony; simply bring out the fullness of an incident and the interval's suspense. Any stress, in Homer, is due to something standing out, any abatement to an intervening silence.

The clear sense of focus does not require us to press any meaning too hard. Even insults and threats (as in the quarrel of Achilles and Agamemnon) are contained within the modulation of the verse and do not degenerate in general confusion. We should, therefore, voice them as coruscations of the occasion rather than realistic outpourings of a furious temper. For Homeric rhythm encompasses any particular thing in a perpetual ebb-and-flow. Nobody—no hero, no god—remains immune. We have a pervasive relativity: any act is no sooner brought about than it is swept away by the next one. Nothing is static and yet nothing exceeds its form, even bliss or horror finds its measure, a general flux deprives glory of its bombast and misery of its abjection.

NOTES

1. *The Making of Homeric Verse: The Collected Papers of Milman Parry*, ed. Adam Parry, Oxford, Clarendon Press: 1971.

2. P. Vivante, *The Epithets in Homer: A Study in Poetic Values*. New Haven, Yale University Press: 1982.

3. "Der Homerische und der Kallimachische Hexameter," in *Wege und früh-griechischen Denkens*, Munich, 1955: 100–156—a version of an essay first published in *Göttinger Nachrichten*, 1926: 197–229. A résumé in English may be found in Fränkel's *Early Greek Poetry and Philosophy*. Trans. M. Hadas and J. Willis, New York: 1975: 30–34. I quote from the 1955 version.

4. G. Pasquali, *Gnomon* 3 (1927): 241–47. Pasquali especially pointed out the way Fränkel transformed negative rules into positive ones. Thus Fränkel explains the prohibition of a caesura at the fourth trochee (Hermann's Bridge) as the incidental reverse effect of the way heavier words gravitate towards the end of the line, covering the caesura at that point. A similar explanation is given for the avoidance of trochaic or dactylic word-ending in the second foot if a word has three or more syllables (Meyer's Law): such words gravitate towards the central caesura. A harmonizing tendency is seen at work. What stands out is the positive force of rhythm, not unexplained inhibitions.

5. *L'Epithète traditionnelle dans Homère. Essai sur un problème de style homérique.* Paris: 1928.

6. Eugene G. O'Neill, Jr. "The Localization of Metrical Word-types in the Greek Hexameter," *Yale Classical Studies* 8 (1942): 105–78.

7. H. N. Porter "The Early Greek Hexameter." *Yale Classical Studies* 12 (1951): 2–63.

Chapter 2

Rhythm and Metre

DEFINITIONS

Whereas metre is admittedly a verse-pattern indicated by a type and number of feet, by rhythm I intend the encompassing movement of the verse as a whole. Rhythm results from the use of feet but is in no way identified with their succession. Through its operation, what would otherwise be a monotonous sequence becomes development. We have meaningful melody, the realization of organic form. Rhythm is more fundamental than metre, prompting the use of certain feet and precipitating the creation of the verse.

It is relatively easy to analyze metre—noting, for instance, the role of dactyls and spondees, fixing their number, pointing out the way they alternate, and establishing the points at which one or the other most frequently occurs. It is much more difficult, if not impossible, to analyze rhythm. Its effect comes from the blending of the words with the metre, the pauses between word-end and word-beginning at certain points of the verse, and from the sense of a forward flow and what instantly checks it. Here are intervals, transitions, and resumptions: balance or suspense before we reach the end of the verse. These subtle modulations can hardly be mapped out.

Rhythm is naturally malleable. It cannot be the result of patchwork or mere construction. It signalizes form in its making, not form as a ready-made mold. Quite apart from any deliberate effect, it testifies organic growth—just as the branch of a tree presents its sinuosities even within a generally given shape. It is thus responsive to moods or undertones of emotion and thought. It must be felt, before it is learned. Its stresses and abatements are too delicate for any precise notation. Look at verse in this rhythmical light, and you will find that it cannot

possibly be presented as a metrical scheme. We might, if at all, think of
a graph marking all kinds of vacillations and undulations up to a final
cadence. Any feature here will be significant of life: a sudden initial
motion will suggest a resolute starting point, a pause will convey
hesitation, a steady even stretch will reflect achievement and objectivity.
Whatever the topic at hand, we are made to feel the informing process.
The beginning is vaguely prophetic of the end, and the end comes as a
desired response. We have a sense of potentialities finding their
realization.

   We are reminded of the relation between a tune and its words, or of
words that suggest a tune. Rhythm is inconceivable without meaning. It
draws its articulations from the words, while giving them a heightened
power through their position in the verse. Here is another reason why
rhythm is quite different from metre: we might compose, for instance, a
correct hexameter insofar as feet are concerned, and yet such a
hexameter might make no sense at all; but a feeling of rhythm can only
arise with the perception of some harmony between the words and the
thought. It is, more particularly, the role of rhythm to resolve the tension
between the analytical word divisions and the metrical sound blocks
bridged over them. As a result, meaningful music supersedes both the
literalness of meaning and the rigidity of the metrical measure.

   We may put this truth of rhythm to the test by reciting a verse of
Homer in various ways. Recite it, first, by simply taking into account
each separate word according to its individual accent, and the verse will
sound like a clumsy sentence. Recite it, next, by merely scanning the
metrical feet without marking the separations between words, and you
will have a smooth but mechanical succession of dactyls and spondees.
Recite it, finally, in a way that respects word-division and pauses as well
as metre, and as a result, meaning will be harmonized with sound. H. N.
Porter observes:

By minimizing the concept of the foot and by stressing the colometric structure
it has been possible to omit that awkward period in which the student places a
strong stress-accent on the arses and pauses after every foot. If a beginner
pauses after every colon, his pauses at least generally coincide with a word end,
and often with a phrase-division.[1]

EXAMPLES

   Consider the first verse of the Iliad. I mark the central and minor
caesuras that are an essential feature of rhythm: Μῆνιν ἄειδε,/ θεά, ||
Πηληϊάδεω/ ᾽Αχιλῆος. Attempting to reproduce the effect of the four
cola, we may translate: The wrath now sing,/ o goddess, || the wrath of
Pelides/ Achilles. I repeat the word "wrath" to bring out the impact of

the central caesura: a heightening and subsiding of the voice most
notable at this point.

The third foot bridges the end of θεά [goddess], and the beginning
of Πηληϊάδεω [Pelides]. At this point there is very often a pause in the
sense and always the sound unit of a single foot extending over a word-
end and a word-beginning. The rhythmical value of the phenomenon is
plain. It means that, at this crucial point in the middle of the verse, a
fusion of sounds obliterates the division of word from word and, vice
versa, the inherent pause of sense injects distinction into this very fusion.
We accordingly emphasize the final syllable of θεά while lingering on
the initial syllable of Πηληϊάδεω. Both unity and differentiation are
given their role all at once. There is overriding harmony. This, we
realize, is no matter-of-fact announcement. Our voice, checking itself as
if in wonder, welds together in one breath two quite disparate things:
Achilles and the Muse.

But such an accomplishment is not all. There is reverberation. The
upward movement of the verse determined by the central caesura is also
reflected in the resulting halves. Consider the minor caesuras as marked
above. In the first half-verse "the wrath sing, o goddess," the initial
rising stress of the imperative abates somewhat in the vocative
"goddess," and at the end there is a similar though much slighter
abatement from "Pelides" to "Achilles." The two half-verses thus
rehearse, on a minor scale, the melody which the whole verse plays out
full scale. The rhythm of the whole is reflected in the parts and the parts
prefigure the whole. There is an organic symmetry, not an artificially
superimposed pattern. It is as if a form in embryo attained completion.

Now repeat the same verse again and again. The utterance
constitutes one moment filled with self-contained energy. If we simply
said "Sing, o goddess, the wrath of Achilles," we would merely have a
matter-of-fact statement. We would have a similarly unsatisfactory
effect if we made up a hexameter of the same literal meaning, but
without the rhythmical caesuras. For instance, consider Μῆνιν κλείετε,
Μοῦσαι, θείου Πηλείωνος or Μῆνιν κλείετε, Μοῦσαι, Πηλεΐδεω
'Αχιλῆος. Single words so coinciding with feet would appear as
separate blocks, held where they are by the mere requirements of syntax
and metre, and we would have versification rather than real verse. The
order of words is equally important. If we should reverse it and try to
build a verse starting with the hero's name (e.g., Πηλεΐδεω 'Αχιλῆος
ἀείδετε νῦν μοι, Μοῦσαι/ οὐλομένην τὴν μῆνιν), we would miss the
rising and subsiding flow leading up to its spacious cadence.

As it is, the μῆνις opens the line with a tremendous, sudden impact
and the final Πηληϊάδεω 'Αχιλῆος does not so much serve to explain

whose wrath it is, as to let the violence subside in the hero's well-rounded name and take its quiet place as an object of song. The verse thus acquires infinite suggestion: we might read into it the shock of experience and its translation into form, or commotion stilled into memory, or the way an explosive deed comes to rest in the solemnity of a name. The spell of rhythm tunes us to an infinite fringe of implications, removing us from factual description. The wrath of Achilles inhabits our mind even before we learn the details of the situation.

In this appreciation of rhythm, we should not be misled by such terms as "colon" or "caesura": we should not take them in a purely technical sense, as if they were peculiarly applicable to Homeric verse. These terms have a much broader frame of reference than their technical ring might suggest. They are concerned with characteristics of all speech: position and order of words, intervals, pauses, silences, transitions, and resumptions. A modulation stands out; significant as it is in any act of speech, it is naturally predominant wherever the utterance itself (and not any external point) is the principal focus. Such is eminently the case in poetry. In this respect Homeric verse is no different from any other. Here we may even pass over the difference between quantitative and accentual verse. While the forms naturally differ, this idea of rhythm remains essentially the same.

Take the verse: "To be, or not to be, that is the question." As in Homer, we may mark four cola or units of rhythmic meaning:

To be, / or not to be, ‖ that is / the question.

The first colon "to be" incisively uplifts us with a sense of discovery; then, introduced by the hesitating *or*, the second one "or not to be" holds us, mid-verse, in high suspense. We are then brought down to earth, in third place, by the objective "that is"; and the final colon, "the question," sets us to rest with the realization of the dilemma. However we may analyze the verse, the internal interplay brings us well beyond the speculative contents.

We might picture an actor playing out each phrase with a posture, a gesture, a pose—passing from puzzlement to a firm grip of the problem. As for us, we may forego the acting, and yet realize each phrase as an actual state of being, as a condition of existence that has its own independent justification. In the reading of the verse, we should let out this undercurrent. We do not have a mere statement, but a cognitive process. Thus a first impression becomes a thought and leads to an idea.

To clarify the point, try alternative forms of verse again. If we had "the question is: to be, or not to be," we would have the flat proposition of a problem, as if we were students introduced to a theme of discussion. Or, if we had "to be or not to be: on this I wonder," we would merely bring out a point of gratuitous speculation, casually made relevant. As it is, the verse of Hamlet appears inevitably right: a vital train of thought has its light, natural starting point and (at the end of the line) it is presented in its objectivity. Though contents and context could not be more different from Homer, we are reminded of the way in which Homeric verse often draws its brisk inception to a final stillness.

IMPLICATIONS IN CRITICISM

These considerations speak to common sense. They are so plain that they might be considered naive. And yet it is imperative to bear them in mind: an intimate appreciation of rhythm is a prerequisite to any general appreciation of poetry; even the loftiest poetic vision would lose its force, unless at the bottom it drew sustenance from those perceptions which we find in the essence of verse.

And yet here we fly in the face of inveterate prejudice. A basic flaw in the study of poetry consists in separating, or even opposing, verse-form and meaning. Poetry is thus confused with versification, as though we were to assume a neutral subject-matter on the one hand and, on the other, the task of putting it into verse. Hence the *Gradus ad Parnassum* or the dictionaries of rhyming words—the habit of equating poetry to verse-composition in contrast to prose. There is no need to illustrate this equivocation. It comes from confusing the spirit with the letter. How easy it is! An obvious external feature is taken for granted and deemed to be the essence of a thing, without any attempt to find out why.

Homer has suffered most from this misconception. The very form of Homeric verse produced the impression and illusion of an artificial fitness. Here was an apparently flawless welding of language and metre, a pervasive evenness of style, a unique rarity of obscurities or corrupt passages undermining the straightforward sense: such reasons contributed to the notion of a craft so perfected that any subject-matter could naturally be adapted to the verse-form. As a result, students take the form for granted. If asked why the poet chose one word rather than another or why he gave it a certain position in the verse, they are at a loss and are tempted to find in the metre the ultimate reason. The trimeters of Greek tragedy, for instance, or the hexameters of Virgil have a more fitful music, more prone to special effects, more conditioned by deliberate shifts of meaning. The verse appears less inevitable than it is in Homer and the process more transparent.

It is no wonder that the student should be perplexed. For scholarship seems to confirm this simplistic view: what scholars have emphasized is not so much the genius of the language as the peculiarly striking capacity of fitting the form of diction to the metre. It has been so ever since the scientific study of the language gained ground in the latter part of the last century. The discovery of facts did not go hand in hand with their interpretation. Thus the grammatical richness of forms, their heterogeneous nature and the blending of dialects were taken as signs of an artificial and conventional language whose unifying principle was to be found in the requirements of the Homeric hexameter.

The specious scientific reasons hardly conceal a plain absurdity. For how shall we account, on their terms, for the very rise of Homeric poetry *qua* poetry? If the fine and subtle textures of rhythm are disregarded, we are left with a grossly standardized pattern. The hexameter, in fact, is taken for granted. Its rules are laid down and expounded, but not justified or traced back to any underlying poetic reason. Here is a mold found, none knows where or how, and yet proclaimed as the mainspring of Homeric poetry. Derived from conjectural prototypes and tentatively explored in its possible developments, the process of versification is supposed to have lasted centuries and to abut in Homer as its ultimate spokesman.

This obvious half-truth is misleading. What always holds true concerning the influence of the past upon the present is so exaggerated and distorted here that we are left in limbo: no Homeric present exists. All we have is a termination with Homer at its dead end. There cannot even be any question of influence where no point of focus is there to receive it, and the vivid present is quite diluted in its antecedents.

Such an approach dispenses us from any research in depth; it ignores the meaning of rhythm. For the verse-form appeared to neutralize the problem of poetry. Anything in the poems—any phrase, or thought—could be seen as an exemplar, a record, a sediment of experience, a thing taking epic status by finding its place in the hexameter. Hence we find many oddities in accounts of Homeric poetry. We hear of "poetic language": but what does "poetic" mean here? Nothing qualitative, but simply a matter of fact: a word or phrase that mostly occurs in Homer; or we might say "epic," or why not "hexametric"?

This view of Homeric verse came to a head in the work of Milman Parry. His papers might be read, in part, as a handbook of Homeric versification. Overwhelmed by the massive array of metrical formulas, the unprepared reader is surprised and balks at the idea that Homer is made up of clichés. He would look for exceptions: but the exceptions are too few to impair the system. What then? How counter Parry's formulaic system? The answer lies in the interpretation of the facts. The very array of Parry's typical verses challenges the imagination and calls for a different approach.

By emphasizing rhythm rather than metre, we may get closer to the creative moment. For rhythm, unlike metre, is no common currency that can easily be adapted through the ages. It must have its period of dynamic emergence and development. It arises, like a tune, from the felicity of a disposition and the propitiousness of circumstances. It thus points to a certain eventuality in life or history, and not to an indefinite tradition. Look at the matter in this light. What if the creation of Homeric verse took much less time than it is commonly assumed? What if the originality that is denied the poet were assigned to the genius of the language, finding at a certain point its moment of triumph? What if the verse, or the thousands of verses, were to be seen as a form of poetic thought coming into its own and filling its period of time—an achievement in itself and not merely a means of composition?

Parry himself gives us a cue when he writes:

what a marvellous thing the bards succeeded in creating. In allowing themselves to be guided by the material elements of the hexameter and by the metrical values of the words they used, and in constantly looking for facility in the making of verse, they created a style conforming in the highest degree to the rules of thought. The clarity of the sentences of epic poetry is born from the very difficulty of rendering them in the rhythm of the hexameter line.[2]

We are excited to hear about "a style which conforms in the highest degree with the rules of thought"; but Parry never tells us what these rules of thought really are. What does he mean here? His next remark about clarity born from difficulty gives us pause, striking a sympathetic chord. For, surely, this difficulty must be taken in a positive creative sense: it is not the labor of the versifier but the tantalizing pursuit of rhythm in the very perception and presentation of things. When facts are resolved into rhythm, the material obstructions are overcome and a vivifying transparency ensues. We then have the clarity of movement and outline, not the mere plainness of facts.

"Rules of thought," or we might say, "ways and modes of thought" exist at a deeper level than the rules of grammar and syntax which simply crystallize their most obvious features. The correctness of speech must have been a matter of rhythm before it became a matter of logical construction. For at this deep level, thought itself is rhythm and rhythm is thought. This is a reason why we do harm to both the sense and the sound when we labor a point. There is a logic of rhythm that cannot be violated with impunity.

NOTES

1. H. N. Porter. "The Early Greek Hexameter" *Yale Classical Studies* 12 (1951): 2–63.

2. *The Making of Homeric Verse* : *The Collected Papers of Milman Parry*, ed. Adam Parry, Oxford, Clarendon Press: 1971:164.

Chapter 3

Order of Words

GENERAL CONSIDERATIONS

The order of words is intimately connected with rhythm. In enunciating a thought, do we merely choose each word and place it in the order that seems most fitting to our purpose? Or do we not, rather, let ourselves be beckoned by the very material of the words, as if the words furthered the development of our thought? Even the most abstract thought is thus made palpable. Hence comes the aesthetic pleasure of reciting or hearing a well-constructed sentence. The thought itself seems more convincing.

Such is preeminently the case of verse. Each word is a note leading us to a certain conclusion; the articulations of thought pass into the modulations of the verse, and the order of words impresses us as inevitable, natural and immune from any arbitrary twist.

I shall, therefore, take the verse rather than the sentence as my reference point. Just as the syllables or the various sounds within a word constitute its meaning as well as its music, so do the words within the verse. Consider, for instance, how in an opera the song stretches single syllables beyond their customary range and thereby gives an added resonance to the word itself; similarly we enrich the verse inasmuch as we sympathetically heighten or lower our voice in pronouncing a single word. The verse, in other terms, must be seen in its integrity. By being what it is, it sanctions any order of words it may contain. It is up to us to tap its secrets.

Such an approach is not a common one. Parry's basis is the formulas or combinations of formulas, and he does not inquire into the significance of the word-order, satisfied with the formula's metrical value. Others take a mainly syntactic point of view. H. Ammann, seeking the point of emphasis in the sentence, seems to treat Homer as if he were an orator and examines the word-order in terms of common usage or special effect.[1] He thus establishes a basic normal pattern (e.g., the sequence of verb+object with the meaning "to carry") and explains the exceptions by adducing some special point in the passage, invoking "metrical constriction" only as a last resort. Similarly, B. Geiseke notes the end-position of the verb in subordinate sentences and tries to justify any exception through points of syntax and sense.[2] Elsewhere he observes how the verb of a subordinate sentence comes at the end of the verse or, if there is enjambment, it occurs before the central caesura of the next verse, letting the remaining half-verse be filled with a formula. But why is it so? We are left in the dark.

Scholars often sift the evidence for the sake of establishing a rule, but even if valid, such a rule is not by itself sufficient to give us any enlightenment; it remains a blind neutral datum or a restriction unless it is made to yield its reason.   Such is the case when a metrical or grammatical rule, or a combination of both, is used to explain the order of words in verse. The path is thus laid open to one-sided views. What we need is a more nimble approach. A sense of rhythm offers the key. It is not identifiable with either literal construction or metrical scheme; it is inclusive of both meaning and measure. It justifies, on its own strength, the order of words.

Here, then, is a floating essence that is neither discourse nor music, but both at the same time. How shall we come to grips with something so vague and elusive? Give, first, ear to the verse, like someone who has little knowledge of the language or the metre and yet listens most intently to the sequence of sounds, most keen to catch their modulations and read into them any suggestion of meaning: essential instances of rest and movement will come to the fore. Read, thereafter, the same verse with all the knowledge you can muster, and then its meaning—even the literal and explicit meaning—will be filled with the pulse of life.   A contributing factor in Homer is the character of ancient Greek as an inflected language: the case-endings, and not a fixed order of words, distinguish subject and object. If we say in English "Achilles loves Patroclus," Achilles is clearly the subject because his name comes first, whereas in ancient Greek any alternative order is possible. The freer order of words is in itself significant, permitting a variation of tone according to what precedes or follows. In poetry, of course, these variations merge with the rhythm of the verse. But especially Homer's short verse-sentences show them in their pristine quality, unaffected by rhetorical effects; for Homer seldom presses an arbitrary point or detail. Description most often gives way to a sense of position, occurrence, or occasion. He will not, for instance, describe the violence of a wave, but let the wave surge, curve, splash on the shore. Any particular thing is no sooner mentioned than it merges with the moment that brings it to the fore. There is a rhythm in the very appearance of things.

Can this approach tell us what words and phrases come before or after? Can it fix their positions in the verse? No, what we propose to do is elicit a rhythmical, poetic significance in any given verse. For the rhythm traces a trajectory between two points: here are rising, lingering, and abating phases that take their place according to the relative weight of the words succeeding one another. A final noun-epithet phrase will thus bring us down to the objectivity of things; a final verb will rather convey direction and a sense of the next step. We find, for instance "he came to the Achaean swift ships" but "when to the ships they came." We therefore have a narrative meaning as well as the shape of meaning.

My aim is to highlight certain tendencies or intentions and not to discover a rule—to catch a glimpse of the artistic process and not to establish crystallized results. My classifications are thus tentative. They are a means to an end. They are not intended to give a complete account of incontrovertible facts.

VERSES WITH FINAL NOUN-EPITHET PHRASE

Consider the typical Homeric verse Il.1.121 (cf. 18.181; 20. 177, etc.):

τὸν δ' ἠμείβετ'/ ἔπειτα ‖ ποδάρκης/ δῖος ᾿Αχιλλεύς.

To him replied / thereafter ‖ swift-footed / divine Achilles.
Disregard how many times this verse or its like recurs in Homer. Let us take it at its face value and ask: Why such an order of words, why this rhythm, why the hexameter; what poetic sense prompted this form of expression? Such questions are usually ignored, or if any answer is given, it most often begs the question. We are told, for instance, that this verse is an epic equivalent for "Achilles replied," that it is traditional, derived from the combination of two formulas. Similarly disappointing are historical theories about the origins of the hexameter, for they derive one form from another and thus ignore any independent motivation. Our concern is the verse itself, its value and resonance as something actually present.

Notice again how content merges with rhythm. Our voice instantly rises with the two initial words that mark an important narrative point. What follows is ἔπειτα [then, thereafter]. This adverb is superfluous from a literal and narrative viewpoint, but it has a poetic function: coming at the central caesura, it lets us linger mid-verse on the act of replying, bringing a suspense that adds weight to the moment, and introducing a lengthening tone that prepares us for the broader final cadence that contains the hero's name. The epithets let the hero's image unfold. The name by itself would come in too abruptly against the preceding flow, but as it is, an atmosphere anticipates it. The slight caesura after ποδάρκης [swift-footed] enhances this effect.

There is a poetic quality in the mode of expression. An act (such as replying) summons up its agent; a predicate suggests its subject rather than the other way around. A movement or state craves form. Thus, in this verse, the moment of replying is not taken for granted but projects itself into the full-blown image of the hero. There is, as Porter puts it, a pattern of expectancy. Nothing is more delightful to the mind than this sense of positive expectation and fulfillment. We foreshadow before we know, realizing the meaning rather than learning it as a matter of fact. It is not just a question of foreseeing what is going to happen (as often in ordinary life); instead we are let into the creative process. Homer's verse becomes our own as we anticipate the passage of rhythm into words. Especially the weighty noun-epithet phrase is significant here: what might be advantageously left out in point of narrative (even the name of Achilles is not necessary in this respect) takes the largest room. Right from the beginning of the verse the hero looms ahead, as the verb craves its subject—not in the shape of a flimsy "he," but as a full-bodied presence that richly opens up at the end. The verb is not merely a predicate, but a prelude; the name is not merely a subject, but a crowning note.

In order to clarify this effect of rhythm and words, let us try to make up, by way of contrast, a hexameter with a similar literal meaning, but with a different order of words, for example:

Πηλεΐδης δ' 'Αχιλεὺς ἀπαμειβόμενος προσέειπε, or

τὸν δ' 'Αχιλεὺς πόδας ὠκὺς ἀπαμειβόμενος προσέειπε, or

τὸν δ' 'Αχιλεὺς μεγάθυμος ἀπαμειβόμενος προσέειπε.

Such verses, of course, never occur in Homer. But why? Why do they sound so infelicitous? One reason is that the noun-epithet phrase as subject comes at the beginning of the verse; placed there it hardly has any poetic function. It does not finally gather in itself the initial act through the dynamism of the rhythm; or the force of the verb does not lead us to the name with the movement of a falling wave. There is no sense of anticipation, fulfillment, or realization. As it is, the epithets here are quite otiose, ornamental, and superfluous, bearing no rhythmical weight; for the heavy noun-epithet phrase, which is the subject of the sentence, is bluntly followed by the verb as in ordinary narrative, and we are led on by the mere curiosity of knowing what is going to be said next, not by any impulse of anticipation.

Here is a poetic reason why the pattern of τὸν δ' ἠμείβετ' ἔπειτα ποδάρκης δῖος 'Αχιλλεύς is so prevalent in Homer (cf. Il.1.55, 58, 130, 172, 206, etc.). For a classification of such verses, see Milman Parry.[3]

Similarly we have: ἴαχε δῖος ᾿Αχιλλεύς [he cried, divine Achilles, Il.18.228], ἀνέστη δῖος ᾿Αχιλλεύς [he stood up, divine Achilles, ibid. 305], and ἐκέκλετο δῖος ᾿Αχιλλεύς [he called out, divine Achilles, ibid. 343].

Such diction carries us well beyond any notion of metrical formulas for the names of heroes or gods. What stands out is a rhythm applicable to any occurrence materializing into form. Compare a verse like διὰ μὲν ἀσπίδος ἦλθε φαεινῆς ὄβριμον ἔγχος [it went, through the shining shield, the strong spear, Il.3.357; 7.251; 11.435] or διὰ δ᾿ ἔπτατο πικρὸς ὀϊστός [and it flew, the sharp arrow, Il.5.99; 13.587; cf. ibid.592]. Just as in the case of heroes, a movement solidifies and the sense of form comes at the end (cf. Il.5.292; 616; 838; 7.247; 8.137; 11.128, 253; 13.408, 595). If such instances are much rarer, the reason is obvious: weapons, tools, and man-made objects are subjects of a sentence far less frequently than persons; they are mostly rendered with a final noun-epithet phrase in their proper function—as object or instrument of an act (see p. 27).

A magnificent example is the verse that depicts daybreak ἦμος/ δ᾿ ἠριγένεια ‖ φάνη/ ῥοδοδάκτυλος ᾿Ηώς [when, / early-born ‖ she appeared, / the rose-fingered Dawn, Il.1.477 etc.]. From the light initial "when" to the splendidly resounding finale, it is as if we scanned the process itself and not just parts of the verse. Or consider the sunset: ἐν δ᾿ ἔπεσ᾿ / ᾿Ωκεανῷ ‖ λαμπρὸν φάος / ἠελίοιο [and it fell/ into the Ocean, ‖ the bright light/ of the sun, Il.8.485, cf. 1.605]. After marking the actual point of sunset with a sudden instant touch, the verse closes with resonant finality, suggesting a glowing fiery end in its very cadence even more than in the literal meaning of the words, (cf. Il.8.66; 12.177; 15.715; 16.300; Od.4.429, 793; 5.279, 313).

The rhythmical and poetic reasons for a final noun-epithet phrase have their basis in ordinary experience. Thus a sound gains volume before it dissolves in an echo, a figure gains perspicuity before it merges with its space, and the inkling of an action precedes the full sense of its agent. The Homeric sequence of predicate + noun-epithet phrase has a logic of its own; it is not primarily a convenient metrical model.

A proof is Homer's avoidance of an initial noun-epithet phrase in self-contained, end-stopped verses. On the other hand, an initial noun-epithet phrase in the verse is quite regular after enjambment (see p. 39, 56); it has in this case its poetic reason, for it meets our expectation as it comes on the surge released by the preceding verse.

A character's name occurs, of course, very often as subject at the beginning of the verse; but then it usually has no epithet, its function being a narrative one in this case—a function quite different from that at the verse-end, where the noun-epithet phrase gives body to the preceding act. I have explained elsewhere the relative value of these two modes of expression.[4]

This rhythm and word-order find their way through the material. There are fluctuations, no stark polarities, but the tendency is unmistakable. Exceptions are few (cf. Il. 6.323, 9.236). In Il.3.228 τὸν δ᾽ Ἑλένη τανύπεπλος ἀμείβετο, δῖα γυναικῶν [to him flowing-robed Helen replied, divine among women], the final epithet makes all the difference; we are made to feel Helen's presence throughout the verse, vivified by the central verb. In Ἠὼς μὲν κροκόπεπλος ἐκίδνατο πᾶσαν ἐπ᾽ αἶαν [Dawn saffron-robed was spread all over the earth, Il.8.1, cf. 24.695; 19.1], we might give κροκόπεπλος a predicative force: Dawn encompasses the world in the glow of her robe. Elsewhere the metrical quantity of a particular name obstructs or complicates the name's position towards the end of the line. Such is most notably the case of Τηλέμαχος[5] in the recurring line τὴν (or τὸν) δ᾽ αὖ Τηλέμαχος πεπνυμένος ἀντίον ηὔδα [to her (or him) inspired Telemachus spoke face to face, Od.1.213]. But the anomaly is compensated by the use of the epithet "inspired" in a verse always presenting Telemachus in the act of speaking, which in Homer is inseparable from the act of thinking. For Telemachus has newly attained, in the Odyssey, the power to think and speak effectively. The language of the verse implies this role. Rhythm, order of words, and meaning spontaneously concur: through its mere position, the epithet πεπνυμένος acquires a predicative color in characterizing Telemachus. The point is neither deliberate nor matter of fact. Inevitable overtones transpire from the order of words. There is an intelligence of rhythm.

SYNTACTIC VARIETY OF THE FINAL NOUN-EPITHET PHRASE

We have seen, so far, a persistent rhythm that joins a predicate with its subject into one arching moment. But this syntax of predicate and subject is incidental here. We find the same kind of rhythm where the syntax is quite different. This wide-ranging prevalence of the same rhythmical movement is in itself highly significant. We are shown how it holds its ground irrespectively of any particular syntax or special topic. We are dealing, in fact, with a fundamental poetic element and not merely a convenient combination of formulas for subject and predicate to convey in the hexameter such meanings as "Achilles said," and "Menelaus saw him." A mode of perception catches the rhythm of occurrences, whatever they may be.

Consider such verses as the following (Il.3.346, cf. 355; 5.15 etc.):

πρόσθε/ δ᾽ Ἀλέξανδρος ‖ προΐει/ δολιχόσκιον ἔγχος.

First/ did then Alexander ‖ cast / the long-shadowed spear.

Here things are seen in a different perspective than in the previous section—the final noun-epithet phrase represents the object, not the subject, of an act. There is the same arching rhythm, and sense of an active moment that rises and subsides in the field of vision, but the act now materializes in the configuration of what is touched, handled, used. Thus, in our instance, the long final noun-epithet phrase mirrors the lengthening path of the spear traced by the shadow on the earth below. Thus we have "Hector among the foremost carried the all-even shield" (Il.11.63), "Meriones . . . shot upon him the bronze-fitted arrow" (13.650) or "he drew the red-sparkling wine" (16.230), and "the girl brought from the room the shining robe" (Od.6.74). On the other hand, notice in such cases the lack of epithet with the narratively important subject at the beginning of the line. The epithet's sensuous touch comes at the end, highlighting the object.

Verses of this kind are frequent in passages that directly render human acts as they fall into place and touch upon familiar objects. The contour of an object seems to still the passing moment (cf.Il.1.12–14; 2.42–7; 3.262–3; 4.105, 111, 459; Od.1.99, 126–7, 334, 436; 2.259, 260, 299; 3.46,51–54).

Consider Il.1.34:

βῆ δ᾽ ἀκέων/ παρὰ θῖνα ‖ πολυφλοίσβοιο θαλάσσης.

and silent/ he walked by the shore ‖ by the shore of the wide-
roaring/ sea.

In this and the next instance my translation repeats the central word to mark suspense at that point (cf. Il.1.327, 9.182). The brisk initial βῆ [went, walked], is narratively significant in telling us that Chryses is rebuffed and withdraws. But the verse is less and less narrative as it proceeds beyond the central caesura. With the final noun-epithet phrase, we are removed into space, away from the story. Chryses is absorbed in the distance. In Od.1.333 (cf. 16.415, 18.209, 21.64):

στῆ ῥα/ παρὰ σταθμὸν ‖ τέγεος/ πύκα ποιητοῖο.

and she stood/ by the pillar ‖ the pillar of the well-built roof.

there is again a light sudden start, στῆ [stood], which is narratively important: Penelope appears before the suitors. But then the sense of place expands, and we pass to the solid hall that encloses a fleeting, trepidant act. And in Od.1.365 (cf. 11.334, 13.2):

μνηστῆρες δ᾽/ ὁμάδησαν ‖ ἀνὰ μέγαρα / σκιόεντα.

and the suitors/ made clangor ‖ through the hall/ full-of-
shadows.

the suitors, without epithet, are narratively important and open the verse, but they are forthwith left out—their cry vanishes, echoing in the shady hall. The final noun-epithet phrase brings us to a standstill. The epithet prolongs the moment to a vanishing point, as the human outcry is absorbed into the lulling spaces of the hall.

I touch something, and it is palpable; I walk and cover the ground. As I voice such occurrences, I impart a distinctive tone to each respective phase. Just as meaning has its connotations, so does the voice that brings it out have its modulations. Homer gives full value to this basic tendency. In the verses just quoted the final noun-epithet phrases evoke the imagery of things and places that inevitably attend upon any human act. Thus the shadowy hall, the roaring sea, the pillar of the well-built roof, and the long-shadowed spear are unobtrusively integrated into the picture. The epithets are the tersest of definitions. They do not comment or explain and, rather than qualifying, they simply enhance the sheer presence of a thing. Any additional point or external frame of reference would destroy the effect. At the end of the line, we slide off into the world of nature or man-made objects; we are let into the realm of what is pervasively permanent, and we are drawn away from the friction of a particular situation. Thus, in a drawing or painting, the lines do not stop abruptly, but seem to melt into the surrounding atmosphere. Seen in this light, the noun-epithet phrases are the essence of rhythm. Neither making a point nor serving as a metrical stop-gap, they merge the shapes of things into the cadence of the action.

BEYOND THE NOUN-EPITHET PHRASES

Verses that end with a noun-epithet phrase evince, we have seen, a characteristic rhythm, but it would be wrong to identify this rhythm with fixed types of diction. These final noun-epithet phrases are but one aspect of a wider phenomenon. The significance of the cadence or dying fall can be conveyed in many other ways.

First consider some typical verses that have coordinated nouns at the end instead of a noun-epithet phrase. Il.1.193; 11.411 etc:

ἦος ὁ ταῦθ᾽/ ὥρμαινε ‖ κατὰ φρένα / καὶ κατὰ θυμόν.

while these things/ he revolved ‖ in his mind/ and spirit.

Il.5.122; 13. 61; 23. 772:

γυῖα δ᾽ ἔθηκεν/ ἐλαφρά, ‖ πόδας / καὶ χεῖρας ὕπερθεν.

swift did he make/ his limbs, ‖ his feet/ and his hands above.

Od.6.235; 23.162:

ὣς ἄρα τῷ/ κατέχευε ‖ χάριν, / κεφαλῇ τε καὶ ὤμοις.

upon him/ did she shed beauty, ‖ upon his head/ and his
                                                          shoulders.

We could merely have said "he thought," "he became swifter, more beautiful," but these acts or states are rendered in that they take place, they happen and their effect is seen spreading out to the pertinent organs. The end of the verse gives sensuous evidence to this process. Our voice takes an expansive, even tone when mentioning the natural features of body and mind.

Take instances in which a verse contains two sentences. We have not so much a narrative sequence as a process of completion. Il.1.475, Od.9.168, etc:

ἦμος/ δ᾽ ἠέλιος ‖ κατέδυ/ καὶ ἐπὶ κνέφας ἦλθε.

and when/ the sun ‖ sank down/ and thereon darkness came.
Od.2.388, 3.487, etc.:

δύσετο/ τ᾽ ἠέλιος ‖ σκιόωντό τε/ πᾶσαι ἀγυιαί.

then did it set,/ the sun ‖ and enshadowed/ were all the streets.
Od.4. 794, 18.189, etc.:

εὗδε / δ᾽ ἀνακλινθεῖσα, ‖ λύθεν δέ οἱ / ἅψεα πάντα.

and she slept/ leaning back,‖ and loosened were/ all her joints.
Il.5.497, 6.106, etc.:

οἱ / δ᾽ ἐλελίχθησαν ‖ καὶ ἐναντίοι/ ἔσταν Ἀχαιῶν.

and/ about did they turn ‖ and stood/ in face of the Achaeans.
Il.4.504, 5.42, etc.:

δούπησεν δὲ/ πεσών, ‖ ἀράβησε δὲ/ τεύχε᾽ ἐπ᾽ αὐτῷ.

he resounded/ in falling,‖ they clanged upon him,/ his arms.

Even coordinated verbs, without a noun, produce a similar effect of climax and anticlimax rather than a descriptive sequence, as in Il.6.253, 406, etc.:

ἔν τ᾽ ἄρα οἱ / φῦ χειρὶ ‖ ἔπος τ᾽ ἔφατ᾽/ ἔκ τ᾽ ὀνόμαζε.

and he/ clung to his hand, ‖ spoke word/ and called out his
name.

The variety of incident here is a foil to the persistence of one rhythm: sunset and the encompassing darkness; a woman reclining in sleep and her loosening joints; a turning about and a standing face to face; a crash and its sound; a clasping of hands and the attending greetings. All these instances, however different from one another, have something in common. There is always the unity of one moment that arches over the succeeding acts, rising to its climax and then subsiding. What stands out is not the connection of cause and effect but aspects of the same event, or a wholeness that naturally falls into its constituent parts. The verse starts off quickly, letting out the occasion and giving it effect at the tapering end. Again, the final part is less functional from a narrative viewpoint, but it is often more purely poetic in its sensuous and concrete connotations. Here are the enshadowed streets as the sun is setting, the abandon of a woman's limbs as she falls asleep, the sense of an actual position as men turn about or rally, the clang attending upon the crash, and the warmth of "calling by name" as people meet. Facts yield their intimate outline.

Here we may add a few instances in which the two main parts of the verse are sentences that are separate but bound together by a sense of action and reaction, appeal and response, question and answer. For example, Il.4.79:

κὰδ δ᾽ ἔθορ᾽/ἐς μέσσον ‖ θάμβος δ᾽ ἔχεν/εἰσορόωντας.

and she sprang/in their midst; ‖ wonder seized / those who saw.
Od.10. 311:

ἔνθα στὰς/ἐβόησα, ‖ θεὰ δέ μευ/ἔκλυεν αὐδῆς.

standing there/ did I cry; ‖ and the goddess / heeded my voice.
Il.1,43 (cf. 457, 16.527):

ὣς ἔφατ᾽/ εὐχόμενος, ‖ τοῦ δ᾽ ἔκλυε / Φοῖβος Ἀπόλλων.

so did he speak / in prayer; ‖ and him heard / Phoebus Apollo.
(Cf. Il.6.311; 10.285; 23.771; 24. 314; Od.3.385; 6.328; 9.536; 10.481). This last instance lends itself to comment. The impassioned prayer arises and forthwith comes to rest in the calm presence of the listening god. Apollo's angry reaction will come later; for now all we have is the solemn scene in and by itself. The simple, perfect juxtaposition of speaker and hearer has the effect of a bas-relief; with the central caesura as a water-shed, the act of praying traces a curve that joins the two poles in one ideal moment. If we said: "he desperately prayed: the god heard with anger, compassion. . .," we would lose this simple effect. The same would be the case if we injected an emotional crescendo into the Homeric verse, in such a way as to bring out the mood of the characters. As it is, the rhythm resolves all complexities into a matter of movement and poise.

VERSES WITH FINAL VERB, DUE TO FORECAST OF THE VERB

There are many verses in Homer that end with a verb. What then becomes of the dying fall or heavy ending which I have associated with nouns? The roles are reversed, but we still have the same arching movement of the verse, the sense of expectation and fulfillment. The preceding nouns now portend the sequence and anticipate the final verb. As we read or recite, we again project the modulations of meaning.

Consider the following instances and classifications in which the final verb elicits an act that is implied beforehand:
A) Il.3.121: Ἶρις δ᾽ αὖθ᾽ Ἑλένῃ λευκωλένῳ ἄγγελος ἦλθεν (cf. 6.127, 394; 7.98; 11.219, 231, 809; 13.210, 246; 18. 2; 21.151,113; 24.194; Od.6.280; 10.277; 12.374; 16.138) In rendering a meeting of two persons, the nouns (or pronouns) very often come first and the verb

follows. An initial nominative and dative give us an immediate sense of relation between the two; the mere juxtaposition of persons prepares us for the actual approach.

Rhythm and order of words attune us to a poetic logic. In this respect, consider more closely the verse just quoted. Marking the caesuras, we may translate: "and Iris/ to Helen,‖ to the white-armed,/ as messenger came." The names Iris and Helen stand out in a sort of premonitory contiguity, and the epithet "white-armed" adds suspense to the moment before we have the expected final verb. There is tension and release of tension. An alternative order of words would fail to give us this sense of climax and anticlimax. If we had "Iris came to Helen with a message" (e.g.,Ἶρις δ' ἦλθ' Ἑλένῃ λευκωλένῳ ἀγγελέουσα), the incisive moment would turn to loose narrative. If, on the other hand, we had the final noun-epithet phrase, ἦλθεν δ' ἀγγελέουσ' Ἑλένῃ πόδας ὠκέα Ἶρις ["and she came with a message to Helen, swift-footed Iris"], such a phrase would be deprived of its proper function as subject of a simple self-contained, sentence as in ἀπέβη πόδας ὠκέα Ἶρις [and she went, swift-footed Iris].[6] It is a sense of relation that prevails in this verse, and that would be lost or weakened.

B) Il.2.375: ἀλλά μοι/ αἰγίοχος ‖ Κρονίδης Ζεὺς/ ἄλγε' ἔδωκεν [but to me the aegis-bearing Zeus son of Cronos pains inflicted] (cf. 1.2, 445; 4.396; 8.141; 15.719; 18.431; 19. 270; 21. 525; 22.422; 24.241, 741. Od.1.244; 3.136; 4.339, 340, 722; 19. 550, 576). The same tendency is shown here on a wider range, with verbs of giving, bestowing, inflicting, and sending. What stands out is a relation between giver and receiver—often a god giving fortune or misfortune to mortals. A dative often comes first intimating the final giving. Thus, in the verse just quoted, "to me," "upon me" at once presents the speaker as a recipient, then at the center comes the expansive naming of Zeus, and finally the god's actual visitation. A rendering like ἀλλὰ μοι ἄλγεα δῶκε πατὴρ ἀνδρῶν τε θεῶν τε [but to me gave pains the father of gods and of men], with a final epithetic phrase, would hardly suit this context, being appropriate to an ordinary human self-contained act.

In these examples the act of "giving" takes a sense of dispensation and destination that seals the verse. It is not just a matter of metrical convenience in such forms as ἔδωκε, ἔθηκε coming at the end. On the other hand, the ordinary act of giving (i.e., handing out) is often followed by an object—a noun-epithet phrase in the accusative that provides the verse with its expected final cadence or heavier ending (Od.3.50, 51, 53, 63, etc.).

C) There are many other ways in which a sense of relation takes precedence, driving the verb to the end of the verse. The relation is expressed in concrete terms: to bring one thing to bear upon another, to set in place, apply, or put on—to cause anything to happen to someone. Only a few brief hints can be given here to the great variety of meanings that come under this general heading:

Il.1.3: πολλὰς δ' ἰφθίμους ψυχὰς ῎Αϊδι προΐαψεν [many strong souls into Hades it dashed] The heavy strained initial accusatives propel us to the final verb. Such a form as πολλὰς δὲ ψυχὰς προΐαψ' ῎Αϊδι κλυτοπώλῳ would give us a lingering cadence quite unsuitable to the meaning (cf. 6.487).

Il.5.40: πρώτῳ γὰρ στρεφθέντι μεταφένῳ ἐν δόρυ πῆξεν [upon him first as he turned, on the back, the spear did he fix, cf. 5.539; 8. 258; 11.447; 16.772; 17.519; 22.283]. On the other hand, the verse end ἵει δολιχόσκιον ἔγχος (see p.27) draws attention to the act itself, not to its effect.

Od.9.39: Ἰλιόθεν με φέρων ἄνεμος Κικόνεσσι πέλασσεν [from Ilion me . . . did the wind to Ciconians bring near]. Away from . . . towards: the rhythm and the words impart to the verse a forthright direction that can only abut in a final verb. This sense of energy would be lost in such a verse as Ἰλιόθεν δ' ἄνεμος μ' ἔφερεν Κικόνων ἐπὶ γαῖαν (cf. 3.291; 4.500; 5.111; and Il.13.1, 180; 15.28).

Homer says "upon you . . . his heavy hands shall he lay," and not "lay his hands upon you" (Il. 1.89; cf. 567; 24.743; Od.1.254; 13.376; 20.29, 39, 386). Similarly he says, "upon the victuals . . . their hands did they lay" (Il.9.91), not "they laid their hands on the victuals" or, in the arming scenes, "the greaves around his ankles he put," (Il.3.30; cf.332, 336, 339, etc.) not the reverse order. The part of the body mentioned first, summons up in its aftermath the action that is pertinent to it.

Il.13.418: Ἀντιλόχῳ δὲ μάλιστα δαΐφρονι θυμὸν ὄρινε [and to Antilochus most, to the brave one, the spirit he stirred, cf. 14.459, 487; 2.242]. The initial dative reaches out for the final verb through the intervening suspense. An initial verb would fail to produce this effect, suppressing the strong sense of relation (e.g.,Ἀντιλόχῳ δ' ἄρ' ὄρινεν ἐνὶ στήθεσσι φίλον κῆρ).

Il.1.105: Κάλχαντα πρώτιστα κάκ' ὀσσόμενος προσέειπε [and to Kalkhas . . . he said, cf. 320; 5.756]. Such is usually the case when the name of the listener is mentioned. Compare the frequent ὅ σφιν ἐϋφρονέων ἀγορήσατο καὶ μετέειπεν [to them, meaning well, he spoke and said, Il. 1.73]. Here the sense of relation is uppermost.

VERSES WITH FINAL VERB, DUE TO THE TENOR OF THE SENTENCE

For instance, we find, "go to the tents" (Il.1.322) but "when to the tents he went" (Il.618), "he came to the ships" (2.17) but "to the ships may he return" (16.247). There is a hint of the same tendency in English when we say, for example "this is true" or "is this true?" but "how true this is."

Homeric verse is most sensitive to this underlying tone. Consider the following sets of examples:

1) Il.17.156: εἰ γὰρ νῦν Τρώεσσι μένος πολυθαρσὲς ἐνείη [would that in the Trojans a might full of courage were present, cf. 4.289; 18.464; Od.4.697; 6.244].

2) Il.1.39: Σμινθεῦ, εἴ ποτέ τοι χαρίεντ' ἐπὶ νηὸν ἔρεψα [O Smintheus, if ever for you a beauteous temple I roofed, cf. 40, 503; 5.116; 22.83].

3) Il.16.100: ὄφρ' οἶοι Τροίης ἱερὰ κρήδεμνα λύωμεν [so that the two of us alone sacred Ilion may conquer, cf. 2.332; 6.258; 8.513; 16.84, 258, 455; 17.445].

4) Il.7.313: οἱ δ' ὅτε δὴ κλισίησιν ἐν Ἀτρεΐδαο γένοντο [when within the tents of the Atrides they came, cf. 8.60, 180, 343; 9.669; 11.170, 618; 12.143, 373].

Note the recurring verse (Il.1.469) αὐτὰρ ἐπεὶ πόσιος καὶ ἐδητύος ἐξ ἔρον ἕντο [and when of food and of drink their fill they had], instead of ἀλλ' ἐπεὶ ἐξ ἔρον ἕντο ἐδητύος ἠδὲ ποτῆτος (cf. Il.11. 780).

5) Il.1.254: ὦ πόποι, ἦ μέγα πένθος Ἀχαιΐδα γαῖαν ἱκάνει [alas, indeed a great woe to the land of the Achaeans is arriving, cf. 161; 7.124; 8.147; 11.246; 12.318; 13.99;15. 185].

A slight initial touch in these verses impinges upon the direct perception of occurrences: if you start a sentence with "if ever", "when indeed", "would that", you give way to a sense of potentiality before an imagined outcome, and the verb comes naturally at the end of the verse.

It would be futile, however, to try and turn these tendencies into rules by explaining away the exceptions. We do find, most notably, ὅτε [when] immediately followed by a verb. It is a question of degree. The more a goal or a term looms ahead in a temporal sentence, the more likely it is for the verb to come at the end of the verse. On the other hand, the more an act or occurrence is contained in its central moment, the more likely it is that the verse has a nominal ending. Hence comes the frequent end position of the verb in sentences conveying purpose or consequence.[7] Also, verbs of arriving (i.e.,ἄφικανε, ἀφίκοντο) tend to come at the verse end, unlike the verbs of going (i.e., βῆ, εἶσι, κίε).

This last distinction is well-exemplified in Il.1.327–8 (cf.9.182–5):

τὼ δ' ἀέκοντε βάτην παρὰ θῖν' ἁλὸς ἀτρυγέτοιο,
Μυρμιδόνων δ' ἐπί τε κλισίας καὶ νῆας ἱκέσθην.
and unwilling they went by the shore of the unvintaged sea,
to the Myrmidon tents and their ships they came.

Rather than saying "they went, along the sea, to the tents of the Myrmidons," Homer breaks the action into the space which they summon up (cf.1.34; 19.40; Od.13.220). Movement thus blends with place, and the verse invites a lingering contemplative look. The second verse, on the other hand, gives us quite a different feeling. The heavier initial rhythm tapers off at the end, as if to present us immediately with an important goal that is finally attained. There is a resolute drift, not an act that finds rest in its natural space. It therefore seems appropriate that the verb should precede in one instance and follow in the other. At the same time, however, there is expectation and fulfillment in both cases. The opening space of the shore is prefigured by the men's advancing steps no less than the act of arrival by the Myrmidon tents.

Broadening extension or final point of arrival: these distinctions affect the position of the verb and the order of words. It is rare that the verb "I go" comes at the end of the verse. In Il.6.313 (cf. 16.856; 22.361, etc.), Ἕκτωρ δὲ πρὸς δώματ' Ἀλεξάνδροιο βεβήκει, we should note the pluperfect form βεβήκει [and Hector to Alexander's house was going]. It brings out the "aspect" of the verb—not so much a passing movement as a state. Hector is seen as an image even while he walks away. The very weight of the word prompts this effect.

ORDER OF WORDS AND SENSE OF THE MOMENT

It makes a difference, we have seen, whether a verb or a noun comes first in the verse; whether an act anticipates its agent or vice versa; or whether we have a sense of process or of outcome. Here are two different ways of perceiving an event, but in both cases one thing is clear: Homeric verse is responsive to a sense of timing that affects the order of words. By becoming verse, a sentence ceases to be a mere statement. An inner pulse or modulation is revealed. Narrative facts, we are led to suppose, are not the main thing. They are a foil to more basic predisposition: to modes of happening, and to ways of being. Homeric verse, in short, highlights an essential moment.

What do I mean by "essential moment"? Homer's constant focus upon a certain spot and occasion gives us the answer. Such a moment is the immediate realization, before our eyes, of an act or state of being: "I stand my ground," "I step out to go," "I speak out," "I look out," "I am moved." Homer renders such acts in a simple fullness that confers to them their moment of existence by letting them fill the verse. Take such frequently recurring verses as βῆ δὲ διὰ προμάχων κεκορυθμένος αἴθοπι χαλκῷ · [he went through the foremost, clad in flashing bronze, Il.4.495] or καὶ μιν φωνήσας ἔπεα πτερόεντα προσηύδα [and to her speaking out wingèd words did he address, Il.1.201]. Why mention this "flashing bronze"? Why specify "wingèd words" in a simple act of saying? There is no narrative justification. What matters is the balance of weight and lightness in the representation. Each act is given its contour in space and time — neither reduced to one flimsy verb nor expanded into lengthy description.

Such a way of looking at things is nothing strange. Homer brings into the clarity of an art form something of which we are all dimly aware. Consider any act or state of being in your own experience, but cease taking it for granted and dwell upon it imaginatively. It will then appear to be a self-existing moment, not a mere step from one point to another in an indefinite series. The act of going will imply extension and breathing space, the act of speaking will suggest the forming of words and their utterance, and any sensation will seem to emerge and get hold of you. There will always be a point of focus and its fringes, an impulse and its intrinsic occasion; a sheer sense of happening will prevail over the narrative matter. Here the moment itself stands supreme: we get absorbed, for instance, in the incidence of a forward step and not in the interest of where we are going or why.

Are we any nearer to understanding the nature of the moment reflected in Homeric verse? Another general look at the order of words may enlighten us further. Consider the following points:

1. There is, in Homeric verse, an organic quality: the parts relate to one another and to the whole through a necessary, inevitable contiguity or succession. In such a verse as Il.15.442, ὣς φάθ᾽, ὁ δὲ ξυνέηκε, θέων δέ οἱ ἄγχι παρέστη [Ajax so spoke; and he heard and ran and stood at his side], the several verbs are phases of one moment. If a verse contains more acts than one, these cohere as parts of the same movement. Such is often the case in Homer (i.e., Il.1.25, 33, 57, 199, 407, etc.). There is thus a non-Homeric ring in Apollonius Rhodius 3.650 "she walked out from within, and then again she slunk back." Homer does not titillate our curiosity from act to act. There is no surprise. What variations there are come from the modulation of one prevailing strain. Any dissonance would turn us to other matter, away from the pulse of the moment.

2. Therefore, in the verse there is a sense of self-completion, self-development. Each word leans forward, preparing the ground for the next one. Word melts into phrase, phrase into sentence, sentence into verse; and meaning arises from the enveloping moment. Even so, as a moment materializes in real life, the past melts into the present, the

present points to the future, and the moment is a presence that quivers in between.

3. This organic quality, this sense of self-completion and self-development attests a creative spontaneity within the verse. It is as if the verse started and moved to a conclusion on its own strength; for we neither have a purely mechanical sequence nor a deliberate effect. Why do we look out before we see? Why do we reach before we touch? And how do these acts fall into a certain rhythm that is inscribed in the verse no less than in the ways of nature? Such is a compelling moment in real life: it is suddenly a swaying present suspended between past and future—none can say what chemistry composed its poise.

The word "moment" is best taken here in its etymological sense of movement. For any vital movement has all at once its delicate articulations and its decisive forward thrust. It is organic but not contrived, dynamic but not reckless, spontaneous but not casual. Even the most formulaic verse shows the pulse of time at its core; its repetitions sanction this felicity of touch.

SENSE OF THE MOMENT AND SENSE OF NARRATIVE

Any object can be seen in itself as it rises in the field of vision, or it can be observed, described, assigned where it belongs in a certain context. A sense of the moment prevails in the former instance, a narrative interest in the latter. We may thus oppose a representational mode to a narrative one.

These two modes are, however, complementary to each other. No single moment or feature can exist by itself in absolute abstraction; no background, foreground or outer context can have any interest without a central point of focus. There is, nevertheless, a theoretical distinction. Now one mode prevails, now the other. Thus central moments or occasions stand out in our lives, but an intervening narrative is required to sustain them; as in a journey, we notice landmarks, but they could not have any significance without the intervening landscape.

These reflections are also pertinent to any work of literature. But Homer is a case apart. Moments of focus, we have seen, are his hallmark; and yet we may wonder how any story, never mind a whole epic, can be made up of moments. The ordinary reader, however, finds no problem here: the succession of separate moments and the lack of general surveys do not impede the narrative, but rather quicken it and make it more convincing.

In Homer the sense of the moment and the sense of narrative are twin faces of the same phenomenon. We continually pass from one to the other—as when, watching a stream, we hardly distinguish its ripples from the general current. Is the wrath of Achilles a narrative theme or does it spontaneously come up from the movements of dialogue? Is the return of Odysseus treated as a tale or does it arise, rather, from his longing gaze across the sea as he sits on the shore of Calypso's island? Or do we have a story of war and not, rather, the thrust and counter-thrust of the battle-scenes? Moments lead into narrative and narrative breaks into moments.

We might say that Homer leads us back to the very sources of the narrative art. For why do we narrate, why do we give any account of events or situations making up a story? It is not because of any idle fancy, or primarily to instruct or entertain. There is, rather, a point that first stands out and strikes the imagination, a focal moment that suggests other such moments through analogy or contrast; and this concurrence motivates a plot with its environment. I am looking at the matter philosophically and not historically. I am not saying that story-telling originated from a poetic perception of moments. The representational and narrative mode go hand in hand; they ideally coexist. Any single act or state of being is potentially part of a story. Any episodic fact is originally an act or state in the making.

Homer is faced with this twofold aspect of reality all the time. An instinctive sense of focus continually tends to a larger vision, and the larger vision continually returns to a point of focus. The result is a constant unison. It is no question of accommodating two different modes of perception. Homer tunes us, rather, to a more fundamental and concrete perspective—to see how any immediate act or state through its very impact produces a narrative trend, and how the narrative trend cannot be pursued without drawing fresh strength from the impulse of yet another act or state caught in its immediacy.

We have considered, so far, only single moments in end-stopped verse or verse-sentences. But not all verses are of this kind. There is at times, within the verse, a sudden shift of focus; a sentence is cut short and another sentence branches out beyond the verse-end. What is the role of rhythm here? How does it preserve the sense of the moment? We must study, in this connection, the art of enjambment.

NOTES

1. H. Ammann. *Untersuchungen zum homerischen Wortfolge und Satzstruktur*, 1 Teil, Freiburg: 1922; 2 Teil in *Indo-germanische Forschungen*, 1924: 42, 149-78; ibid. 300-22.

2. B. Geiseke. "Über die Wortstellung in abhängingen Sätze bei Homer." In *Jahrbücher für classische Philologie,* 1861. 83:225-32.

3. *The Making of Homeric Verse* : *The Collected Papers of Milman Parry,* ed. Adam Parry, Oxford, Clarendon Press: 1971: 10 ff; 38 ff.

4. P. Vivante, *The Epithets in Homer: A Study in Poetic Values*. New Haven, Yale University Press: 1982: 92-3.

5. *The Making of Homeric Verse: The collected Papers of Milman Parry,* ed. Adam Parry, Oxford, Clarendon Press: 1971: Cf. Ἰδομενεύς, Μηριόνης, Τυδείδης, Σαρπηδών. Parry calls *generic* certain epithets of heroes that belong to less frequent formula types and occupy portions in the middle part of the verse; πεπνυμένος is among them. The name to which these epithets refer often present, like Telemachus, the quantity___ ˘ ˘ __ The material is not always malleable. Here, it checks the tendency to place the noun epithet phrase at the end of the line.

6. Cf. P. Vivante. *The Epithets in Homer*: 86 ff. Il.2.786: Τρωσὶν δ' ἄγγελος ἦλθε ποδήνεμος ὠκέα Ἶρις, is exceptional and less distinctly Homeric. Its occurrence in the *Catalogue of Ships* is perhaps significant.

7. Cf. B. Geiseke, "Über die Wortstellung in abhängingen Sätze bei Homer." In *Jahrbücher für classische Philologie* (1861,83):225–232.

Chapter 4

Enjambment

TIME AND SPACE IN HOMER'S ENJAMBMENT

The singleness of focus which we find in self-contained verses breaks down where enjambment occurs—where, that is to say, the sentence runs on from verse to verse. Why does this running over occur? There must be a reason that is intrinsic to the verse itself, intrinsic to form and contents. We should, in other words, beware of mechanical explanations telling us in some way that the sentence runs over because there is not enough room, or that on the other hand, a verse is self-contained because a complete sentence fits into its metrical length. Such an argument merely begs the question.

There is, indeed, a question of length, but the length is one with the utterance itself. There is a breathing space. One moment of expression spreads over it, or a new development rises from within the unfolding moment and it carries us beyond the limits of the verse. These variations spontaneously arise from modulations of the material at hand—from the way it is imagined or perceived. Enjambment is internal to the thought itself. It is not due to an arbitrary addition that necessarily overlaps, but to an inner development that cannot be contained.

The sense of a shifting focus is neatly brought out where, in an assembly scene, a speaker succeeds another, as in Il.1.68–9:

ἤτοι ὅ γ' ὣς εἰπὼν κατ' ἄρ' ἕζετο· τοῖσι δ' ἀνέστη
Κάλχας Θεστορίδης, οἰωνοπόλων ὄχ' ἄριστος.

thus indeed did he speak, sat down: and among them arose
Kalkhas the son of Thestor, among soothsayers the best.

(cf.1.101, 247; 2.76, 278; 7.354, 365; Od.2.224). In these instances a new character, or position, stands out at the end of the verse—a presence brought out by what precedes and pressing forward into what follows.

The same moment is prolonged beyond the verse boundary. In the passage just quoted, Kalkhas moves on the spur of Achilles. There is an intimacy of connection that would not have been possible in two separate moments, two separate self-contained verses.

Let us look at instances of greater complexity. Remote shifts of focus in time rather than space are signaled by Achilles bidding Agamemnon return Khryseis in Il.1.127 ff.:

> ἀλλὰ σύ μὲν νῦν τήνδε θεῷ πρόες· αὐτὰρ Ἀχαιοὶ
> τριπλῇ τετραπλῇ τ' ἀποτείσομεν, αἴ κέ ποθι Ζεὺς
> δῷσι πόλιν Τροίην εὐτείχεον ἐξαλαπάξαι.

> But do now let her go to the god, and we Achaeans
> shall threefold or fourfold repay you, if ever Zeus
> grant us to conquer the well-walled city of Troy.

Notice how different times find their place within one movement. There is anticipation in the present. The succession of verses still reminds us of time's regular progress; but the enjambment, by running verse into verse, presents this succession as one of thought. Hence comes the tension. We have unity and distinction all at once. Try to recompose the passage into self-contained verse—for instance:

> ἀλλὰ σύ μὲν νῦν τήνδε θεῷ πρόες ὅττι τάχιστα,
> τριπλῇ τετραπλῇ τ' ἀποτείσομεν ἐνθάδ' Ἀχαιοὶ
> αἴ κέ ποθι Ζεὺς δῷσι διαπραθέειν τόδε ἄστυ.

> but do now let her go to the god, as soon as you can.
> We Achaeans shall here repay you threefold and fourfold,
> if Zeus to us ever grant this city's destruction.

The effect would be intolerably weak: a mere proposal and a pious wish. But, as it is, our impression is a different one. The plain, business-like content of the passage is given life by two successive enjambments that mark time's widening range. The present moment reverberates beyond itself. We have realization rather than statement.

Wherever a sense of hope or fear is implicit in the present, it tends to spill out into the next verse which gives it fuller contour. Compare the enjambment in Il.1.340, 509; 2.97; 3.411; 4.415; 5.224, 316; 6. 526; 8.535; 9.242, 244; 12.122; 15.427; 16.81; 20.426; Od.2.33; 4.34; 6.273; 8.241; 9.16–17.

There is a similar motivation where the enjambment marks a shift of focus in space rather than time. Take the passage in which Briseis is led away, Il.1.348 ff.:

> ἡ δ' ἀέκουσ' ἅμα τοῖσι γυνὴ κίεν· αὐτὰρ Ἀχιλλεὺς
> δακρύσας ἑτάρων ἄφαρ ἕζετο νόσφι λιασθείς,
> θῖν' ἐφ' ἁλὸς πολιῆς, ὁρόων ἐπ' ἀπείρονα πόντον.

> unwilling with them the woman went. And Achilles
> in tears away from his friends sat forthwith, far withdrawn

on the bank of the foaming sea, gazing over the infinite waters. Through the enjambment, the scene spaces out while still contained within the same human moment. It is important, in this respect, that Briseis and Achilles should find their places in the same line: Briseis departing and Achilles left to himself are part and parcel of the same picture. Achilles thus stands at the verse's edge. There is suspense; there is tension. What can he do at this point? The broken sentence craves a further opening—where else but in a solitary spot, a long gaze over the whole scenery.

The narrative element is thus absorbed into the rhythms of time and place. There are no details or description of emotions except for "unwilling," "in tears"—light touches at one with the visual presentation of the figures. What contributes most to the powerful effect is the interplay of respective positions, the verse-end suspense, the sudden shift of focus, and the consequent integration of scenery and action. The place itself participates in the moment.

The poet's art may be made clearer by examining possible alternatives without enjambment. The departure of Briseis and the reaction of Achilles might have been coupled in such a verse as:

ἡ δ' ἀέκουσα κίεν· νόσφιν δ' Ἀχιλεὺς ἐλιάσθη.

and unwilling she went; aloof did Achilles withdraw.

We should have had two separate acts in one verse, as in ὡς ἔφατ' εὐχόμενος, τοῦ δ' ἔκλυε Φοῖβος Ἀπόλλων [so did he speak in prayer; and him heard Phoebus Apollo, Il.1.43, etc. (see p.30)]. But the acts of "speaking" and "hearing" are inevitable parts of the same process and thus constitute one moment in one verse; whereas in our passage the going away of Briseis and Achilles' withdrawal are incidental to the narrative. The suggested alternative would thus give a false unnatural effect. It would present, as a self-produced necessary connection, what is really a free narrative development, to which only the enjambment can confer any inner cogency.

Let us try to recompose the contents in separate self-contained verses, for instance:

ἡ δ' ἅμα τοῖς ἀέκουσα   γυνὴ κίε δάκρυ χέουσα.

ἀχνύμενος δ' Ἀχιλεὺς ἑτάρων ἀπάνευθ' ἐλιάσθη,

ἕζετο δ' αὖτ' ἐπὶ θῖν', ὁρόων ἐπ' ἀπείρονα πόντον.

with them unwilling the woman went shedding tears;

Achilles, grieving, away withdrew from his friends,

and he sat on the shore, looking over the infinite sea.

We should indeed have self-contained verses, but hardly presenting us with the rhythm of self-contained unfolding moments—unlike τὼ δ' ἀέκοντε βάτην παρὰ θῖν' ἁλὸς ἀτρυγέτοιο [both unwilling they went by the shore of the unvintaged sea], where we realize movement covering its ground. No, the tenor would be that of reporting successive incidents. We might continue indefinitely in this vein, adding any episode that may seem fitting. Achilles' gaze over the sea would become a casual detail or a realistic touch here. And, in such conditions, the verse should lack, of course, its intrinsic modulation.

We often find such verse-endings as αὐτὰρ Ἀχιλλεύς, αὐτὰρ Ὀδυσσεύς [and Achilles, and Odysseus] bringing out, in many ways, a new development that intimately grows out of what precedes without breaking the integrity of the moment. Compare especially Il.9.628; 16.124, 220; 21.520; 24.3; Od.5.370; 7.81; 8.83, 264, 367, 521; 13.367; 16.177; 18.394; 19.209, 388.

SPATIAL ENCROACHMENT OF FOCUS UPON FOCUS

We sometimes have opposition rather than juxtaposition; things are successively seen in contrasting perspectives, and then several enjambments often follow one another. Such is mostly the case in the battle-scenes, for here body is pitted against body, there is blow and counter-blow; one space continually intrudes on the opposite space. Our first superficial impression is one of confusion, but the confusion is illusory. There is no arbitrary effect. Excitement and turmoil remain quite implicit. The opposing tensions receive their necessary measure, and the verse maintains a sense of balance that sways one way and the other. On the other hand, the moment of the encounter is strenuously prolonged over the points of enjambment.

Consider Il.13.160 ff. Here Meriones strikes at Deiphobus' shield:

> τῆς δ' οὔ τι διήλασεν, ἀλλὰ πολὺ πρὶν
> ἐν καυλῷ ἐάγη δολιχὸν δόρυ· Δηΐφοβος δὲ
> ἀσπίδα ταυρείην σχέθ' ἀπὸ ἕο, δεῖσε δὲ θυμῷ
> ἔγχος Μηριόναο δαΐφρονος· αὐτὰρ ὅ γ' ἥρως
> ἂψ' ἑτάρων εἰς ἔθνος ἐχάζετο.

> and pierced it not, but well before that,
> the tall spear broke in the shaft; and Deiphobus then
> away from himself held the bull-shield, he feared at heart
> the spear of brave Meriones; and he, that hero
> drew back to the throng of his friends.

Taking each verse by itself, we see in turn (a) a blow falling short, its failure left in suspense; (b) a broken spear and a standing figure at the further edge; (c) the same figure parrying the blow and fearing; (d) the broken spear and, again at the edge, the spearmen about to withdraw. Now Deiphobus, now Meriones stand in suspense at the verse-end; a broken spear, and a shield share the field of vision with a human figure.

Each verse is a fragment that craves completion, like the detached slab of a bas-relief; and the sentences, on the other hand, can only compose the scene as a whole through enjambment, by making their way beyond the boundaries of the verse. For the interlacing of bodies in action, compare especially Il.13.527 ff; 16.319 ff., 335 ff., 477 ff; 17.304 ff; 20.278 ff. The ebb-and-flow of battle continually drives a figure toward the edge of the verse, in the imminence of a further blow: Il.4.489; 5.38, 308; 6. 63, 65; 8.158, 268, 324; 11.91, 153, 216, 497; 13.396, 528, 615, 618; 14.409; 15.434, 688; 16.116, 289, 307, 319, 321, 337, 359, 401, 413, 579; 17.277, 306, 580; 20.395, 474, 497; 21.144; 22.35. Or what stands out is a weapon: 4.448; 5.66; 6.10; 7.260; 11.377; 12.184, 404; 13.507, 519, 651; 14.451,. or, similarly a part of the body: 4.525; 11.97; 12.185; 16.349, 740; 17.385.

Why the enjambment in all these cases? Consider again the passage just quoted above and imagine how we might render its contents in smooth self-contained verse, for instance:

He pierced not the shield, he failed well before he could do it.
For in its shaft his spear was suddenly shattered:
Deiphobus parried the blow, holding against it his shield:
deprived of his spear, brave Meriones withdrew.

Such verses, if they can be called verses, would be quite devoid of energy. Or we might render the contents discursively, in prose: "Meriones struck with his spear, but was checked by the shield which Deiphobus was holding firmly against the fearful blow coming upon him. As a result Meriones' spear was shattered, and the hero was obliged to withdraw"; we would then have mere description and comment. In neither case could justice be done to the suspense within the movement, to the climax and anti-climax of the action. Homer's enjambment implies what we might wish to emphasize with adventitious remarks.

We are shown how Homer looks at the battle. We have a continuous interdependence of opposing figures. Respective focus can never be forgotten. The sense of position is just as strong as that of action. There is point and counterpoint rather than comparative description, stroke and counter-stroke rather than relative strength and weakness. Thus, in our passage, it is not so much a question of Meriones and Deiphobus as heroes as of the clash itself. These heroes are equally strong. Chance meets chance and a hair's breadth wins the day. It is a matter of where and when—a point which the enjambment often brings out. The rhetoric of battle, on the other hand, would rather emphasize a hero's special valor—a sort of emphasis that appears alien to Homer.

RELATION OF THE PARTS TO THE WHOLE

This kind of enjambment may be seen at work within the same object of representation. Such is especially the case in presenting a human or animal body whose parts appear to have each a life of its own and they concur to a general effect. Intimate contiguity and resulting unity of impact are brought out well in Il.16.517 ff:

> ἕλκος μὲν γὰρ ἔχω τόδε καρτερόν, ἀμφὶ δέ μοι χεὶρ
> ὀξείης ὀδύνῃσιν ἐλήλαται, οὐδέ μοι αἷμα
> τερσῆναι δύναται, βαρύθει δέ μοι ὦμος ὑπ' αὐτοῦ.
> a strong wound here I have, and my arm
> through and through by sharp pains is pierced, nor my blood
> can be stanched, weighed down is my shoulder under the
> impact.

(cf. 10.83 ff; 15.607 ff; 19.365 ff; Od.10.496 ff.) Glaucus, in this passage, presents his wound as a state that encompasses him from point to point. At the verse-ends the arm, and the blood are points of both suspense and connection, articulating the process down to the effect of the burdening shoulder. The enjambment, as always, singles out a detail and draws it all at once into a larger movement. We thus have a moment that prolongs itself from verse to verse, remaining one and the same through its distinctive phases. Any sharp sensation has this effect: as it increases in intensity, it expands beyond any single recognizable point.

The enjambment here highlights a part or aspect of the body. The suffering is dramatized. The pain itself is a happening and the affected part is the field upon which it takes place. If single end-stopped verses had been used respectively for arm, blood and shoulder, we would have had a mere series of symptoms. If, on the other hand, we had been given a more general description, we would have missed the sense of the moment. Suppose Glaucus said, "I have a wound in my arm; I bleed; I am sick. . . .": his words would have been pathetic, but nerveless.

There is a similar forcefulness when Ajax says (Il. 13.78 ff.):

> οὕτω νῦν καὶ ἐμοὶ περὶ δουρὶ χεῖρες ἄαπτοι
> μαιμῶσιν, καὶ μοι μένος ὦρορε, νέρθε δὲ ποσσίν
> ἔσσυμαι . . .
> even to me round the spear my irresistible hands
> are raging, my might is astir, down below on my feet
> I rush along . . .

One pulse of energy runs through these verses, but this energy is no formless excess: hands and feet give it contour by occurring at the point of enjambment. For the verse-ends are points of focus which this energetic flow must reach and overcome, lest it dissipate into vague exuberance. Each verse is like a space within the body—one space drawn into the other and thus constituting one moment of self-assertion. Compare similar instances in Il.7.21; 11.811–13; 22.451–53; Od.4.704–5 (=Il.17.695–6); 19.471.

Or consider cases in which an inner organ, (heart, spirit) stands in similar position, as when Achilles is incensed by Agamemnon (Il.1.188 ff.):

ὡς φάτο· Πηλεΐωνι δ' ἄχος γένετ', ἐν δέ οἱ ἦτορ
στήθεσσιν λασίοισι διάνδιχα μερμήριξεν.

so he spoke; grief rose in Achilles, within him his heart
in his shaggy breast wavered one way and the other.

Achilles' grief cannot be contained, and his heart stands out at the verse-end checking the outburst whilst letting it spill into the next verse. Even the mind becomes space: first there is room for the rising grief or anger, and then for the wavering heart. The enjambment marks the tension with which these separate parts melt into each other, constituting one quivering moment.

Remarkable though they are, such instances only bring out more fully the poet's normal form of expression. (cf. Il.1.103; 14.38; 16.162; 19.319, 21.542, 571; 22.169, 288; Od.4.539, 548; 6.155; 7.82; 10. 497 (= 4.539); 19.516; 23.85)

In rendering human or animal states of being, the idea of a body and its parts is seldom absent in Homer. Note the function of limb or inner organ in the examples quoted above. It would not have been like Homer to say of Achilles, "he grieved, he was angry, he wavered" or to let Ajax cry out, "I am excited, I rush, I am carried away." Homer does not normally have any series of coordinated verbs loosely running on from verse to verse. He must let some concrete feature intervene somewhere, and this often happens at the point of enjambment. Points of sensuous focus emerge at the edges, stemming the narrative flow and yet injecting it with fresh physical energy.

Through the enjambment disparate things are kept in chime. A narrative segment becomes configuration: removed from surrounding incident and circumstance, it unfolds and takes place on its own strength. We have a framing design that arises spontaneously from the material; a moment that cannot be contained within one verse is given its breathing space.

BROADER CONFIGURATIONS

At times we find a much wider field of vision. Even an indefinite space can be given form through the interplay of focal points that stand out near and far. Take Il.4.423 ff:

ὡς δ' ὅτ' ἐν αἰγιαλῷ πολυηχέϊ κῦμα θαλάσσης

ὄρνυτ' ἐπασσύτερον Ζεφύρου ὕπο κινήσαντος·
πόντῳ μέν τε πρῶτα κορύσσεται, αὐτὰρ ἔπειτα
χέρσῳ ῥηγνύμενον μέγαλα βρέμει, ἀμφὶ δέ τ' ἄκρας
κυρτὸν ἐὸν κορυφοῦται, ἀποπτύει δ' ἁλὸς ἄχνην.
as when on the echoing shore the waves of the sea
rise one after the other under the spur of the Westwind;
far out at sea does a wave first crest, and thereafter
it breaks on the land with great roar, and round the headlands
swelling it arches itself, and spews forth the foam of the brine.

(cf. 2.144 ff., 209 ff., 394 ff.; 9.4ff; 13.795 ff.; 15.381 ff.) A movement running to and fro from verse to verse touches upon scattered points and gathers them into one vision. Our eye turns from the wave to the dry-land and then to the projecting rocks, finally returning to the wave as it breaks into spewing foam. The enjambments contribute to the effect by marking the transitions: see how the wave is first held in momentary suspense before we watch it driven by the wind, how again it is checked for an instant before it roars on the land, how at last the outlying rocks at once constitute the edge of the verse and of the scenery. Description is transformed into dramatic interplay. Separate features and separate successive acts are made to participate in one moment. Motion, sound and place respond to one another and hold the picture in one encompassing wholeness. The unifying impact is so strong that it strains the language accordingly: κῦμα is both one wave and many, the adjective ἐπασσύτερον [one after the other] is irregularly used in the singular. It is as if the same wave were seen immediately present, then emerging out at sea, and finally breaking on distant rocks. We have a poetic logic; disparate elements are one simultaneous happening. May we not recognize here our own impression of a seascape: the moving surf, birds flying, a ship sailing—all making sense as aspects of a vivid present?

On a grander scale, the enjambments bring out an interpenetration of the elements in Od.5.291 ff. (cf. 9.67.ff; 12.313 ff.):

ὣς εἰπὼν σύναγεν νεφέλας, ἐτάραξε δὲ πόντον
χερσὶ τρίαιναν ἑλών· πάσας δ' ὀρόθυνεν ἀέλλας
παντοίων ἀνέμων, σὺν δὲ νεφέεσσι κάλυψε
γαῖαν ὁμοῦ καὶ πόντον· ὀρώρει δ' οὐρανόθεν νύξ.
So he spoke and assembled the clouds, stirred up the sea
in his hands taking the trident, and roused all the blasts
of all the winds, and he encompassed with clouds
at once the earth and the waters; night arose from the sky.

Here it is the god Poseidon that causes the storm; but from the poetic point of view, the action of the god has no other purpose than to bring together the various phenomena: a stroke of the hand touches matter into motion. He stirs, he rouses, he encompasses: each active transitive verb comes near the verse-end and spills its effect on the next line. Mighty natural forces intermix as easily as simple act joins act; and the enjambments maintain the sense of a developing contour to which the descent of night confers its conclusion.

These configurations of natural phenomena, for all their sweeping breadth, are kept in focus through the interplay of enjambments that check the movement of the verse at an ultimate point of intensity and make it spill into the next phase. The way Homer presents the state of wounded Glaucus (see p. 44) is similar; the hero's body is a field of action upon which sharp pain encroaches. His arm, his blood, are marked off by the enjambment as spots where the moment of suffering must dwell before encompassing the whole person; and the effect of the burdening shoulder is not unlike the descent of night in the storm scene quoted above. The moment grows upon us from point to point, remaining one and the same.

ACTION AND ITS SPACE THROUGH ENJAMBMENT

We have seen how nothing is mentioned or described in Homer unless brought out by a present moment. This observation also applies to any general view of things—scenery, a crowd, a battle—for we always find, in such cases, a strong sense of movement or position. Things are seen converging, diverging or taking place in respect to one another. Rather than mere description we have drama, interplay, relation; there is a suggestion of a whole and its parts, a point of focus and a periphery. Here, again, the enjambments mark spatial transitions from spot to spot, designing a frame upon which each verse-end impinges and thus pressing the occurrence in a different direction. Take Il.12.177 ff:

πάντῃ γὰρ περὶ τεῖχος ὀρώρει θεσπιδαὲς πῦρ
λάϊνον· Ἀργεῖοι δὲ καὶ ἀχνύμενοί περ ἀνάγκῃ
νηῶν ἠμύνοντο· θεοὶ δ' ἀκαχήατο θυμὸν
πάντες, ὅσοι Δαναοῖσι μάχης ἐπιτάρροθοι ἦσαν.

all over round the wall a god-kindled fire had risen
in a rain of stones; and the Achaeans in their grief were
                                              perforce
defending their ships; and the gods at heart were distressed,
all who took side with the Danaans.

(cf. ibid. 35 ff.; 13.339 ff.; 15.312 ff.; 19.362 ff.). Even here we may, again, admire the plain absence of description. There are three poles (the wall, the Achaeans, the gods) and through enjambment they interpenetrate one another. The picture emerges spontaneously through related actions and states of being which the verse and the enjambment enclose within a contour. We might have expected, in this general view, some abundance of detail and the atmosphere of the struggle. But no, a concentric composition is sufficient. Place and action cohere. There is one animated space from heaven to earth. This effect would surely be lost if we had an account of the opposing forces.

RESONANCES

The enjambment may also mark a repercussion that goes its own way, beyond the space of the verse. The repercussion is at one with what precedes. If I say "he cried out, and his voice resounded far away," the voice is part and parcel of the crying. In the second sentence, we have a repercussion, and not a different occurrence joined, however intimately, with the preceding one.

This kind of bond is common, we have seen, in end-stopped verses that contain two sentences (see p. 30). Relevant here is a verse such as Il.12.338: τόσσος γὰρ κτύπος ἦεν, ἀϋτὴ δ' οὐρανὸν ἷκε [such was the uproar, and the war-cry reached up to the sky]. But the sense of repercussion may develop on its own account and bring us beyond the boundaries of the verse, as in Il.2.333 (cf. 16.276):

ὣς ἔφατ', Ἀργεῖοι δὲ μέγ' ἴαχον, ἀμφὶ δὲ νῆες
σμερδαλέον κονάβησαν ἀϋσάντων ὑπ' Ἀχαιῶν.
so he spoke, and the Achaeans cried out, and the ships all
                                                                    around
in fearful fashion reechoed at the voice of the Achaeans.

Arising from the enjambment, the second verse mirrors throughout its length the expanding wave of sound, and the echo acquires greater relief than the original cry. Compare the glitter of bronze (11.44; 4.431; 10.143), the clang of armor (21.254; 13.497), a cloud of dust (2.150; 23.265), a perfume (Od.5.59, cf. Il.14.173-4).

We still have, in such cases, a spatial enjambment: a tense moment is given its breathing space, and its effect spreads abroad. But the space is now absorbed into an aspect of what is happening—a repercussion, a sound, a perfume. The effect introduced by the enjambment may thus take greater relief than the occasion from which it originates. Homer naturally elicits the implicit force of occurrences, and this force forthwith finds its own way of manifesting itself. We thus find similes that follow directly upon the first term of comparison and, through enjambment, start from within a certain verse, expanding into the next one—as in Il.2.394 "and the Achaeans roared as when a wave/ high upon a bank. . . ." (cf.3.151; 4.130, 482).

More often, however, the effect comes as a culmination that closes the verse. One or more enjambments precede, a flow of occurrences or conditions run into one another and are crowned by a final touch. Thus Od.6.43–5 renders the abode of the gods:

οὔτ' ἀνέμοισι τινάσσεται, οὔτε ποτ' ὄμβρῳ
δεύεται οὔτε χιὼν ἐπιπίλναται, ἀλλὰ μάλ' αἴθρη
πέπταται ἀνέφελος, λευκὴ δ' ἐπιδέδρομεν αἴγλη.

neither by winds is it shaken or storms,
no rain or snow ever comes, but broadly the heavens
spread out without cloud, a radiant glow runs all over.

Compare such verse-ends as "and a shining calm was around" (10.94), "and a roar comes up from the sea" (Il.2.210), "and the whole field resounds" (ibid. 463), "and a light is seen from afar" (ibid. 456), "and the earth ran with blood" (4.451).

Homeric enjambment is symptomatic of Homeric poetry: that time-pulse or sense of focus which is characteristic of end-stopped verses is seen operating on a wider range. A feeling of unison always binds an occurrence with its immediate circumstance. We hardly find it elsewhere. What in Homer is eventuality becomes an abstracted impression in others. This is the reason why there is a non-Homeric ring about, say, Apollonius Rhodius 3.749–50:

οὐδὲ κυνῶν ὑλακὴ ἔτ' ἀνὰ πτόλιν, οὐ θρόος ἦεν
ἠχήεις · σιγῇ δὲ μελαινομένην ἔχεν ὀρφνην.

there was no barking of dogs through the city, no sound
with its echo; silence held the blackening night.

or Virgil, Ecl. 1.82–3:

et iam summa procul villarum culmina fumant
maioresque cadunt altis de montibus umbrae.
even now far away the tops of the houses are smoking
and down from the heights of the mountains are falling the
                                                    lengthening shadows.

Apollonius' lines dramatize Medea's solitude on the eve of her bringing help to Jason; those of Virgil come after an invitation to take rest at the end of the day. There is no immediate, necessary connection with the context. The night or evening scenery tends to constitute a descriptive theme. Such a leisurely manner is unlike Homer. His ease always conceals an underlying movement and tension: sentence leans upon sentence and verse upon verse through a sympathetic contact that sets things in motion. There is always a resonance from point to point; and the enjambments here considered do no more than bring it into greater evidence.

RUN-OVER WORDS

A particular kind of enjambment is presented by so-called run-over words. It again implies extension in time or space, but here the extension is confined to a single point—no more than an accentuation or pause that introduces us further ahead.

A "run-over" word starts a new verse, but belongs grammatically to the preceding one which, however, is already complete in itself. The initial οὐλομένην in Il.1.2 is such a word, agreeing with the previous Μῆνιν and again picking it up:

Μῆνιν ἄειδε, θεά, Πηληϊάδεω Ἀχιλῆος
οὐλομένην, ἣ μυρί' Ἀχαιοῖς ἄλγε' ἔθηκε.
Sing, o goddess, the wrath of Pelides Achilles—
that ruinous (or accursed) one which caused infinite woes to
the Achaeans.

Why the run-over word? We cannot merely say that it is "connective." For any word is connective, but it must also have a more concrete quality besides the obvious function of "connecting." Indeed no such connection is necessary here: we could simply have a relative sentence, for example, ἣ γὰρ δή ποτε μυρί' Ἀχαιοῖς ἄλγε' ἔθηκε [which indeed caused infinite pains]. Nor can we say that the word is emphatic, for the gravity of the wrath is sufficiently explained and such an exclamatory interruption would ring hollow.

What stands out is a renewed sense of presence—a concrete, image-making function. Placed where it is, the word οὐλομένην is at once a reverberation and a new overture. The relative and other sentences that follow are indeed impressive in themselves, but they develop and extend what is implicit already, being foreshadowed by the preceding image. We have the sense of a mighty event gaining ground. The wrath inhabits our imagination, even before we learn its antecedents.

It is typical of Homer to have a run-over adjective followed, as it is here, by a relative sentence. Anything can be so portrayed: Il.2.112, 309, 325; 3.387; 4.106; 5.63, 88, 126, 403, 457, 735, 739; 6.13, 290, 314; 7.220; 8. 177; 9.19, 124, 129; 10.44, 293; 11.33; 12.5, 464; 13.398, 440; 14.172, 220, 349; 15. 705; 19.383; 21. 401; 22. 323; 24. 341, 449; Od.4.228; 5.45. 323; 7.235; 8.373, 448; 9.197; 14.226,521; 19.18; 21.391; 23.17; 24.3.

The run-over word, in these instances, displaces the relative sentence, driving it further along the line and injecting it with its weight. We have both objectivity of focus and relative detail. What stands out is a prolonged presence of the thing itself and not a thin descriptive qualification. In Il.5.735 (8.386), for instance:

πέπλον μὲν κατέχευεν ἑανὸν πατρὸς ἐπ οὔδει
ποικίλον, ὃν ῥ' αὐτὴ ποιήσατο καὶ κάμε χερσίν.

she dropped on her father's floor her delicate robe
many-colored one, which she had made and wrought with her
hands.

the run-over adjective with its sequence ("many-colored, which . . .") upholds the robe-image—an effect that would be lost if we simply had "the robe which she made and richly embroidered" (e.g., ὃν ῥ' αὐτὴ κάμε χερσίν ἔπασσέ τε ποικίλα πολλά). As it is, we have a more concrete rendering. The workmanship of Athena is not additional information, but part and parcel of the robe.

This quality of run-over words may be better appreciated by comparing examples in which they do not occur. Verses that start with a relative have quite a different tone. They explain rather than portray, or they contain some informative detail that may be taken for granted: Il.1.64 "a soothsayer. . . /who might tell us why Apollo is so angry," ibid.70: "Kalkhas . . . / who knew present and past and future" (cf. 162, 258, 321). Hence, verses starting with a relative are most frequent in catalogues (as in the *Catalogue of Ships* or the *Nekuia*). We miss, in these cases, the sense of a qualifying detail that emanates from the thing itself, rather than resulting from the narrative.

We similarly find causative sentences following a run-over word. In Il.5.835–9 Athena pulls Sthenelos down from his chariot and mounts it herself by the side of Diomedes:

μέγα δ' ἔβραχε φήγινος ἄξων
βριθοσύνῃ· δεινὴν γὰρ ἄγεν θεὸν ἄνδρα τ' ἄριστον.

and loud did it rattle, the axle of oak
under the weight; for it carried the dread goddess and the
strongest of men.

The massive run-over word βριθοσύνη again summons up the presence of the goddess; and the inroad of the chariot draws force from the impact. A more regular construction would have missed the point for example, βεβρίθει γὰρ ἄγων δεινὴν θεὸν ἄνδρα τ' ἄριστον [for it was weighed down in carrying the goddess]. We would merely have had an explanation of the occurrence. But, as it is, we have the occurrence itself and its sudden pressure.

With similar directness, a causative particle (γάρ, ἐπεί) often follows a run-over word (Il.1.9, 12, 63, 114, 342). And again (as in the

case of relative sentences) those verses that start out with a causal
sentence usually let us dwell upon a reason; they justify, generalize,
expound, or point to something beyond the immediate. Such is the case
in Il.1.54–6:

τῇ δεκατῃ δ' ἀγορήνδε καλέσσατο λαὸν Ἀχιλλεύς·
τῷ γὰρ ἐπὶ φρεσὶ θῆκε θεὰ λευκώλενος Ἥρη·
κήδετο γὰρ Δαναῶν, ὅτι ῥα θνῄσκοντας ὁρᾶτο.

on the tenth day did Achilles assemble the people;
for she put the thought in his mind, the goddess Hera
                                                              white-armed,
for she cared for the Danaans, in that she saw them dying.

(cf. ibid. 80, 152, 154, 177, 260). The position of γὰρ here determines
the tone and significance of the verse. Where the particle occurs
initially, we have a moment of thought that conditions the statement;
where it comes later, the idea of causality is integrated to the occasion
itself and, if (as often), a stop follows, the cause is rendered as a dying
fall that concludes the verse. Two different modes of perception prompt
two different types of verse. It is a question of rhythm rather than
syntax.

In most cases, however, there is no need of any relative or causal
sentence. The run-over word produces suspense, and the next step
comes dramatically—as in Il.4.496–7 (15.574):

στῆ δὲ μάλ' ἐγγὺς ἰὼν καὶ ἀκόντισε δουρὶ φαεινῷ
ἀμφὶ ἓ παπτήνας· ὑπὸ δὲ Τρῶες κεκάδοντο.

and he stood coming close, and threw with his shining spear,
glancing around him; thereunder the Trojans retreated.

"Glancing around him": where or why is the hero looking around him?
Why do we have this run-over phrase? It is superfluous from a strictly
narrative viewpoint, but it highlights the hero's figure and position so that
the retreating Trojans and all the rest are a foil to his presence. For other
similarly used participles, compare: Il.5.330; 6.509, 514; 7.61, 272;
11.571, 811.

Any striking connotation can thus find its place. In Il.1.14–15:

στέμματ' ἔχων ἐν χερσὶν ἑκηβόλου Ἀπόλλωνος
χρυσέῳ ἀνὰ σκήπτρῳ, καὶ λίσσετο πάντας Ἀχαιούς.

holding up in his hands the wreath of far-shooting Apollo,
upon his golden staff, and all the Achaeans did he implore.

The run-over phrase "upon his golden staff" has an essential resonance,
though it is not literally necessary. The fact that the priest is holding the
wreath of the god is further realized in a sort of after-glow, so that the
subsequent act of prayer comes under its impact. The priest's apparel
blends with his appeal. This immediacy would be lost if we had a more
detailed description; it would also be lost if one sentence ran through the

whole verse—for example, αὐτίκα δ' ἐν μέσσοισιν ἐλίσσετο πάντας
Ἀχαιούς [and at once in their midst he besought all the Achaeans].

A run-over word often suggests more than it explains or describes.
It always implies some basic existential link by simply occurring where it
does—at the crucial point where one verse has just faded away and the
next one is about to begin. So positioned, it looks backward and
forward. We are given pause. There is at times a kind of suspense that
suggests the pathos of the occasion. In Il.11.356 (5.310), for instance:

στῆ δὲ γνὺξ ἐριπὼν καὶ ἐρείσατο χειρὶ παχείῃ
γαίης· ἀμφὶ δὲ ὄσσε κελαινὴ νὺξ ἐκάλυψε.
still staying up he sank on his knees, he leaned with strong hand
on the earth, and dark night encompassed his eyes.

the run-over word γαίης [on the earth] evokes once more the hero's hold
on this earth, before a death-like swoon blanks him out. It is as if the
verse itself reached out for a last breathing space. Compare the sense of
death in 13.544; 17.478; 22.435. Or take Il.1.51–2:

αὐτὰρ ἔπειτ' αὐτοῖσι βέλος ἐχεπευκὲς ἐφιεὶς
βάλλ'· αἰεὶ δὲ πυραὶ νεκύων καίοντο θαμειαί.
and then launching upon them the sharp-piercing arrows
he struck, and ever the pyres were burning one next to the
                                                                    other.

We need not give an unnecessary emphasis to the run-over βάλλ' [he
struck], but the word's position dramatically opens up a desolate view in
the grave cadence of the verse. No such effect would be possible if we
had separate sentences in separate verses as in e.g. αὐτὰρ ἔπειτ'
αὐτοῖσι βέλος ἐχεπευκὲς ἐφῆκε,/ αἰεὶ δ' αὖτε πυραὶ νεκύων καίοντο
θαμειαί [and then upon them the sharp-piercing arrows he launched,/
and ever there the pyres were burning one next to the other].

There is a like sense of helpless finality in other verses that similarly
come to a full stop after a run-over word. Such is the case in Il.17.196–7,
dealing with Peleus and his arms:

ὁ δ' ἄρα ᾧ παιδὶ ὄπασσε
γηράς· ἀλλ' οὐχ υἱὸς ἐν ἔντεσι πατρὸς ἐγήρα.
and to his son did he give them
grown old; but in them his son grew not old.

(cf. 5.157–8; 6.240–1, 457–8; 8.64–5) Presented in the same way is the
pathetic brittleness of shadows that flutter around Tiresias in Hades,
Od.10.495:

τῷ καὶ τεθνηῶτι νόον πόρε Περσεφόνεια
οἴῳ πεπνῦσθαι· τοὶ δὲ σκιαὶ ἀΐσσουσι.
to him even dead Persephone granted his senses—

he alone inspired; the others phantom-like flutter.

These shades of meaning cannot, of course, be deliberate. They rise from the very rhythm and construction of the sentences. For there is a spontaneous interplay of positions and points of focus; there is, in other words, the logic of things. Look at a solitary shape against a vaguer background, listen to a deep-pitched note followed by a lighter sequence, and you will have something of the same impression as that given by a run-over word at the head of the verse. It is as if Homer's style was fashioned to bring out a moment of stress and its resonance: thus a verse leads us to a run-over word and its echo. Here we have basic conditions of perception, transitions and harmonies which the poet appropriates into his art.

Or look at the matter in terms of an unfolding thought: there are advances, stops, and resumptions. When any particular thing is developed into a theme of thought, we cannot lose hold of it and we may often return to it, as if starting anew: "to die, to sleep,/ to sleep, perchance to dream." It is not usual to bring out such repetitions ("anaphora") explicitly, but the possibility is always there. Compare in Homer Il.21.157–8 (2.849–50):

αὐτὰρ ἐμοὶ γενεὴ ἐξ Ἀξιοῦ εὐρὺ ῥέοντος,

Ἀξιοῦ, ὃς κάλλιστον ὕδωρ ἐπὶ γαῖαν ἵησι.

as for me, my lineage is from Axios broad-flowing,

Axios, that upon earth sheds the most beautiful water.

(cf. Il.6.154, 396; 7.138; 21.86; Od.1.51) The repeated name, if nothing else, further embodies the thought of the river: how much weaker would have been such a verse as ὃς ποταμῶν κάλλιστος ὕδωρ ἐπὶ γαῖαν ἵησι [which, fairest of streams, sheds its water on earth]. The preceding verse leaves its echo behind. There is resonance in a name.

VERSE-FILLING NAMES

We are so tuned to the sense of a present moment in Homeric verse that even made up of mere names and epithets a verse affects us with the same kind of tune. Take Il.5.628–9:

Τληπόλεμον δ' Ἡρακλεΐδην, ἠΰν τε μέγαν τε

ὦρσεν ἐπ' ἀντιθέῳ Σαρπηδόνι μοῖρα κραταιή.

Tlepolemos-son-of-Herakles, the great and mighty,

him against godlike Sarpedon stirred powerful Fate.

Suddenly the figure of Tlepolemos, in the accusative, is presented as object of imminent action, and we are held in suspense (cf. ibid. 49; 10.3; 15.576; 23.35; Od.23.153).

Elsewhere, the verse-filling name is subject of the action that follows in the next verse as in Il.7.13:

Γλαῦκος δ' Ἱππολόχοιο πάϊς, Λυκίων ἀγὸς ἀνδρῶν,
Ἰφίνοον βάλε δουρί.
Glaucus-son-of-Hippolochus, of the Lycians the leader
struck Iphinoos with his spear.
Make a long pause at the verse-end, give the verse its full vocal value;
and "Glaucus" will no longer be a mere name, but a hero's presence, a
body poised for action. The whole verse will ring with anticipation (cf.
6.5; 12.182; 13.701; 14.442; 16.593). We find more than one name in
3.136; 6.119; 7.58; 8.333; 11.833; 16.760; Od.4.280; 7. 231; 15.301; 23.
297.

Or two names in different cases, subject and object, fill the verse,
portending what one hero does to the other, as in Il. 5.76: Εὐρύπυλος δ'
Εὐαιμονίδης Ὑψήνορα δῖον. This effect cannot be rendered in
English. The syntax and the rhythm of the verse are a prelude to what is
coming (cf. 6.203, 216; 7.311; 9.590; 12.387; 15.419; 16.358, 463;
17.312; Od.3.279). A most notable example is Il.5.1:
ἔνθ' αὖ Τυδεΐδη Διομήδεϊ Παλλὰς Ἀθήνη
δῶκε μένος καὶ θάρσος.
then to Tydeides Diomedes Pallas Athena
gave might and courage.
The first verse, again, is fraught with implicit meaning. Not only it
highlights the presence of hero and goddess side by side, but it intimates
the closest relation and communion between them—a sort of affinity that
is going to be a central theme in this part of the poem.

Why is any character named with such fullness and prominence?
These name-filled verses often signal a new start against the preceding
background. Tlepolemus is presented all at once after mentioning the
general plight (5.627), Glaucus after Hector and Paris as a pair (6.1–12),
and Athena and Diomedes after the engagements of the preceding book.
There is always, in any case, a sense of resumption that immediately
blends with the forward looking rhythm of the verse. What thus stands
out is a sense of position at a certain point, not the relative importance of
a character. Why is it that Paris is often mentioned with a full verse,
αὐτὰρ Ἀλέξανδρος, Ἑλένης πόσις ἠϋκόμοιο [and Alexander the
husband of Helen fair-tressed, cf. Il.11.369, 505; 8.82; 3.329]? It is not
because of any special merit. The reason is, rather, a striking occasion:
his arrow-shot breaks the regular flow of encounters, his initiatives are
one-sided and conspicuous. The verse marks a vantage-ground, not a
celebration. We are shown once more where Homer's interest lies: in a
sense of the immediate, not in the need to honor especially this or that
hero.

Elsewhere, a proper name with a mention of place constitutes the verse, and the verb (often a verb of rest) comes in the next one, as in Il.3.230–31:

'Ιδομενεὺς δ' ἑτέρωθεν ἐνὶ Κρήτεσσι θεὸς ὣς
ἕστηκ', ἀμφὶ δέ μιν Κρητῶν ἀγοὶ ἠγερέθονται.
on the other side Idomeneus like a god in the midst of the
                                                           Cretans
stands out; and around him Crete's chieftains are gathered.

Again isolate the verse, making a pause where it ends: we have a vivid presence, a commanding image;   then comes, as expected, the overlapping verb "stands out" which in turn conditions the sequel "they are gathered around him."   A spontaneous movement composes the scene, producing a clear forceful outline which would not have been possible if we took a merely descriptive view of the contents, saying for instance: "Idomeneus is on the other side, standing out like a god." It is essentially the rhythm and the enjambment that are responsible for this unfolding visualization (cf. Il.12.1; 7.113; 16.700; 17.665; 23.59; Od.7.321; 18.239).   Or with a mere pronoun: Il.12.131; 7.229, 296.

Such is the inner energy of the verse that the sense of action is intrinsic to it, even if there is no verb, not even a verb coming in the next verse through enjambment.   In Il. 4.253, for instance, 'Ιδομενεὺς μὲν ἐνὶ προμάχοις, συΐ εἴκελος ἀλκήν [Idomeneus in the midst of the foremost like a boar in his strength] there is no need to supply a verb, no need to posit an anacolouthon: Idomeneus' stance or action is implicit in the sense of position that blends with the very movement of the verse (cf. Il.8.261 ff.; 11.56, 833; Od.11.606 ff.).

It is quite a different effect when the name-filled verse follows—as in Il.1.489:

αὐτὰρ ὁ μήνιε νηυσὶ παρήμενος ὠκυπόροισι
διογενὴς Πηλῆος υἱός, πόδας ὠκὺς 'Αχιλλεύς.
he indulged his wrath as he sat by the fast-sailing ships
the god-born son of Peleus swift-footed Achilles.

The hero's presence unfolds majestically in the second verse, but here it suggests rest, not imminent action (cf. ibid. 556; 7.325; 5.721; Od.10.136–7; 11.85; 20.388).   Such finality of touch is most evident in Od.6.17: Athena enters Nausicaa's chamber

ᾧ ἔνι κούρη
κοιμᾶτ' ἀθανάτῃσι φυὴν καὶ εἶδος ὁμοίη
Ναυσικάα, θυγάτηρ μεγαλήτορος 'Αλκινόοιο.
                              wherein the girl
was resting like to the immortals in shape and looks

Nausicaa the daughter of Alcinous the great-hearted.
Repeat the last verse paying attention to its expansive name-giving resonance. This final effect is one of perfect stillness and composure.

Compare the role of a final noun-epithet phrase in end-stopped verses—how the rhythm of the verse comes to rest in the solidity of a character's name (see p. 23 ff). But now this function of a noun-epithet phrase extends to a whole verse. The same effect obtains on a larger scale: two or more verses trace the same arching rhythm, which each single verse rehearses in its own limited way. Consider Od.11.6 ff. (12.148 ff.):

ἡμῖν δ' αὖ μετόπισθε νεὸς κυανοπρῴροιο
ἵκμενον οὖρον ἵει πλησίστιον ἐσθλὸν ἑταῖρον
Κίρκη ἐϋπλόκαμος δεινὴ θεὸς αὐδήεσσα.
and to us on the wake of the dark-prowed ship
she sent a driving sail-swelling wind, an excellent friend,
Circe of the lovely tresses, the dread many-voiced goddess.

And, side by side with this passage, also consider Il.1.479 (cf. Od.2.420) τοῖσιν δ' ἵκμενον οὖρον ἵει ἑκάεργες 'Απόλλων [to us a driving wind did he send, far-shooting Apollo]. There is, in both cases, the same inevitable sequence: a spot out at sea, a speeding wind, a presiding agent. The ampler version expands what is implicit in the narrower one, as if any single colon of an end-stopped verse could produce, on its own strength, another self-standing verse. The amplification is a spontaneous one. Incidents seem inscribed in the rhythm of things before they become narrative details.

Whether the name-filled verse follows or precedes, whether it anticipates what is imminent or resumes what is just past, it always suggests some vital activity, and mere names vibrate with the fluid sense of an adjacent verb. Such is the case even where name-filled verses follow one another as objects of a verb. In Il.13.4 ff., for instance, Zeus turns his gaze far and wide "looking at the land of the horse-tending Thracians/and the close-fighting Mysians and the bright Hippemolgi/drinkers of milk, and the Abians most righteous of men." We are made to feel that these people are brought into the picture by the divine gaze cast upon them. Similarly, in the battle-scenes, are the names of victims struck by a hero's blow (Il.8.274 ff.; 16.694 ff.; Cf. Il.1.263 ff.; 13.92 ff.). There is always the sense of a range that widens, subsides, and comes to a stop.

Homer never presents us with a static list of names. In the *Catalogue of Ships* people and their leaders are always presented in the act of sailing, coming, or arriving; and the names with their epithets arrest images in movement. Most notable in this respect are the names of cities or countries, as in Il.2.496 ff.: "those that inhabited Hyria and

Aulis-the rocky/ and Skhoinos and Scolos and many-ridged Eteonos/and
Thespia and Grais and broad-spaced Mycalessos." It is the fact of
"inhabiting" that summons up the name-filled verses. We are made to
realize that there was life in all these places. Each verse adds to the
sense of an inhabited world and a wide-spread civilization.

ENJAMBMENT IN SUBORDINATE SENTENCES

A quality of Homeric enjambment is to highlight a subordinate
sentence by letting it fill a separate verse. In Il.1.19, for instance, "may
the gods grant it to you . . . / to conquer the city of Priam and make a fair
return," the action of conquering and returning is made to appear as
hanging by itself in the future; it is not the mere object of the governing
verb. Or, read a few lines later (27) "may I never find you again by the
hollow ships/ either loitering now or returning hereafter": the participial
clause acquires a certain independence and sharpness of contour.

This kind of enjambment is of course very frequent: Il.1.23, 60, 77,
151, 171. It is indeed so frequent that it is hardly noticeable, but it
greatly contributes to the sense of perspective in time and space. The
purely syntactic construction appears relieved of its mechanical
dimension and takes a greater transparency. The verse itself comes into
play here, regulating the sequence of sentences and assigning to each its
place and timing.

Here we may single out some notable instances in which the
enjambment of a subordinate sentence marks a shift of focus in time or
space. These instances differ from those studied earlier (see p. 39 ff.).
Here we do not pass from one thing to another; the same act or state of
being persists from verse to verse, but it is suddenly seen from a different
point of view.

I shall list these instances according to the syntax of the subordinate
sentences:

A) *Final Sentences*
Consider Il.5.690–91:

> ἀλλὰ παρήϊξεν, λελιημένος ὄφρα τάχιστα
> ὤσαιτ' Ἀργείους.
> But he swept by in an urge that most swiftly
> he might repel the Achaeans.

The verse-end ὄφρα τάχιστα [that most swiftly] brings the purpose to
the verge of being realized. There is suspense. The point of enjambment
is like the point at which we again take breath in pursuing the same effort
(cf. 4.465; 9.621; 13.326; 18.344; Od.1.85; 3.421; 4.473, 737; 6.32, 289;
15.293).

Or, the time thus envisaged is further removed into the future—as in Il.2.2–5 (cf. 1.509, 558):

Δία δ' οὐκ ἔχε νήδυμς ὕπνος,
ἀλλ' ὅ γε μερμήριζε κατὰ φρένα ὡς 'Αχιλῆα
τιμήσῃ, ὀλέσῃ δὲ πολέας ἐπὶ νηυσὶν 'Αχαιῶν.

but on Zeus no sweet sleep could come,
but in his mind he revolved how to Achilles
he might do honor and destroy many a man by the ships of the
Achaeans.

The hero's name gives us pause at the verse-end, and forthwith the thought branches off into what will ensue. It is interesting that the famous plan of Zeus—a central theme of the Iliad—should be so expressed as a moment's thought that through enjambment spills into the next verse.

We find a more intimate strain in Od.18.160ff. (cf. ibid. 347; 20.80). Athena inspires Penelope:

μνηστήρεσσι φανῆναι ὅπως πετάσειε μάλιστα
θυμὸν μνηστήρων . . .

before the suitors to appear, most utterly to open up
their heart's desire . . .

The enjambment is essential to the situation as it spontaneously unfolds. It integrates the appearing of Penelope with the emotions it stirs up. A crowning moment spills out from verse to verse. One might expand at length on the plan of Athena, the desire of the suitors or the state of Penelope; but these things are only lightly touched upon, merged with the effect of the enjambment. It would be quite unlike Homer to say "wishing to stir up the suitors, Athena had Penelope appear before them." Even Athena's influence is no more than a way to make the situation immediately palpable. If, on the other hand, it had been a question of Penelope's own initiative, explanations would have been necessary. As it is, we have the event itself with its inner logic. The motivation inextricably blends with the act.

It is characteristic of Homer to render an effect or consequence at one with its cause. He does not abstract a purpose or a plan, but he sees it all at once in the actuality of what is happening. Resolution goes hand in hand with action. Hence comes the frequency of enjambment in the sentences that denote purpose (cf. Il.1.118; 5.2; 6.230, 357; 7.79, 334; 8.110; 9.257; 12.390; 15.232; 16.524; 19.173, 231; 22.342, 443; 24.680; Od.1.88; 4.294; 6.218; 9.16; 12.333; 14.45; 16.25; 17.6; 20.80). In all such instances, the enjambment implies a further purport within the same representational frame. The sense of purpose shades off into that of time and vice versa. Note how the frequent conjunction ὄφρα means both "until" and "in order that."

These expressions of purpose are symptomatic of a pervasive Homeric quality, for we do not find in Homer any explanatory introduction or summing up. Any full-blown event bears in itself the suggestion of why it happens and whither it is leading. Such a trend is even mirrored in the configuration of the plot. The initial scenes of the Iliad and the Odyssey are in themselves prophetic of the final dé-nouement.

B) *Temporal Sentences*
The conjunction "when" often introduces enjambment at a critical juncture in time. Thus Achilles, when about to rejoin the battle, says (Il.18.114–6, cf. 22.365–6):

νῦν δ' εἶμ', ὄφρα φίλης κεφαλῆς ὀλετῆρα κιχείω,
Ἕκτορα· κῆρα δ' ἐγὼ τότε δέξομαι, ὁππότε κεν δὴ
Ζεὺς ἐθέλῃ τελέσαι ἠδ' ἀθάνατοι θεοὶ ἄλλοι.

I shall go now and come on the killer of the man I most
                                                                        loved—
on Hector; my doom I shall then receive when indeed
Zeus shall bring it about and all the gods along with him.

This "when" tells us of time running out, before the eternal dispensations of the gods set in. In all such cases there is, more or less, the sense of a turning point before the outcome is reached (cf. Il.1.163, 242; 3.173; 4.229, 351; 6.454; 9.702; 13.817; 14.504; 16.62; 19.295; Od.3.237; 8.342, 444; 11.375; 16.11; 18.252; 19.125, 168; 23.257).

"Until" has a similar effect. In Il.7.376–78(=395–97) Priam proposes a truce:

παύσασθαι πολέμοιο δυσηχέος, εἰς ὅ κε νεκροὺς
κήομεν · ὕστερον αὖτε μαχησόμεθ', εἰς ὅ κε δαίμων
ἄμμε διακρίνῃ, δώῃ δ' ἑτέροισί γε νίκην.

to cease from ill-boding war, until the dead
we may bury; thereafter again we shall fight till a god
may part us and grant victory to either side.

The enjambment here projects duration up to some real or imagined solution (cf. Il.5.557; 7.30; 9.48; 12.281; 14.77; 16.840; 21.133, 531; Od.2.99,19.144; 24;134; 7.276, 319; 9.465; 12.420; 13.59; 16.450; 20.20; 21.357; 22.58).

Or, the meaning is rather "as long as." In Il.9.609–10 Achilles declares that, by the ships, he will enjoy his Zeus-given portion:

εἰς ὅ κ' ἀϋτμὴ
ἐν στήθεσσι μένῃ καὶ μοι φίλα γούνατ' ὀρώρῃ.

                                                                        as long as breath
abides in my chest and my knees have power to move.

The enjambment gives us the sense of a term that expires, but the interim is filled with life. The idea of time would not have been so forcible, if Achilles had just said: "as long as I am alive" (cf. Od.3.353; 17.390).

The difference between enjambment and the lack of it is especially brought out with verbs of waiting. In Od. 11.152–3 Odysseus awaits his mother's shade. He says:

αὐτὰρ ἐγὼν αὐτοῦ μένον ἔμπεδον, ὄφρ' ἐπὶ μήτηρ
ἤλυθε.
Right there did I steadfastly stay, till my mother
came.

The sense of waiting is concrete here—a state existing on its own account and not merely in terms of what is expected. To wait is to stay, remain, abide: we do not forget the actual vantage ground upon which we stand and the moment that finally dawns upon it (cf. ibid.351; 6.295;.9.138; Il.4.334; 7.415). On the other hand, the lack of enjambment conveys a mere waiting for something to happen, as in Il.9.191 δέγμενος Αἰακίδην, ὁπότε λήξειεν ἀείδων [waiting for Achilles to finish his singing, cf. 18.524; 2.794; Od.20.386].

Quite generally a temporal phrase without enjambment is much more factual: "when they came" (Il.2.432; 3.15), "remember when" (Il.15.18; 21.396), "the day when" (Il.2.743, 189), "whenever" (Il. 1.80; 15.207). The temporal sentence here initiates the verse or, in any case, remains contained within it. These differences of meaning are a question of rhythm rather than syntax or vocabulary. Homer's verse naturally brings out the time-value of the action.

C) *Relative Sentences*

Enjambment tends to occur where the relative sentence has a dramatic bearing on its subject and projects his, or her, life into other times. Thus Andromache tells Hector (Il.6.407–9):

οὐδ' ἐλεαίρεις
παῖδα τε νηπίαχον καὶ ἔμ' ἄμμορον, ἥ τάχα χήρη
σεῦ ἔσομαι.
nor do you pity
the infant child and me hapless who soon a widow
away from you shall remain.

The shifts of focus open up, in the last verse, to the terrible eventualities of an imminent future. The word "widow" at the verse-end seems to cry out, and the truncated relative sentence presses to be completed. It is as though, through the enjambment, the future were already contained in the present moment. We would obviously miss this force of expression if there were no enjambment—if the verse ended, for instance, with ἥν σύ

γε λείπεις [whom you abandon].   See other striking examples in
ibid.452; 1.505; 10.88; 14.85; 16.460; 22.60; 24.85, 204; Od.2.48.
    Or consider, in Il.22.431–3, Hecuba crying over Hector:
        τέκνον, ἐγὼ δειλή· τί νυ βείομαι αἰνὰ παθοῦσα,
        σεῦ ἀποτεθνηῶτος; ὅ μοι νύκτας τε καὶ ἦμαρ
        εὐχωλὴ κατὰ ἄστυ πελέσκεο.
        O my child, woe is me, wherefore shall I live in this pain
        you being dead—you who each night and day
        were my glory in the city.
Why is the enjambment so effective?   It lets the past flow into the
desolate present (cf. 24.729, 744).
    The death of any hero may similarly prompt the mention of his past
and again, the enjambment of a relative sentence adds a particular
poignancy—as in Il.4.474, where Ajax strikes down Simoeisios "whom
once his mother/on her way down from Ida on the banks of Simois/ gave
birth to" (6.21;7.9; 5.612).   There is, of course, no such effect in 16.175
where a catalogue of Myrmidons mentions Menesthios "whom the
daughter of Peleus fair Polydore begot" (cf. 11.222 ff.; 17.78).
    A sense of strong attachment rooted in the past seems to favor this
kind of enjambment.   In Il.17.583 we have Phainops "who above all
strangers/ was dear to Hector" (cf.5.325, 535; 9.521; 15.438).   Such is the
case in rendering the relation between a god and a favorite mortal.   Most
notably, in Il.15.254 ff., Apollo cries out to Hector:
        θάρσει νῦν· τοῖόν τοι ἀοσσητῆρα Κρονίων
        ἐξ Ἴδης προέηκε παρεστάμεναι καὶ ἀμύνειν,
        Φοῖβον Ἀπόλλωνα χρυσάορον, ὅς σε πάρος περ
        ῥύομ', ὁμῶς αὐτόν τε καὶ αἰπεινὸν πτολίεθρν.
        Have courage now; such a helper to you did Zeus
        send forth down from Ida to assist and defend you—
        even Apollo gold-sworded—me, who ever before
        am out to save you—both you and your lofty city.
(cf.1.86; 10.278; 23.782; Od.13.300)
    More generally, this kind of enjambment may be appreciated in
contrast with examples that lack it.   For it gives to the relative sentence
the sense of a condition, a plight, a state that is pertinently typical quite
apart from the narrative.   Thus, in Il.2.293 ff., Odysseus sympathizes
with the Achaeans who desire to return home "for he grieves away from
his wife, any man whom the storms/ keep back"; and in 14.198 Hera
asks Aphrodite "give me love and desire with which/ you subdue gods
and men."   In both cases, however different they are from each other, we
are removed into the world at large.   Hence such an enjambment is
frequent in similes such as in Il.3.151: "like cicadas that through the for-

est/. . . shed their beautiful voice"; and in 5.5: "like the star that most bright/shines dipped in the waters of Ocean." In reference to a hero, some endowment will generically stand out, as when Calkhas fears Agamemnon, "that man who over all the Achaeans/holds high sway." Whereas the absence of enjambment denotes a purely factual characterization (cf. p. 51), these instances carry us beyond a mere fact or circumstance, bestowing upon the relative sentence a particular strain and wider range. Though less incisively than in the instances quoted earlier, a sense of other times and places comes into the picture (compare Il.1.234, 238; 3.61; 5.522, 525; 9.74, 553; 10.184; 12.146, 226, 228, 445; 13.103, 390; 15.80; 16.353, 483, 514, 752; 17.164; 19.259; 21.464; Od.2.124; 9.107, 110; 11.200; 12.39; 13.213, 336; 14.3; 15.359; 21.68).

No list of examples, however, can here do justice to Homer's art. The only way is to read at length, paying attention to how far each verse is self-contained, how far it looks backward and forward. It is a matter of degree rather than clear-cut definition. There is the self-sustained lingering of an act, there is at the same time connection or development. Now the one and then the other prevails. Homer's rectilinear style is never a mere addition of fact to fact; we are always kept in chime with the inner pulse of what is happening.

The enjambments of subordinate sentences give us a cue. Whenever a sense of hope or fear is implicit in the present, it tends to spill out into the next verse. Even a delineation of static objects may be given a forward tension: we find, in Od.2.342, wine-jars "against the wall in a row, if ever Odysseus/ should return" (cf. ibid.351; 1.115). The enjambment is expected, natural; and yet its effect is surprising—as when a vague anticipation suddenly seems to be on the verge of realization.

Syntactical classifications are hardly adequate here. What we might term as a conditional or final clause is quite absorbed into the passage from verse to verse. The enjambment gives it a different ring. Such verse-ends as "if ever," and "if perchance" remove us from any particular syntactical acceptation here, enhancing the pure sense of time: what was an undercurrent comes out into the open and implicit possibilities loom ahead (cf. Il.1.340; 2.97; 4.415, 224; 6.526; 12.122).

Homer's enjambment of subordinate sentences ought to be seen in these basic terms. Any act or state worth mentioning either finds its point of focus in one verse or breaks beyond it on the strength of an inner tension. In the latter case, we do not have any particular deliberate effect, but we are shown how moments swell with a sense of destination and actions are prolonged by an inner purpose.

CONNECTIONS OF THOUGHT

Generally in poetry we often find an enjambment or run-over phrase prompted by the need to emphasize an idea or bring out a pure transition of thought. Such is the case, for instance, in Virgil, Aen. 1.25–27:

> necdum etiam causae irarum saevique dolores
> exciderant animo; manet alta mente repostum
> iudicium Paridis.

> nor had the cause of her wrath and bitter grief
> as yet subsided; there stays deep-rooted in her mind
> the judgment of Paris.

Or such is Milton, *Paradise Lost* 1.1–3:

> Of Man's first disobedience and the fruit
> of that forbidden tree whose mortal taste
> brought death.

or (ibid. 65–66):

> Regions of sorrow, doleful shades, where peace
> and rest can never dwell.

In such instances, any sense of time or space is absorbed into mental configurations: the passage from one thing to another is prompted by affinities or contrasts of meaning, not by diverging or converging movements. Such thoughts may indeed constitute in turn an imaginary world of their own, but we do not find the immediate concrete sense of here and there or now and then. Hence comes a tone that is unlike Homer. The suspense between verse and verse is like that of a verdict. The gravity of an issue supplants the tension of an act.

We may wonder whether the Homeric poems present examples of a similar kind. Homer is certainly capable of dealing with concepts and ideas, but the question is whether he so mentions them as to constitute a climax at the verse-end and let their implications spill over in pure transitions of thought. We should hardly expect this to be the case. It is, at least, unusual. For in Homer even a thought or an idea must have its way of happening and manifesting itself somewhere, somewhen. It must have, therefore, its concrete setting, dramatic incidence, and its point or moment of friction.

Take Il.1.167–8, Achilles saying to Agamemnon:

> σοὶ τὸ γέρας πολὺ μεῖζον, ἐγὼ δ' ὀλίγον τε φίλον τε
> ἔρχομ' ἔχων ἐπὶ νῆας.

> To you goes the far greater meed, while I with what little is
> > mine
> go back to my ships.

See how the contrast between the two is expressed in terms of place and movement: Agamemnon lords it in his domain, while Achilles withdraws to the ships, and the enjambment, as frequently, underlines a shift of focus. We might have expected a direct contrast between Agamemnon's greed and Achilles' forbearance. But no: the sense of concrete visualization was too strong. It is true that a few lines earlier (149) Achilles voices his full-blown moral indignation: ὤ μοι, ἀναιδείην ἐπιειμένε, κερδαλεόφρον [alas, o you in shamelessness clothed, o gain-minded man], but again we fall short of any emphatic abstraction that might be prolonged into the next lines. Through the vocative all judgment is immediately embodied, transfused into the actual presence of a man.

Or consider Il.9.628–9. The mission to persuade Achilles having failed, Ajax counsels to give up and return to the waiting Achaeans:

οἵ που νῦν ἕαται ποτιδέγμενοι· αὐτὰρ Ἀχιλλεὺς
ἄγριον ἐν στήθεσσι θέτο μεγαλήτορα θυμόν.

there do they sit as they wait, but Achilles
has set to cruelty the pride of spirit within him.

The anxiety of the Achaeans is presented by their sitting in expectation, the cruelty of Achilles by his aloofness. The verse-end αὐτὰρ Ἀχιλλεὺς [but Achilles] that so often marks a shift of focus in place or time (cf. p. 42), is enough here to highlight the extent of a moral dilemma. This concrete sense of mutual positions often implies a polarity of attitudes (cf. Il.1.282, 318; 9.301; 11.664; Od.1.55).

Impassioned speech always involves swift transitions from thought to thought; but these transitions must have, in Homer, their foothold on some real occasion and thus lead us from verse to verse through the very fact of covering their ground or occurring in their time-span. Thus, in Il.24.33, Apollo cries out:

σχέτλιοί ἐστε, θεοί, δηλήμονες· οὔ νύ ποθ' ὑμῖν
Ἕκτωρ μηρί ' ἔκηε...

You are cruel, o gods, full of harm. Did not ever to you
Hector make sacrifice?

We are on high ground here: the harshness of the gods in contrast with a man's piety. We might expect some moral or religious idea at the verse-end (e.g., οὐ χάρις ὑμῖν, οὐ θέμις ἥδε): but what prompts the enjambment is simply a shifting time-perspective. In many other ways a spatial or temporal enjambment adds poignancy to what would otherwise be a mere contrast of opposites. Thus Patroclus' shade says to Achilles: "never more shall we counsel together, but my doom/ my dreadful doom gapes around me" (Il.23.78); Hector says to Paris: "the people are fighting and dying; it is for your sake that the battle/ is aflame all round the city" (6.328); and Agamemnon tells the Achaeans: "our wives and

children wait for us back at home, and our task/ just lags unfinished"
(2.137). Compare for instance, 24.66; 2.297, 342; 15.553.

There is little room in Homer for digressive abstractions. The
closest we get to an abstracting enjambment is perhaps Il.3.43–5, where
Hector taunts Paris:

ἦ που καγχαλόωσι κάρη κομόωντες Ἀχαιοί,

φάντες ἀριστῆα πρόμον ἔμμεναι, οὕνεκα καλὸν

εἶδος ἔπ', ἀλλ' οὐκ ἔστι βίη φρεσὶν οὐδέ τις ἀλκή.

Indeed they must be laughing the long-haired Achaeans
deeming a prince is their champion, because a beauteous
shape is upon him, but no strength in his midriff nor courage.

The exceptional position of καλὸν agreeing with εἶδος in the next line
opposes the beauty of Paris to his weakness. But even here we do not
have a full abstraction. Homer does not say κάλλος [beauty]. The word
εἶδος denotes an aspect of the body. The swift transition from looks to
midriff does not let us get away from the hero's actual presence.
Compare the enjambment of ἴς [force] in Il.12.320, and νόημα [thought]
in 24.40.

Does not the *Odyssey*, rather than the *Iliad*, present us with
connections of thought emphasizing ideas and moral values? We might
think that such is the case, for in the *Odyssey* localities that are far apart
come into play. Different periods of time are borne in mind, perspectives
lengthen, and hopes extend into an indefinite future. Memory colors the
past with old loves and loyalties, and emotions solidify into ideals
through a sense of faithfulness, constancy, and belief.

All the same, the poet's mode of expression remains essentially the
same. It reveals itself capable of bringing into focus even what is
elusively removed from the present; and the same kind of enjambment
prevails. Take Od.19.363 ff: Euryclea is about to wash the old beggar
and exclaims:

ὤ μοι ἐγὼ σέο, τέκνον, ἀμήχανος· ἦ σε περὶ Ζεὺς

ἀνθρώπων ἔχθαιρε θεουδέα θυμόν ἔχοντα.

Ah me most helpless, o child, for your sake; upon you did
                                                                          Zeus
        most of all cast his hate—you endowed with a god-fearing
                                                                          spirit.

Again, we have an imponderable antinomy: punishment and innocence.
And there is also, to boot, the idea of Odysseus' past life. But Euryclea's
apostrophe resolves this complexity by simply exposing what is now and
what went before in their concrete relation with each other. Zeus, at the
verse-end, holds us in momentary suspense as easily as in the battle-
scenes of the *Iliad*, a warrior or a weapon that is about to deal a deadly

blow (cf.15.449; 16.337, 460 etc.), except this is a different sort of blow reaching back into the past.

A few lines later (367–8), still addressing an imaginary Odysseus, Euryclea recalls his offerings to Zeus:

ἀρώμενος ἦος ἵκοιο
γῆράς τε λιπαρὸν θρέψαιό τε φαίδιμον υἱόν.

praying that you might come
to rich old age and rear your bright-looking son.

The enjambment here is literally the same as many in the *Iliad* (see p. 58 ff.), but it suggests a lifetime: what is immediate purpose there is indefinite hope here.

Or consider Penelope's solitary grief. It is treated dramatically, never made into a theme of discourse. But when presented in itself as an engrossing experience, it is set in intimate connection with some concrete incident or object that, through enjambment, projects its significance into indefinite time. Thus, hearing Phemius' song about Troy, Penelope tells him (Od.1.340–2):

ταύτης δ' ἀποπαύε' ἀοιδῆς
λυγρῆς, ἥ τέ μοι αἰεὶ ἐνὶ στήθεσσι φίλον κῆρ
τείρει.

but cease now from this song,
the woeful song that does ever the heart within me
consume.

The song and its echo here become an embodiment of time.

Elsewhere, in resignation, she retires to her chambers saying (17.102–4; 19.595–7):

λέξομαι εἰς εὐνήν, ἥ μοι στονόεσσα τέτυκται
αἰεὶ δάκρυσ' ἐμοῖσι πεφυρμένη, ἐξ οὗ Ὀδυσσεὺς
οἴχεθ'.

I shall lie down on my bed, a place that is full of my sighs
always soiled with my tears, since the day when Odysseus
departed.

The enjambment internalizes the sense of time, ἐξ οὗ Ὀδυσσεὺς [since Odysseus] is not a mere date: the verse tapering into the name of Odysseus blends his absence and memory with the sense of a deserted spot.

Compare the way Penelope is described to Telemachus by Eumaeus (16.37–39; 11.181–3):

καὶ λίην κείνη γε μένει τετληότι θυμῷ
σοῖσιν ἐνὶ μεγάροισιν· ὀϊζυραὶ δέ οἱ αἰεὶ
φθίνουσιν νύκτες τε καὶ ἤματα δάκρυ χεούσῃ

even too much she resists with steadfast suffering spirit

in your halls; and ever in anguish upon her
vanish the nights and days in the midst of her tears.

Note the singular way in which ὀϊζυραί [woeful, in anguish] at the
verse-end, agrees with νύκτες [nights] in the next line—a sad cadence
forthwith prolonged into indefinite time and filling the spot where
Penelope abides. We have concentrated focus. The enjambment
effectively binds experience with time and place. What stands out is
Penelope's actual presence, not any sublimation of her state.

GENERAL REMARKS

We have been explaining all along that a verse worthy of the name
must always have a certain rhythm that modulates the meaning into a
sense of time; it can never be equated to a merely versified, or metrical,
sentence. We have proof in the cases of enjambment. For an enjambed
verse, by definition, does not coincide with a sentence; it need not make
any grammatical or syntactical sense, but there is one thing it must
convey: a development in time. Again take Od.19.363:

ὤ μοι ἐγὼ σέο, τέκνον, ἀμήχανος· ἦ σε περὶ Ζεὺς . . .
Ah me helpless, o child, for your sake. Zeus most upon you. . .

The cry of despair, the god's name as an agent, and the indication of the
victim ("upon you") summon up suspense and anticipation—the first
inkling of an event not yet expressed, a tense vibration.

Verse adumbrates meanings which a sentence as such cannot
possibly do. Thus the punctuation of ordinary syntax necessarily ignores
the pause or suspense at the verse-end and, conversely, the verse brings
together what a full-stop may separate within its bounds. Here are
distinctions and combinations that lie beyond the pale of narrative or
discourse. While the sentences explain what is happening or what we are
dealing with, each verse in turn occupies us in a different way: we linger
on the self-evidence of things which the verse contains; we are carried
forward by the rhythm and magnetic contiguities of meaning. The verse,
in other words, sharpens our insight into the aspect of a thing or the mode
of an action, without necessarily identifying what that particular action or
thing happens to be. Therefore, in looking at any object, we may notice
zones of low or high relief—zones that do not tell us what that object
literally is (whether, for instance, an animal, a plant or a rock), but afford
insight into form, color, texture, and existence.

Consider, in this respect, passages in which enjambment is
particularly frequent—the battle-scenes, for instance (see p. 42 ff.). The
tale of who wins and who loses easily results from the construction of
sentences and the connection of incidents. More important from a poetic

point of view is the function of verse itself and, especially, enjambment:
what stands out is the poise of bodies facing each other within the space
of the line, the suspense before the clash, and the integration of purpose
to action. We get absorbed into rest and movement or space and time,
not the narrative fortune of the encounter.

These remarks may be applied to poetry quite generally. Take a
passage as far removed from Homer as possible—a passage in Hamlet's
famous soliloquy (3.1.60ff):

> To die, to sleep—
> No more; and say by a sleep we end
> the heart-ache and the thousand natural shocks
> the flesh is heir to. 'Tis a consummation
> devoutly to be wished.

Just as sheer suspense and movement break through the details of a
Homeric battle-scene, so do pulses of thought break through the
argument of whether it is better to live or die. We have in both cases an
effect of verse and enjambment, not of sentence-structure. Let us look at
each verse in this light.

"No more; and say by a sleep we end": the initial "no more" is
rounded off by the final "we end." We have no sentence, but the sense of
finality is driven to an extreme point. Here is absolute standstill, nothing
beyond.

"The heart-ache and the thousand natural shocks": set aside for a
while the fact that this is an object clause to the preceding verb "we end";
let the verse stand out on its own strength in that it renders so forcibly a
basic animal condition. We dwell on ideas, and yet we look ahead: what
are these shocks?

"The flesh is heir to. 'Tis a consummation": separated though they
are by a full-stop, these two phrases are set in intimate connection by
belonging to the same verse. For "The flesh is heir to" makes us think of
what it entails to be born and "consummation" intimates a summing up, a
conclusion, a sense of what life is all about. We forget the literal
meaning required by the sentence: "an outcome to be desired."

To appreciate this passage more clearly, consider different
alternatives. We might easily recompose it into smooth end-stopped
verses, and we would then have a series of flat statements. Or we might
put it into prose through well constructed sentences, and we would have
a thin piece of reasoning. Again, insert into your prose pauses,
interjections, all sorts of realistic touches, and you will have a disordered,
deranged effect. It is the verse that makes the difference, for it provides
the timing. It is, at each turn, a breathing space for thought, curbing the
sentences to its own measure, and sweeping the terms of the argument
into vital moments of apprehension. It hardly matters what the outcome

of the dilemma will be. Throughout Hamlet's speech the contentious points are little more than a fabric upon which the imagination plays. What stands out is the train of thought.

While Hamlet's speech renders a mental process, we mostly find action in Homer, but from opposite ends the two converge. In both, the verse projects into broader vistas what the sentences construe in view of a particular purpose: the very rhythm, for one thing, transforms the contents into an existential beat, inducing us to look at things as points of focus in time and space rather than objects in their specific settings. Hamlet's arguments no less than the proceedings of a Homeric scene become a foil to a sense of presence and transience. But in Homer this effect is far more pervasive. It springs from the very subject-matter: action continually absorbed into moments to which the verse gives their timing.

Chapter 5

Time and Verse

THE SENSE OF TIME IN THE EXPRESSION OF OCCURRENCES

Any sentence or statement more or less conveys a sense of time: we say, or at least imply, that something is, exists, happens, occurs and develops. Even an abstract thought has a way of manifesting itself. A time-element penetrates, however subtly, into anything we think or say. Here we find a vivifying influence. The more we realize it, the stronger is the sense of truth in our mode of expression: things cease to be crystallized and taken for granted; they are brought to the fore by the occasion that gives them life, drawn to participate in the reality of experience, and seem to be made actually present. Any occurrence may thus be felt as really occurring, incisively taking place and expanding. It is as if time sustained its course, whatever the narrative purpose might be.

This sense of time is preeminent in Homer. We have seen how it is highlighted by the very rhythm of his verse. When a verse is self-contained, it marks a developing moment in its beginning, middle and end; when there is enjambment, a complication lets the moment spill into the next verse. We have, in any case, a process: the meaning of the sentence has its timing, it is acted out, and it is presented as an occurrence in the making.

Everywhere in Homer the narrative is actualized. He will not say "the assembly met" or "took place" but "the heralds called out, and swiftly the people assembled"—not "they had their meal" or "they sat at a banquet" but "upon the laid-out victuals they set their hands"—not "they boarded the ship and set out" but "they drew the swift ship into the sea divine"—not "he rose from bed and got ready" but "he put on the soft mantle . . . and under his glistening feet he fastened the beautiful sandals"—not "they made love" but "they took, embedded, the pleasure of love." Compare "he stepped over the threshold" rather than "he entered the house"; "to sail the watery paths" or "move on the sea's broad back" rather than "sail across" or "make a sea-journey." A flowing outline always replaces the fixity of ascertained facts, producing a vivid effect. We have the feeling of something that actually happens taking shape—representation rather than mere statement or report of events.

Or, consider the matter from a different angle. Where occurrences are rendered in their essential flow, there is little room for crystallization or abstraction of general terms. It is remarkable that in a poem like the *Iliad*, there is no term for "army" used in the nominative as a subject of description. For the word στρατός (cf. Il.1.10, 53, 318 etc.) is mostly an accusative in a spatial sense as in: "they reached the wide host of the Achaeans," "he rushed through the host," and "to wander through the host." An army, in other words, is not an institutionalized entity, but something actually reached and visualized, a presence, a teeming space into which someone enters and moves. Similarly the battle is often presented as a force that drifts to and fro: "massively hither and thither the battle swinged through the plain" (Il.6.2, cf.11.216; 12.35; 13.337, 339, etc.). Compare the characteristic Homeric phrase πολέμοιο γεφύρας (Il.4.371, etc.). What are these "passages of war"? However interpreted, they are suggestive in this sense. Thus "to glance over the passages of war" evokes a field of vision and the movement within it— spaces emptied and filled by the throng, men that break resisting barriers and resist in their turn. No wonder advance, retreat, and approach are constantly highlighted. Note those verses that swiftly convey the instant clash: "when they were close, upon one another advancing," "when into one spot, converging, they came," "and they at once turned around and stood in front of the Achaeans." We have the movement itself, not an engagement or encounter taking place.

The ground is cleared of superfluities. It is as if the action created its own space and space had the function of containing the action. Hence, also, there are no abstract futile comments or descriptions. The design is at once simple and decisively significant. Things àre made tangible, palpable. We see what is happening rather than learn about it.

NATURE OF THE RESULTING VIVIDNESS

This Homeric immediacy has always been admired since antiquity. But what does it have to do with any special sense of time, you may object. Do we not have here a talent abundantly found elsewhere? Do we not praise in any author the gift to make things come alive? Here, after all, is a freshness of touch and a vivacity of expression that are prompted by the occasion and realized by any gifted writer or speaker.

Distinctive of Homer is the vast scale on which this talent is made manifest. Here is a form of realization that is not usually sustained for long. What in other authors is a special effect comes in Homer from an encompassing style. Epic poems generally, or novels, have passages that are particularly lively and dramatic, but these passages stand out against the prolixity of a detailed background; however, in Homer it is the foreground that always prevails, everything equally shares its portion of existence as it is brought to the fore in the field of action.

How can we explain this Homeric evenness, this pervasive quality whereby any detail takes a life of its own? From beginning to end there is a sprightly but steady pace. From step to step, a vital pulse keeps us on the same level of realization. There are no highs or lows. If certain scenes stand out for their special pathos, the reason is that they actually take place where they do, not prompted by some intervening inspiration, but by witnessing—as in an interlude—the surrounding action. On the other hand, an unprepared reader might have little taste for the lengthy battle scenes; but not on close inspection. For we never have a stale account of warlike exploits. What absorbs us, through its very recurrence, is the incisiveness of outline—the continuous resilience and abatement, rise and fall, climax and anticlimax. Mirrored here is the ebb-and-flow of life.

How then shall we explain a perfection that is so naturally self-consistent? We could hardly credit Homer with superhuman poetic powers. We may, if anything, highlight the genius of the language or the effectiveness of style. On the other hand, to extol the epic oral tradition means to beg the question by transferring the problem somewhere else, unless we admit that the force of inertia or of habit provides a satisfactory answer. We should take the form of expression at its own face value.

The problem is to find a philosophical reason for Homer's style. We shall not make much advance by simply dwelling on Homer's vividness and illustrating it with countless examples. The question is: what kind of poetic insight lies at the source? For surely here is no mannerism, no empty phraseology. Any vital style must be true to life. The very flow of Homeric narrative reflects the flux of existence.

Homer's vividness or immediacy is due to decisive focus upon a moment of action or rest. Throughout the poems there is an instinctive sense of focus that seizes upon any act or state of being, letting it achieve an instant fullness before passing away. I have amply illustrated this process. Take any verse from the mainstream of the action, for instance, Il.1.6: ἐξ οὗ δὴ τὰ πρῶτα διαστήτην ἐρίσαντε [from the instant when

first they stood asunder in strife], or ibid. 33: ὣς ἔφατ', ἔδδεισεν ὁ'ὁ
γέρων καὶ ἐπείθετο μύθῳ [so he spoke; and he shuddered, the old
man; and followed his word]. The verse highlights a moment and lets it
subside. There is a lingering modulation. The time-element intimately
suffuses a step in the narrative. We have both the occurrence and its
music.

The action is made up of such moments. What sustains it and gives
it life is a continuous sense of time, subtending the succeeding moments.
There is no need to heighten or slow down the tone. There is no need for
any special effect. Quite naturally, the verse-rhythm spells out the
appropriate timing. A throb of life thus inevitably finds its way, quite
apart from any deliberate point.

We may try to imagine the poetic process in its larger range—how
an initial insight proved forceful and pervasive, summoning up its
likeness from occasion to occasion and precipitating the work of composition. There was at the beginning the perception of a vital moment
materializing into imagery—a moment arising, lingering both in its
fullness and lightness, and finding its pertinent dimension in the balance
of the verse. Hence came a communicative stress. The same mode of
perception and expression passed from verse to verse and from scene to
scene. The development of an encompassing style went hand in hand
with the portrayal of the action and the conception of the story.

THE HOMERIC MOMENT

The concept of "moment" may prove useful in trying to account for
Homer's immediacy. How can we render an occurrence simultaneously
conveying the sense of its actually taking place? If, for instance, I simply
say "he walked," I merely give an informative item or detail. If I say "he
walked erect, defiantly, briskly," I let the sense of time be smothered by
description. If I emphasize the time-element and say "he walked for a
while" or "he walked at length," I separate and abstract the idea of time
from the act itself. On the other hand, such a verse as (Il.1.34) βῆ
δ'ἀκέων παρὰ θῖνα πολυφλοίσβοιο θαλάσσης [and in silence he
walked by the shore of the wide-roaring sea] gives us quite a different
effect. The verse itself, with its rhythm carries us along, conveying a
vital space that is one with the act of walking. No descriptive detail
distracts us. The walker, the walk, and the place conspire in unfolding
the moment. For "silent" (ἀκέων) hardly detaches itself from the verb;
and the sea-shore here is no description of place but affords a
magnificent extension and cadence to the advancing act.

The Homeric moment or what we might call a "verse-moment"—
presents us with one single process; one sweep which we apprehend all

at once in its beginning, middle and end. A unity of movement runs through the various articulations. More than one act may be contained in one verse, and yet this unity remains unimpaired. It is the warmth of one encounter that is evoked in the verse ἐν τ' ἄρα οἱ φῦ χειρὶ ἔπος τ' ἔφατ' ἔκ τ' ὀνόμαζε [she clung to his hand and spoke and called him by name (Il.6.253, 406, etc.]; there is the vibration of one shot in λίγξε βιός, νευρὴ δὲ μέγ' ἴαχεν, ἆλτο δ' ὀϊστὸς [the bow twanged and loud rang the string and out leapt the arrow, Il.4.125]; and there is one striking occasion in θάμβησεν δ' Ἀχιλεύς, μετὰ δ' ἐτράπετ', αὐτίκα δ' ἔγνω [amazed was Achilles, he turned, and instantly knew Il.1.199]. In these cases the forthright rhythm integrates the parts into one moment, we have direction rather than narrative detail.

Such a moment can also include any time-span that can immediately be apprehended. It need not be taken literally as the briefest instant. There is the same sense of a moment, say, in the gathering of an assembly, in the advance of an army or in the act of a man's arriving to a certain spot. Complex events are naturally simplified into the beat of one verse.

What matters, in a Homeric moment, is the inner rhythm that makes us realize a materializing impact. There must be movement, but not necessarily a literal movement. For, unless taken for granted, any state of things is what it is through an internal development that sustains it. There is an unfolding meaning, an implicit movement which we identify with a momentary actual duration. Even a state of rest and stillness is given its movement. Take for instance Il.9.190, Πάτροκλος δέ οἱ οἶος ἐναντίος ἧστο σιωπῇ. Achilles, we are told, was singing, "and Patroclus, before him, alone, was sitting in silence." We should not merely read the verse as an additional point of interest in the narrative. Homer tunes us to a different mode. Through the music of the verse, a simple juxtaposition or face-to-face presence gives us pause. Patroclus sits, absorbed in the moment; and his sitting is at once poise, expectation, suspense. This state will abide until interrupted by the arrival of the visitors. We thus have a posture delicately balanced between one event and another; a moment that acquires its fullness before it vanishes.

Much depends on rhythm. The verse just quoted shows it. It coruscates in the middle pause (οἶος) highlighting the hero's solitary presence and it forthwith concludes with a final silence (σιωπῇ). If we had, say, Πάτροκλος δὲ σιωπῇ ἐναντίος ἔζετ' Ἀχιλλεῖ [and Patroclus in silence was sitting in front of Achilles], the verse would fail in this respect: we would have description, not a sense of the developing moment. What we need is both forcefulness of focus and harmony— impact and modulation, energy and nuance. Obviously no mere report of an occurrence, even if metrical, necessarily achieves this effect. If I say "he came to see me and told me," I hardly render the actual incidence of the act, I mainly point out the interest of the occasion. If, on the other hand, I say "he stood before me and said" (cf. Il.12.60; 17.338, etc.), the outline is stronger, more immediate, more concrete; and I give a truer sense of the moment.

There are times when we feel a perfect coincidence of focus, meaning, and rhythm. Something strikes our senses, we give it its breathing space and meaning comes spontaneously—as a realization, not a predetermined notion that is put into words. Verse, at its best, comes closest to this achievement. It tunes us to the moment within the incident. It is as if its rhythm marked the vibration of time—a sense of time that runs through any act or state of being.

EXPECTATION AND FULFILLMENT

A moment so conceived imparts direction. It finds its logic in the quickening and subsiding movement of the verse. If its rhythm is so forceful, the reason is that it relates to nature itself. Thus we breathe in and out, a sound has its echo, a footstep its rise and fall, any effort its point of stress and relaxation. The pulse of life is no other. Art gives this rhythm a self-conscious form, but we all live by it.

The movement of Homer's verse is often so compelling and transparent that we might almost guess the contents even without knowing the literal meaning of the words. Take, for instance, the frequent verse ὡς ἔφατ' οἱ δ' ἄρα τοῦ μάλα μὲν κλύον ἠδ' ἐπίθοντο (Il.7.379; 9.79, etc.). Do not be satisfied with a mere translation: "So he spoke; they heard and obeyed." Give the verse its full sweep and widening range. It takes off briskly with a commanding voice (ὡς ἔφατ '); in the middle the voice fans out, it is heard, it is present (μάλα μὲν κλύον); and finally it imposes itself, it is obeyed (ἠδ' ἐπίθοντο). We have a movement that reaches out and comes to its term, a blow that has its inevitable repercussion. It is as if the verse itself were the field of action, as if a cry ran through it gathering momentum and then vanishing away.

No casual or arbitrary connection of narrative details, even if versified, could achieve this effect. We have an organic quality. For the parts stand in strict natural relation to one another, each word necessitates the next one through a basic affinity of meaning (as "to speak," "to hear," "to obey"), nothing is forced or adventitious, and thus we have an impression of inevitability. But the factual objective meaning needs to be touched into life. Here, rhythm is the catalyst. Suggested by the organic process itself, it holds in balance a vital moment.

A sign of this organic quality is that sense of expectation and fulfillment which I have tried to highlight in Homeric verse. How do we apprehend it? First we have an intimation of what is to come, then a sense of actuality, and finally the gleam of a vanishing contour: a dawning realization and its aftermath. We are predisposed to the poet's mode of perception, for the movement of the verse strikes a sympathetic chord in our very being. Affinities rooted in nature come into play.

This sense of expectation and fulfillment brings us to the heart of the matter. It is quite different from the hypnotizing response to a repeated metrical pattern. Each instance is both unique and typical. Freedom blends with form. We thus know what to expect, though there are possibilities of infinite modification and nuance. We are, on the other hand, in initial suspense, but not from perplexity; this is, rather, the suspense of a growing awareness—as when, say, we perceive the shape of a sea-wave accentuating its developing curve. We thus have both certainty and suspense—a present clarity and a forward tension, a sense of immediacy and also a presentiment. The moment impinges on the solidity of things; they seem relieved of their status to participate in the problematic progress of time.

Homeric verse constantly suggests these ideas. Light at the beginning and graver towards the end, it swells and tapers off. Its sharp sudden start stirs up expectation, and its prolonged close strikes a tone of fulfillment. It makes no difference whether a final noun brings the act to a resonant standstill, a final verb gives vent to a preceding strain, or consecutive verbs flow to an inevitable conclusion. We always have a moment that gathers consistency, a thing drawn to its occasion and effect. Homer says, for instance, "all astir was the throng, and the earth gave a groan underneath" (Il.2.295), "thus from under their feet the dust rose up in a mass" (3.13), "a fire burns . . . and the glow appears from afar" (2.456), and "down sank the sun, and enshadowed were all the streets" (Od.2.388, etc.). We hardly have, in such instances, a connection of cause and effect, but fleeting aspects of the same phenomenon as it emerges and passes away. The verse does not coldly subject one separate fact to another. Its movement lets one phase melt into the next and, while completing itself, it also completes our perception.

Compare the way in which the verse spaces out after an initial "so he (she) spoke," even when there is a strongly negative or hostile reaction on the part of the hearer (Il.1.33, 188, 568, etc.). The moment blossoms out even here. We do not have any abrupt or violent transition within the line, as in Apollonius Rhodius (cf. 3.367, 382, 398). To bring out a retort, Homer starts a new line (Il.1.148, 292, etc.). The verse exerts its sway, checking the abruptness of incident and the looseness of chance.

The general effect is one of intensity and calm at the same time: the urge of necessity goes hand in hand with spontaneous development. For the connections are both natural and forceful. I thus observe a cloud and its shadow (cf. Od.9.68), wind pressing upon the grass (cf. Il.2.148), a splashing wave resounding on the shore (cf. 4.425), a foot and the ground it covers up (cf. 13.18), a hand and the object it holds (cf. 1.219). The verse gives a form to these basic moments. There is a sense of emerging and taking shape. What we dimly expect to hear or see is made into the very stuff of perception and realized as imagery.

Homeric verse stimulates perception. It is not so much a narrative medium as a mode of realization. If we listen to it, we get closer to the actual pulse of vital moments, away from stolid facts and their alleged purport. Where someone is going can be easily ascertained; but the going itself, the moving body, the advancing step and its rhythm never cease giving us pause. Homer's verse taps this mystery. Instance after instance, it extracts a basic keynote. Without any imitative intention and through the same dynamism of form, it does justice to the most disparate things: a wind's blowing, a lion's leap, a hero's onslaught, the sweep of a wave on the shore. The rhythm highlights the same movement everywhere. We are tuned to wider harmonies than any detailed observation might afford.

We have a phenomenon of nature. Consider any momentary physical effort and imagine, as in a curve, the degrees of mounting and dwindling intensity. One degree prefigures the next, without determining it in advance. There is a steady but quivering progress, quite unlike that of a motor-engine. A vital process is at work here: a stress that intensifies before loosening its hold. Verse, and Homeric verse in particular, appropriates this spontaneous rhythm, injecting into a sentence the energy of nature. One word summons up the next through the arching sequence. It is not just a question of syntax and versification. Rhythm exerts a magnetic power in drawing the parts to one another. Sensuous affinities intervene. We divine the drift before we parse the words; and then the literal meaning comes enriched with an existential flavor, as if it emerged from the depth of matter set into motion.

To know and not to know, to wonder; to expect and then reach a crowning conclusion: Homeric verse attunes us to this inward activity. Nothing is more congenial to the mind and the senses. Here, to think is to realize and discover. The way things happen outside us is seen conforming to the direction of our very thought. We get excited by this harmony. It is as if perception were made prophetic. Thus, in a verse of Homer, the opening word is a premonition of the sequence. Time and again the same process is realized: things move and take an inevitable shape, a form arises that meets our own sense of form.

But the effect is reciprocal. If we are stirred to fresh insight, the verse of Homer reveals, on its part, a new transparency. Remote crystallized details of the subject-matter are released of their impenetrability and made into elements of the rhythmic process. What matters is not so much their curiosity as their position, their relative lightness or heaviness in the sustaining flow. What is, for instance, the "four-bossed helmet" which Agamemnon puts on his head in Il.11.41? It suffices that the epithet gives Agamemnon's gesture its appropriate weight.

There is tension and poise even in the most ordinary act. The rhythm gives us the coruscation of what literally occurs: a sense of flight, for instance, rather than a bird that flies. The effect is elusive and shadow-like, but essential. It touches us to the quick, like a familiar intonation that arises above what is being said. In reciting Homeric verse, we similarly experience a thrill of recognition. Our inmost dispositions come into play. It is as if we rehearsed each time the process of coming to be. Thus quite naturally potentialities tend to realization; therefore, in the verse, we have a prelude and high suspense before the final delivery.

The rhythm suggests what the sentence makes explicit: a pent-up energy coming to fruition. Hence everything moves and comes alive. Nothing is mentioned but its occasion brings it to the fore and gives it focus: any act must have its incidence, any step its space, any gesture its reach, any sound its resonance. There are no static facts, but actualizations. As we let the verse pass by, not ours is the interest of the voracious reader. We listen, we visualize. The moment of the verse opens up and lingers in its full clarity—a vantage-ground between what is just past and what lies ahead. Expectation and fulfillment—or potentiality and realization, are only the most obvious aspects. The actual pulse of life comes into play. It affects us more than any outward shock or titillation.

FORMS OF EXPRESSION

Homer's poetic phrases embody the rhythmical qualities of focus and movement: an act is both what it literally is and an occurrence that develops in its own right. For instance, a phrase like, "he spoke wingèd words," at the same time tells us that a character is speaking and does justice to the nature of the utterance itself.

A characteristic of these phrases is the combination of brevity and fullness. They are neither too long nor too short. Their focus naturally requires brevity, while their movement develops into fullness. We are thus as much as possible removed from both flimsiness and verbosity. We touch upon the occasion, but let it linger in its moment. It is as if the intrinsic time-span of the verse is made manifest in the words. Much of Homer's poetic diction could be viewed in this light. We might thus realize a truly poetic reason for many forms of expression that are usually explained away as ornamentation. The word "poetic" is too often used as a mere term of classification; to earmark any idiom that does not normally occur in prose or in ordinary speech.

Take the meaning "he went." We often find the phrase βῆ δ' ἴμεν, βῆ δ' ἰέναι at the beginning of the verse as in Il.17.657: βῆ δ' ἰέναι ὡς τίς τε λέων ἀπὸ μεσσαύλοιο [and he stepped out like a lion out of a steading, cf.15.483; 24.347, etc.]. The initial momentary aorist confers an opening impetus; a sudden spurt, often an absolute sense of movement. Contrast the instances of a final pluperfect, as in Il.13.156: Δηΐφοβος δ' ἐν τοῖσι μέγα φρονέων ἐβεβήκει [Deiphobos among them in high thoughts was going, cf. 6.495, 513, etc.]. The long final pluperfect gives us, instead, the sense of a movement that settles into form. Thus, in the verses just quoted, we see, on one hand, Menelaus hastening as if committed to some fatal mission and, on the other hand, Deiphobus similarly moving but gathered in himself as a prepossessing figure. βῆ δ' ἰέναι is instant motion, and ἐβεβήκει is motion in its composure.

What stands out is the "aspect" of the verb, with its distinction of a momentary or durative or perfective sense. But Homer taps the expressive value of the grammatical form, eliciting a poetic suggestion. Thus, in our instances, the distinction is made palpable according to whether the movement evokes an image or an instant tension; whether it vibrates and vanishes forthwith or we see it taking place in the field of vision. There is, in other words, a quality within the act—a mode of being, a sensuous connotation. We have no such descriptive distinction as, say, between "striding" and "walking." The motion itself is paramount with its degrees of weight and lightness, sharpness and fullness.

These values of expression are exemplified in many other ways. Take again the meaning "he went." Homer similarly brings out its actuality by highlighting the feet, as in Il.15.405: τὸν μὲν ἄρ' ὡς εἰπόντα πόδες φέρον [and he spoke; and his feet bore him away, cf. Od.23.2; 15.555; Il.17.700; 18.148; 5.885; 13.515, 75]. Feet that thus carry the body give us a tangible sense of motion and the concrete active moment.

We also find the knees as agents of mobility (Il.9.610; 11.477; 22.388; 21.302; 6.511), hands that act (Il.13.75; 16.244; 23.627, 587; Od.20.237 = 21.202), and eyes that see (Il.23.477, 463; Od.12.232; Il.17.679; 14.286). Very often an inner organ (θυμός, κῆρ, ἦτορ, κραδίη, φρήν) prompts or localizes an emotion or thought, as in Il.12.407 θυμὸς ἐέλπετο [and his spirit hoped, cf. 1.103, 173, etc.].

Elsewhere the part of the body or the inner organ is not subject, but complement to the verb: "to go with one's feet" (cf. Il.5.745; 13.18, etc.), "to seize or touch with one's hand" (cf. Il.1.210; 3.385, etc.), "to see with one's eyes" (Il.1.587; 3.28, etc.), "to think in one's spirit" (cf. Il.1.193, 256, etc.). These complements are not pleonastic, nor do they have any special point. For instance, in the verse, ὦ πόποι, ἦ μέγα θαῦμα τόδ' ὀφθαλμοῖσιν ὁρῶμαι (Il.13.99, etc.), it is the seeing itself that stands out and we need not translate "I see with my own eyes." Similarly, ἧος ὁ ταῦθ' ὥρμαινε κατὰ φρένα καὶ κατὰ θυμόν [while these things he revolved in his mind and his spirit, Il.1.193, etc.], need not convey any particular intensity: the revolving, the pondering itself has its weight, takes its time and runs its pertinent course (while . . .).

These points of focus remove us from the thin narrative thread. A foot that moves, a hand that touches, a thought that revolves in the midriff—all instances of this kind have no special relevance, they rather impede the forthright drift of discourse. Here the moment is arrested, it turns upon itself, is released from any ulterior purpose, and we have an occurrence in its essence and consequently the expression thickens, it takes a form that maintains itself whatever the outward circumstances may be. Even so, but more elusively, the rhythm of the verse is applicable to all manner of contents.

There is a mode of perception in this style. The very idea of time is affected: experience is dramatized rather than described, central moments replace detailed situations. Take Il.3.33-5:

ὡς δ' ὅτε τίς τε δράκοντα ἰδὼν παλίνορσος ἀπέστη
οὔρεος ἐν βήσσῃς, ὑπό τε τρόμος ἔλλαβε γυῖα,
ἂψ' δ' ἀνεχώρησεν, ὦχρός τε μιν εἷλε παρειάς.

as when a man sees a lion and backward he shrinks
in the dale of a mountain, and a tremor seizes his limbs;
back again he withdraws, and paleness besets his cheeks.

Tremor seizes the limbs, and paleness invades the cheeks: an act or state is rendered as a force, and the verse-end thus brings out a final overwhelming effect. We see the experience materializing on its own account. If we had, say, "he shudders, he panics, he turns pale, he shrieks," the sense of the moment would obviously get diluted into description.

We very frequently find this kind of phrase at the verse-end: "and wonder seized them in seeing" (Il.3.342, etc.), "and pale fear seized them" (Il.7.479, etc.), "and fierce anger seized her" (Il.4.23, etc.), "and sweet desire now takes me" (Il.3.446, cf. Od.22.500, etc.), "reverence holds me as I see" (Od.4.75, etc.). In such instances, a final effect similarly crowns the moment. We have an event and its repercussion. Whether or not a part of the body or inner organ is mentioned, there is a momentary focus; and the form of expression swells, revolving upon itself.

In such a verse as Il.4.79: κὰδ' δ' ἔθοϱ' ἐς μέσσον· θάμβος δ' ἔχεν εἰςοϱόωντας [down she leapt in the middle, and wonder held those who saw], the phrasing reaches the utmost fullness and simplicity all at once. The verse thus acts as a filter. Any addition, it seems, would destroy the directness of the effect; any subtraction would weaken it. There is nothing but an event and its repercussion—a moment that suddenly materializes and fill its space. In other terms, we have a central focus whose influence expands to a certain proportion: if this expansion exceeded its measure, the sense of focus would be lost and if, on the other hand, the expansion were cut short, the focus would be reduced to a mere negligible point. Thus the verse has its vital space. Its limits give body to the inherent fullness. Even so any movement is checked by the measure of its inner energy: there is both a centripetal and centrifugal force, expansion and contraction at the same time.

Just as language, with its words, highlights points of focus out of the mass of existence, so does Homeric verse carry out this process on a more conscious, transparent level. The very narrative is conceived so that it continually comes upon essential moments of existence or activity. Here the verse takes its time to give them a momentary but universal relevance. Familiar things thus arrest the attention, taking their portion of life and experience—things that we might just barely mention or subject to long and tedious description. Homer lets them linger, float in their poetic moment. The treatment is forthright and full. The logic of perception embodied in the verse could not have it otherwise.

How and when are these fuller forms of expression used? A veritable poetic syntax arises from the way they occur wherever their fullness is unimpeded by a supervening construction. We are reminded of the use of epithets (see p. 1).

Consider the meaning "he died." When forthrightly expressed in an independent sentence, it is regularly rendered in such phrases as "death encompassed him" (Il.5.553; 16.502, etc.), "darkness covered his eyes" (4.461, 503, etc.), "the spirit left him" (4.470; 12.386, etc.) and a variety of phrases conveying how the body fell or the ghost sped to Hades (4.504; 5.58; 6.422, etc.). We do not find, on the other hand, the simple indicative "he died" (θάνε, ἔθανε) in this central function, while its other moods occur in subordinate clauses: "let him die," "if you die," "may he not die," (Il.3.102; 4.170; Od.15.359, etc.)[1].

Compare "he fell asleep." We have "Athena shed sleep on his eyes" (Od.5.492), and "upon her eyelids Athena poured sweet sleep" (Od.1.363–4; 20.54; 19.590, etc.). These phrases highlight sleep itself. On the other hand, the verbs of sleeping (εὕδω, δαρθάνω, ἰαύω, ἀωτέω, ἄεσα) refer to sleeping in a certain place. Note Od.7.285–6:

ἐκβὰς ἐν θάμνοισι κατέδραθον, ἀμφὶ δὲ φύλλα
ἠφυσάμην· ὕπνον δὲ θεὸς κατ' ἀπείρονα χεῦεν.

getting out in a thicket I lay; a bedding of leaves
I heaped up; and a god shed upon me infinite sleep.

The verb means no more than "to lie down," but the final phrase, closing the verse, renders the magic effect of sleep.

"He grieved": note "grief came to him" (cf. Il.1.188; Od.21.412, etc.), "grief comes to the heart and spirit" (cf. Il.8.147; 16.516, etc.), "grief encompassed the midriff" (Il.8.124; 17.83), and "a dark cloud of grief encompassed him" (Il.18.22; Od.24.315; Il.17.591). The corresponding verbs (ἄχομαι, ἄχνυμαι, ἀχεύω) are rare except in the participle. They do not normally render the moment of grief; exceptionally, νῦν δ' ἄχομαι [now I grieve] in Od.18.256 =19.129. But we do have θυμὸς. . . ἄχνυται [the spirit grieves] (Od.14.169–70; Il.14.38–39, cf. 6.523–4). The stress of the inner organ is equivalent to that of the feeling itself.

Similarly the spirit or heart hopes, wills, rejoices, and desires; whereas the corresponding verb, when used as direct predicate of the person, seems inadequate to convey the full moment of these emotions. Most notable is a phrase of the type θυμὸς ἐποτρύνει καὶ ἀνώγει [the spirit stirs and commands Il.15.43, cf.8.322; 18.90], that conveys the moment of will and resolution in a way in which the verbs ἐθέλω, βούλομαι could hardly do. Any act entails an intransitive as well as a transitive dimension, it is a present state and not only a sign leading forward. Thus, feeling implies an inner throb as well as a disposition or relation; an act of going is not only motion in a certain direction but also a foot that steps out, its sound, its tread on the ground.

Bruno Snell, in a brilliant book, pointed out how Homer gives prominence to single limbs and inner organs, lacking a general abstract concept of body and mind. But there is, above all, a poetic reason. These organs and parts of the body are points of focus whereby an act or state of being materializes. The moment thus acquires a fleeting fullness, and the very articulations of the verse reflect the phases of the moment. A verse as in Il.5.122:

γυῖα δ' ἔθηκεν ἐλαφρά, πόδας καὶ χεῖρας ὕπερθεν.

and she quickened his limbs—his feet and his hands above.

evinces the sense of swiftness far more effectively than if I said "he
suddenly became swifter," "his body was made nimble." Limbs, feet,
and hands become the sinews of the verse, as if the rhythm were one with
that of a body in swift motion. Nor is it simply a question of the human
or animal frame. We similarly find waves rather than the sea, a
promontory rather than land, a tree rather than a forest, a hall rather than
a house, a ridge or summit rather than a mountain. What stands out is
always a feature or point of focus which some action or state brings to
the fore.

    Are we any closer to understanding the connection between the
sense of time and the use of formulas? There is a time-span in the
rhythmical outline that encompasses the verse, and the resulting moment
tends to condense the expressive material into a formula. There,
recurring formulas keep us in focus; they inject into the verse a perpetual
time-beat that must ever be true to itself. Here is a pure sense of
occurrence and recurrence regardless of any particular topic. Without
these condensations of expression, the point of focus should be lost.
Predicative attributes or parenthetic characterizations and comments
would disrupt the integrity of the moment. But, as it is, the formula or,
rather the persistent sense of form, preserves the pulse of time.
    Or, look at the matter in broader terms. Think of a song and its
tune. The notes of music arise above the narrative or discursive thread.
Their repetitions and developments remove us into a pure sequence of
time, and yet they seem to run in unison with the words. We may read
the words into the music, but it is not necessary. The tune itself may
seem self-sufficient; it pleases us by abstracting from the episodic
contents a fluid quality and carrying us along an emotional flow that is
released from the details of incident and discourse. The coherence of the
music makes up for the narrative variety. Things seem spirited away into
the simplifying flux of existence. On quite a different level and with the
necessary modifications, we may apply a similar reasoning to Homer and
his formulaic language. Homeric rhythm soars above the narrative; but
unlike the case of a song and its tune, it affects the narrative literal
phrases, impressing upon them its form and making them suggestive of
time. What is more or less true of all poetry is compellingly true of
Homer: so pervasive is the rhythm that it transforms the linguistic
material. A sense of time absorbs the narrative as much as possible.
There is a tempo in each verse, each scene and indeed in the composition
as a whole. Here formulas and themes are indispensable. Their
recurrences maintain the time-continuum; or, rather, they emerge from
the way the story is conceived. There is no makeshift chronology, no

rambling tale. The action grows upon us and draws us into its momentum as surely as the succession of night and day. The ever-renewed time-beat suggests identities or analogies of form in the shaping of events or, vice versa, the perception of events in their essence suggests the rhythm of salient moments.

Rather than a repertory of formulas, we have an inborn sense of form that, wherever possible, renders any narrative fact in the outline of a self-contained process. Consider, in this respect, some formulaic verses that are quite different in meaning from one another: "when the early-born rose-fingered dawn appeared," "under the glistening feet he bound the beautiful sandals," "upon the ready-made victuals they laid their hands," "at once speaking out he addressed to him wingèd words." Diverse as they are, what do these examples all have in common? The essential meaning is always bared of adventitious details; the formulas with their epithets enhance the sense of form in what is presented in the moment of an act or actual state of being. It would have been, on the other hand, quite unlike Homer to say, for instance, what the weather was like at the time of dawn, what kind of food the men ate for their meal, to describe a speaker's demeanor while speaking, or specify the garments which any character might be wearing. Such details would obliterate the vivid moment. For the same reason, Homer seldom *describes* a character.

The formulas, on the other hand, would be quite intolerable in any ordinary narrative. It would be ridiculous to say, for instance, "I was waiting for the early-born, rose-fingered dawn to appear" or "I remembered his wingèd words." The vitality of the Homeric formulas comes from the way they are always integrated with a certain moment that opens up and vanishes forthwith, conferring to it solidity in its very transience. Here is a reason why we never weary of them, and their very frequency delights us. They are vivid points of focus for the evolving action, not items of description.

The formulas are thus quite poor in point of descriptive interest, but they are essential as points of striking identity and recognition. They sharply establish the presence of a thing the moment we get into touch with it. This realization is more important than it might seem. It has a gratifying effect: the familiarity of things blends with changing circumstances and even what is most marvellous takes a human dimension. By highlighting a permanent time-beat and form in the very heart of change, Homer accentuates a sense of truth which is common to us all. For any present perception is, unwittingly, loaded with the memory of countless identical perceptions that have preceded it: we contemplate a summer's day and all our past summers are implicit in the present perception. Any sense of freshness or novel excitement comes from the ever renewed context of the inveterate experience, rather than from any new peculiarity we may notice or discover. Things as old as rocks light up at each turn. We might even say that this new vivacity is largely due to the way the newness blends with what has so often been repeated. Something strange or peculiar would not affect us so deeply.

PARATAXIS

Just as moments follow one another, so do sentences. When this correspondence takes shape, the syntax is resolved into a nimble display of immediate, successive representations. Thus, we often find in Homer sequences of short self-contained sentences. Their close juxtaposition is determined by the underlying continuity of time, their brevity is one with the moment they each single out along this continuity. The very form of expression evolves accordingly: we have a fullness of form that cannot be diluted into descriptive length, a brevity that needs its weight in order to be significant.

The coordinative arrangement of sentences in Homer is commonly recognized. "Parataxis," or coordination, is opposed to "hypotaxis," or subordination. Here is an important distinction: on the one hand we have things seen in themselves with a natural implicitness of connection and, on the other, things construed as parts of a greater whole, tracing cause or effect and thus subjected to a superimposed structure. The ancients already drew attention to this distinction. Aristotle and Demetrius pointed to the loosely strung style of the early logographers (λέξις εἰρομένη or, διηρημένη) opposing it to the rounded off periods of the later orators (λέξις κατεστραμμένη).

These categories, however, ought not be applied too literally. Since such distinctions are usually made in historical terms, we are led to believe that an earlier simplicity is followed by later complexity; whereas things do not necessarily conform to this pattern. Moreover, even quite apart from the question of earlier or later, classification tends to become an end in itself. Once a class is established, it is treated as a fact and taken for granted. No further explanation is needed. A thing appears sufficiently accounted for insofar as it lends itself to being classified. Its further individual merits are disregarded. Such is the case of Homer's parataxis. If we ask why Homer so coordinates his sentences, we get a reply that begs the question: parataxis exemplifies a primitive age; it is the style of early epic, the hallmark of oral composition. We thus miss any interest in the *raison d' être* of such a style, any inquiry into the intrinsic quality of so rendering thoughts and events. The reasons adduced are external ones: the condition of the times, the social and cultural milieu. Thus Parry tells us that, as an "oral poet," Homer must necessarily proceed by adding one thing to another, since the urgency of instant performance prevents him from thinking ahead.

As a matter of fact, Homer is quite capable of construing complex hypotactic periods (see especially Il.15.53–64; 22.59–65, 66–71, 111–21; 24.290–5, 582–6; Od.5.33–40; 7.189–96; 16.328–32, 376–82). Such passages warn us against facile assumptions. In any case, a real style is no fixed model. It has a life of its own. It is what it is by realizing its potentialities. We should look at it positively, not negatively—on the strength of its achievements and not in view of what it does not do. If Homer coordinates his sentences, it must be for a vital reason. The question is: on the basis of what expressive value does Homer compose in this way? What elements of the action does he so single out and join one to the other? There is surely a creative principle at work, not a makeshift habit.

What lies at the source is a sense of focus in the sentence. It is not emphasis. It is nothing deliberate. It is, rather, a native capacity to seize the ripe moment and let it extend across the line. A salient incident is thus touched off: it has its rising climax, its vanishing cadence; and points of focus necessarily emerge next to one another, excluding the entanglements of adventitious matter. If any circumstance is mentioned, it is to take place in the main sequence and participate in the forward movement. The process is maintained from sentence to sentence, from verse to verse.

Moments thus presented next to one another produce self-developing creative sequences. The juxtaposition, once started, is seldom arbitrary or just casual and passive. An act is no sooner given its setting than it summons up the next, as if the sequence were inscribed in the very order of things: "he went . . . he arrived . . . he found . . .", "he took . . . he held . . . he carried." What makes such a treatment forcible is the combined effect of sentence and verse. For the sentence conveys a compelling energy of meaning, the verse holds it in momentary suspense; and we thus get the impression that time and action move on at the same tune. Homer's paratactic style is the triumph of pure perception. It signals the act itself and by itself—its irruption in the field of vision, its taking place and shape, and its effect in touching off a sequence of events.

We may wonder at how so simple a style could encompass the whole complex human contents of the poems. There was no plan, no story thought out in advance and later composed into scenes, or broken into succeeding moments. It was, rather, the other way around. The dynamic thrust of Homeric sentences gives us a cue. The primary impulse must have come from a dramatic suggestion within the material at hand—from sheer sense of happening, a perception of how events come into the wake of one another, how precipitating is the effect, how any occurrence must have its logic insofar as it is visualized, experienced, and realized. Some general idea of the action certainly loomed ahead, but what carried conviction was the vital friction of succeeding moments—each of them so immediate and yet so prophetic of the imminent outcome.

Consider, in this light, the opening scenes of the *Iliad* (1.12 ff.). The arrival of Chryses immediately absorbs us, blending all detail into one visual impression. Tightness of contour produces suspense, full-blooded presence gives a sense of the next step: standing out where he is, what else can Chryses do but address the Achaeans? We next see him rebuffed, yielding, walking away and praying, as a priest to his god. The narrative is again gathered into inevitable succession; the verse giving each step its proper ground and moment. Thus we necessarily anticipate the next scene: Apollo listens, descends, and approaches. Once more, there is pressure of sentence on sentence; one verse leans on the next and, once or twice, a slight enjambment lets the moment expand. There is therefore growing awareness of the god's presence: see how each step brings him into further evidence—in the clang of his bow, his body's motion, his mysterious impact equated to the coming of night.

Dialogue, on the other hand, presents things through the speaker's eye and not in their actual immediacy. But, in Homeric dialogue, we find a similar pace, a similarly pressing relation of sentence to sentence. Thus, in the ensuing assembly, events are realized by being set against one another. "Go away, if your spirit so moves you", Agamemnon says to Achilles, "I shall not beg you to stay. . . . Phoebus Apollo now takes Chryseis away from me, I shall send her off in my ships. . . .but lovely-cheeked Briseis I shall seize, I myself going up to your tent. . . ." The whole scene of the quarrel is filled with similar movement. It is largely a question of seizing and giving up, overcoming and yielding. Such material acts are the backbone. Again we have points of focus, assertive moments. By projecting them, the characters widen the range and intensify the momentum. One step provokes the next, things seem to be set in motion on their own account. The style lets loose both a course of action and a train of thought; to speak is to act and give rein to boundless ambition. The style coheres with the occasion. It does not leave room to abstract pleading or peroration of cause against cause. The sense of right and wrong is sunk in the connections of sentences.

This kind of "parataxis" is a style *sui generis*. It is ultimately due to a force that is internal to any act or state—a force that inevitably expands and forges its way forward from moment to moment in a vital continuity of time. The sentences run on, activated by this inner pulse.

This style is obviously quite different from that of the annalist who records facts one after the other in a foreordained chronological order. Nor is it the style of the story-teller who, whether arbitrarily or casually, keeps adding any interesting detail: "there was a king. . . .his palace was on a hill. . . .a moat ran round it. . . ." The annalist sets a record: the storyteller works out a plot. Both are removed from the immediate sense of action, bypass the single moment and its effect, and ignore the magnetism of sentence on sentence. There is hardly any parallel to Homer. We might perhaps compare the train of thought in a lyric poem: inward moments succeeding one another in the unbroken duration of the poet's inner experience. But Homer applies this treatment of time to the gritty material of external events; and, as a result, these events are no longer just external, but seem quickened by the heart-beat of the action.

Homer's coordination of sentences is one with the sense of continuous time in the action. "Paratactic" and "rectilinear" style are aspects of the same phenomenon. What determines both is a sense of concrete focus that allows no paraphrase, no general survey or random description. Each successive act fills the space of representation; we are faced with an unfolding present as when, traveling, we watch successive sceneries, tracing consistencies of form and color. With a similar pace the action runs its course. If there is an intermission or truce, it is accounted for and its duration specified. If there is a digression, it takes the same step as the mainstream and participates in the same kind of movement. Deeper down than the plot there is a vital continuity of time—energy transmitted by each concrete moment and imparted to the poems as a whole. Here is a style that cannot give up the basic conditions of existence—the ground on which to move, the breathing-space in which to live. It is as if the laws of existence appropriated the narrative, transforming any episode into a way of happening, being, developing.

Style in this broader sense cannot be merely "paratactic." It also leads us far beyond any narrow category or hallmark of an epoch, let alone any idiosyncrasy or personal mannerism. We may, if anything, refer to language itself in this Homeric phase. Here grammar, as well as syntax, shows the independence of single elements. Consider in this regard the individual force of the parts of speech: the article as a pronoun, the preposition as an adverb, the epithet as a name, and the aspect of the verb. Here the single word has a concrete value rather than an auxiliary function. The same trend is seen in sentences. The poet draws out an inherent significance, tapping on the genius of the language. A good syntactical example is the lack, or rarity, of a proper passive construction at this stage. The "passive" is admittedly a secondary development. This circumstance is in keeping with Homeric poetry that so persistently brings out an active moment. Consider Il.1.194-5:

ἦλθε δ' Ἀθήνη
οὐρανόθεν· πρὸ γὰρ ἧκε θεὰ λευκώλενος Ἥρη.

down came Athena
from heaven; the goddess sent her, Hera white-armed.

(cf. 208; 6.399; 19.168; 20.319; 21.299, 376, 384; Od.2.11; 18.207) Here the act of sending (or any other transitive act) must be a self-standing moment and not an explanation. In these instances, a possible passive construction is checked by the vivid resilience of the occasion.

Style turns to advantage what is at its disposal. Thus Homer touches on the phase in which the independence of word or phrase still subsists and yet gives way to a sense of development: momentary resilience bends to the overriding narrative flow and the flow is checked by any salient point. We have neither stark juxtaposition nor complication, no static presentation nor any running to a conclusion. We are released both from subordinating constructions and from the stolidity of things that are taken for granted. What holds sway is the unbiased hold of spontaneous connections.

DURATION OF THE ACTION, COMPOSITION

A unique feature of the *Iliad* and the *Odyssey* is the brief duration of the action. In the *Iliad*, a week of fighting is framed by intervals at the beginning and end; In the *Odyssey*, six days see the return and restoration of Odysseus in Ithaca, preceded by some thirty days in all for Telemachus' quest and Odysseus' reaching the Phaeacians. But what really matters is not so much the number of days as the fact that the action is conceived in terms of days.

This brevity of duration is extraordinary, especially considering the large scale of the poems. There is no parallel to Homer in this respect. How could anyone fail to find a connection here with Homer's focus on simple continuous moments? Such a continuity of concrete moments would obviously be unthinkable in any narrative covering long indefinite periods of time. How could the *Aeneid*, for instance, or *Gilgamesh* be composed in this way? How could any novel or biography present us with successive moments in the lifelong career of its hero? We would flounder in a morass of countless details.

We should not suppose, however, that the poet added moment to moment, completing one day after the other. The poems themselves tell us otherwise. Just take any page, and a certain scene will stand out in its individuality, naturally linking with its context and hardly requiring any chronological cross-references to be understood. What comes most instantly to mind when we think of Homer is always a certain specific scene; this is the way the ancients referred to the *Iliad* and the *Odyssey*, quite apart from any arrangement of the parts.

The various scenes integrate one another rather than prolong the narrative thread. We should look at the work of composition in a qualitative and not a quantitative sense—not as a construction conceived through additions, but as a process of creative expansion. At what point did it all start, at what point did it end, and how long did it take? Such questions are not relevant to the nature of the work. We cannot assume any strict chronology here. The initial scene of the wrath, though preeminent, need not have been the first. Right from the beginning, or at any stage, such scenes as that of Hector and Andromache or Achilles and Priam must have been present in the poet's mind. Any of the battle-scenes must have been similarly rehearsed again and again quite apart from any chronological order, much as a sculptor essays a body time after time. Here were haunting instances of action or pathos, each presenting itself in its susceptibilities and potentialities. A wider range of associations, like a penumbra, opened up at the margins.

The plot sequence eludes us more often than not. There is, for instance, no obvious reason why the *aristeia* of Diomedes, in book 5 of the *Iliad*, should come long before Agamemnon's in book 11; but it takes place here because this book and the next one touch particularly on the question of who is a god or a man—a question especially relevant to Diomedes as a character. The chronological arrangement of incidents must be viewed in this light: what determines the place of a passage within the context and not a narrative plausibility. Thersites echoes Achilles; the duel of Hector and Ajax takes up that of Paris and Menelaus the day before; and the onslaught of Asios and Sarpedon in book 12 prefigures that of Hector: the series of advances and retreats in the long day of books 11–18 brings out the general ebb-and-flow of war and the individual encounters cluster together in condensing the deadly beat of the fighting: here we need not see a "retarding effect" in the consummation of the plot.

Or, again, why does the scene of Hector and Andromache take place early in the poem and not toward the end, preceding Hector's death, as a last farewell that would have been more satisfactory from a narrative point of view? For Homer, the scene rightly occurs where it does. For it follows closely upon the other intimate scenes in which Hector speaks to Hecuba, Paris, and Helen; it thus constitutes a climax in the inner life of Troy. A vantage-ground opens up to past and future while the war rages all round. What first mattered was not where to fit any scene, but how a scene might irradiate and summon up analogies.

Rather than being steps in a story, such happenings set in motion a sequence or a kindred wave of like eventualities. The same tale of plunder is found in the scene of the wrath as elsewhere throughout the *Iliad* (1.164; 2.226 ff., 6.414 ff.); the same echo runs through such speeches as those of Andromache and Briseis; the same successions of thrust and counter-thrust make up the account of war; the same emotions persistently affect the Trojans and Achaeans; and the same returns involve other heroes as well as Odysseus. Indeed much of Homer is the accosting of like to like. Hence the similes. We have, so far, one fluid level of representation.

How then shall we account for the narrative element in its Homeric form? It is not imposed from without, rather it arises from the depth of the material. Consider, in this connection, an essential part of the plot: Patroclus slain, the revenge of Achilles, the death of Hector. Here is a theme of thought that runs through the battle-scenes of the *Iliad*: again and again a hero is slain, a friend or relative comes to avenge and retrieve the body, and another death takes place. In Il.11.248, for instance: "when Koon saw. . .overwhelming grief covered his eyes for his brother's fall. . .he stood at the side with his spear. . .and hit Agamemnon. . . ." See especially such close sequences as 13.384–403, 410–420, 427–469, 518–526. The similes show the same drama enacted far and wide in the world of nature. Thus, in Il.18.316 ff., Achilles mourns over Patroclus, intensely moaning "like a well-maned lion, whose whelps a hunter has taken away from the forest thicket; in grief he returns to it, hither and thither he wanders to trace the man . . ." (cf. 16.259; 17.4, 133). A persisting, prepossessive imagery thus stands out. Achilles and Patroclus gather in themselves a drama that is carried out in countless other instances. But, in their case, the scale and setting are different. What the battle-scenes present in a moment's immediacy is shown here in a wider perspective. Achilles is absent, he receives the news of his friend's death, the preparation for his revenge takes time and, in the interval, grief sinks deep into his mind bringing about an inner change and transformation. In other words, the experience of one moment expands, it fills a series of days, and the march of events falls in unison with it.

Or take what from a narrative point of view might be regarded as a central element in the *Iliad*: the plan of Zeus, his promise to Thetis that Achilles shall be vindicated. This theme was hardly such as to inspire the poet. It operates, if at all, in the background. It does not have in itself any dramatic or poetic power. On the other hand, such scenes as Achilles and Thetis on the shore in books 1 and 18 must have loomed large in the poet's imagination: the first one showing the humiliated hero, the second showing him crushed with grief for Patroclus' death, and in both the divine mother sitting beside him, as if to console him for being born. Here the plot is intimated from within the action. So visually effective and intensely significant, these scenes by themselves suggest the events that brought them about and those that will follow. As for the plan of Zeus, it becomes a feeble backdrop. Things could have happened the same way without it.

   No less evident in the *Odyssey* than in the *Iliad* is this potentiality of the material: the sheer presence and disposition of things producing a time sequence. The *Odyssey* is no thin long narrative of a hero's return. We are presented, rather, with a basic idea set before us in concrete terms: a sea to be crossed; a land to be reached; and the very juxtaposition is a challenge, a condition for action.
   We first see Odysseus as he longingly looks over the sea from Calypso's shore, in a posture that anticipates his further sailing. But, from beginning to end, the effort of braving the seas is rehearsed again and again: Telemachus sets sail on his father's quest, then come the sea-journeys recounted by Nestor and Menelaus, and last but not least, Odysseus' sea-faring is echoed again in the tales he tells Eumaeus and Penelope disguised as an old beggar. There are, on the other hand, the lands touched by the sea, but safely settled: the banqueting halls of Ithaca, Pylos, Sparta, and Scheria. Here life is at ease, but there is a common concern for Odysseus: where is he? Will he return? The *Odyssey* brings us to the last phase of this separation. Ithaca is waiting, Odysseus is approaching; the years dwindle to days, moments. And yet we do not have the sense of a brief sweeping success, for these days and moments come charged with the burden of like days and moments in the past. When Odysseus is finally brought back to Ithaca, he does not know where he is—as if his return were yet another landing.
   It was a stroke of genius not to give Odysseus' adventures as straight narrative but to place them on Odysseus' lips as one night's performance among the Phaeacians—a performance that was not the least of his feats, crowning them all by establishing his image and identity. But how is the sense of time conveyed in Odysseus' tale? Chronology is here no more relevant than any realistic geography. What prevails is, again, the concrete moment, the concrete spot. We have, as in the battle-scenes of the *Iliad*, a sheer sense of occurrence and recurrence: landing and setting sail, welcomes and rejections, calm seas and storms, steadfast rowing and wind-blown sails. A self-perpetuating form absorbs the adventurous details: here is what all wandering at sea is about. Furthermore the same rhythmical treatment is maintained in Ithaca itself. We might expect a complicated strategy in beating the suitors; but no, we have three successive banquet scenes (in books 17,18,20) in which the disguised

Odysseus comes progressively into focus—up to the point when, arrows in hand, he stands out self-revealed in a final confrontation.

Both in the *Iliad* and the *Odyssey* we have a brief tract of time seething with activity. There are no external frames of reference. Connections with mythical or historical cycles are scanty and, in any case, they do not play any relevant role in the action. The Homeric moments have thus no other connection with the outside than the day in which they occur. By highlighting a succession of days, the internal time-beat of the action could be brought into harmony with an objective sense of time—the time of nature that has no particular regard for any action.

But a problem now arises. Whatever else they do, the Homeric poems give us a sense of voluminous human experience. We have an impression of indefinite duration. How then can we make these Homeric moments compatible with the time continuum? How can we realize all at once both the highlights and the steady continuity? Even the duration of a single day is forbidding in this respect: countless incidents pass by unobserved and forgotten. There is incompatibility between the excitement of the instant and the leveling flow of existence. The antinomy can only be resolved by letting the central moments stand out in themselves and yet be supreme instances of like moments that have come before and will come again.

It may help to consider in the same light our own experience of life. If we survey the ordinary acts of living (such as to get up or have a meal), we naturally condense them in their respective types, and countless variables are set aside. If we take a more serious look, the same condensation applies to the most momentous occasions: a great sorrow; a great love becomes a dominant note and tends to absorb all minor notes of the same kind. Time here is shown in its essence: its quantitative duration is abridged, its significance is enlarged. Such a process of abridgment and enlargement is the reason why we have an impression of surprising brevity when looking back at our past life; and yet imponderable experiences are summoned up that seem to imply immeasurable time. What our memory evokes is not a sequence of episodes, but a pregnant material that expands on its own account.

Similar reflections are prompted by Homer. The Homeric action is only a matter of days, and yet the burden of cumulative moments gives a sense of indefinite time. Homer's language strongly contributes to this effect: recurring phrases and typical scenes constantly convey this condensation. For any moment—any act or state—comes up voluminously: a phrase like "he plied into swiftness his knees" does not only render the act of running as a narrative detail, but solemnizes it, condensing into its outline all other instances of running. As Bergson puts it: "a runner's countless successive positions are condensed into one symbolic pose which our eyes perceive and art reproduces; it becomes for all to see the image of a man that runs."[2]

Anything in Homer suggests recurrence, rhythm. It follows that any tract of human experience appears engrossed, enlarged. We are tuned to look at things *sub species aeternitatis*. And yet nothing in the poems is symbolic. Nowhere do we find the air-tight pattern of allegory or parable. The sense of time is too strong; it does not allow any crystallization. As a result, we focus on any single concrete act presented to our view; and yet we are constantly lifted above it. Though we are always within the pale of a certain moment and a certain day, the very time-beat tunes us to a widening perspective and we lose track of any limited duration.

SENSE OF FOCUS AND SENSE OF TRUTH

Homer's sense of focus is also a sense of truth. When an act is individualized in its essential simplicity, it is also universalized. It becomes typical. It stirs up analogies the world over. Just as there is a greater cognitive range in individual insight than in a collective body of opinion, so is the truth of experience reflected more strongly in an authentic moment of life than in a general survey.

Take Il.20.154 ff.: "Achilles . . . sprang like a lion . . . whom men strive to slay . . . glaring he is driven forward by his spirit . . . even so his might and spirit stirred Achilles" (cf. 12.41, 299, etc.). What more self-evident than this forward leap? What more striking than the senses so merged into one burst of energy? Homer recognizes the same spirit in hero and animal. By simply highlighting an act, he cuts across the boundaries of class and species. A sense of focus shows the way: no prejudice obscures it—no dichotomy of "soul" and "body," no conventional distinction of high and low, no adventitious interest. What stands out is position, movement. There treatment is dynamic, not descriptive: Homer would never say that Achilles is as strong as a lion, but instead "he sprang as a lion springs."

Flashes of perception present us with a sympathetic view of nature. Here anything may find its place as long as it is fully and clearly brought into play by a typical moment—at rest or in motion, emerging or subsiding, rising or falling. A tree that withstands the storm or one that is felled by foresters reflects the same destiny as a resisting or falling warrior; the stillness of clouds in a momentarily windless sky is suggested by an army's precarious stance; a sudden respite in the struggle summons up the view from a mountaintop at the moment a cloud is swept away. What prompts the analogy is the very process of the occurrence, whenever a movement attains form or form dissolves into movement. Such is, for instance, the case when the poet renders the curving of a wave (Il.4.424), birds on the wing (2.464), a sound's echo (16.633), the convergence of torrents (4.452), melting snow (Od.19.204). If these things affect us, the reason is that they strike a common chord by highlighting a moment with which we may sympathetically identify.

The Homeric similes bring to a head a strain that runs through the poems. Where rhythm is so identical with phrase and sentence, what stands out is a process rather than a static fact. We are made to disregard the stolidity of incident and look at the flow that brings a thing into play. Literal connotations and narrative connections are thus left out; in their stead, the flowing outline, the shimmering design draw us to analogies in the nature of things. Over and above his story, Homer continually brings us back to the ways of existence. Even where similes do not occur, there is always the potentiality of a simile. It is as if things ceased to exist in their peculiarities, as separate objects of curious interest. By being always integrated into an essential moment of action, they are made symbolic of their native function in a world where occurrences become recurrence, image begets image, and action summons up its likeness.

Homer's clarity resides in the rise of form. It is not a matter of descriptive accuracy but self-evidence, outright presence in the field of vision. Things simply stand out; what matters is their exposure to the moment that sets them off. They seem released from the conditions of a particular status: a hero, an animal, a tree, a mountain, and an island share the same daylight evidence. While form gives them fixity, the highlighting moment touches them with life.

Especially as regards the human action, the influence of such a style was immense, for we are always brought back to immediate instances of resilience and abatement, surviving or dying, winning or losing, resisting or escaping, being present or absent. There is a mighty interplay rather than *parti pris*, the truth of things rather than one-sided glorification. Rhythm itself pointed the way: the stress of the moment impinged upon hierarchical status. We find in ever-widening spheres the signs of an implicit philosophy or a wisdom as yet unaware of itself.

The mythical material is, to begin with, greatly abridged, the main action being conceived in human terms. We may most particularly appreciate the Homeric touch when it is put to the test in dealing with the mythical or fantastic elements that inevitably come up. If such elements are impervious to Homeric art, they are, if at all, treated as briefly as possible: the metamorphoses of Proteus only takes two lines (Od.4.456–7), similarly the Chimera (Il.6.180–2). Where the material is malleable, Homer reduces the uncanny features to natural movements: is Scamander a river or a god when he fights Achilles (Il.21.136 ff.)? The ambiguity is resolved in the arching wave that takes the form of a projecting body: and the current's bull-like roar, μεμυκώς ἠΰτε ταῦρος (237), keeps us within the pale of nature, even while lightly reminding us of rivers traditionally personified as bulls. Or consider Scylla and Charybdis (Od.12.226 ff.). When Odysseus reaches them, he hardly finds the monsters described in advance by Circe. Charybdis is invisible in her whirlpool; she is a chasm showing the dark bottom when she swirls downward and a seething cauldron when surging upwards. As for Scylla, Odysseus' eyes grow weary looking at her misty cliff, until six of his companions are jolted out of the boat, the monster itself only shown in the effect of human bodies lifted up, falling, and perishing in the cave below. Here we find again the art of the similes: incongruous things brought to the level of natural phenomena. Elsewhere the mythical story cannot be altered, but it is bypassed by a humanizing touch: the Cyclops leads the life of a shepherd, Circe grows into a hostess and lover.

Even where a myth is faced in its fullness, it seems mellowed by an Ionian feeling for natural processes. Such is the case of the love scene between Hera and Zeus, the ἱερὸς γάμος of Il.14.153 ff.: there is Hera's ointment "whose perfume spreads over the earth and high up into the sky"; her earrings "from which loveliness shines out abundant"; the pine tree "whose stem shoots up to heaven"; and there is the floral couch— indeed a miraculous thing, and yet rendered as natural growth quickening into sudden luxuriance. Similarly, the conventional flight of gods is not as striking as the leaves that tremble under their feet, the spell of Aphrodite's girdle not as vivid as the fact that it is a real object— something to be touched, handled, worn. Such things as the tremor of a leaf or the upward sweep of a tree have a vibrant effect. We realize them rather than just learn about them. For occurrence blends with shape, a time-rhythm penetrates the material; and the sublimity of gods finds common ground with the naturalness of experience.

Another effect of the same outlook concerns the relation between gods and mortals. Homer makes credible what is usually taken for granted or explained away as a question of belief. Consider, again, any act or state in its instant fullness. What kind of force, what energy lies at its source? The phenomenon gives us pause: we have, all at once, clarity of focus and implicit mystery.

Consider, in this respect, the phrases in which a part of the body or an inner organ is the subject, especially those that designate an act of the will. We have, for instance, the frequent type "my spirit bids me" (Il.18.90; cf. 7.74; 8.322, etc.). But Homer could also say "a god bids me" (cf. Il.15.725; 16. 691, etc.). The two alternatives are actually combined in Il.9.703, cf. Od.3.26–27; 12.38; Il.15.725; 24.194; 7.199. Both cases point to an active principle: it is as if spirit were a god and, by the same token, a god were made manifest in the driving spirit. In any case, a vital impulse is implied. We are obviously lifted above mere casualness, reflex or habit. What, indeed, can be more wonderful than a thought that suddenly comes up, forthwith transformed into resolution, speech, action?

Or, take the instances in which a hero shows renewed strength. In Il.5.1 ff. Athena bestows courage and might upon Diomedes (cf. ibid. 513; 10.482, etc.), but elsewhere it is his own might that stirs a hero (20.174; 5.136, cf. 5.506; 16.602). Again we find both kinds of perception fused with each other into one moment: in Il.13.73–80 the two Ajaxes are touched into new vigor by Poseidon, but they feel a spontaneous resilience taking hold of their heart and limbs. The Homeric gods refrain from unnatural influences, they mostly quicken inborn potentialities.

While the thought of death decisively separates mortals and immortals, the dividing line vanishes in the moment of action. Considerations of status and hierarchy are excluded from the immediacy of a crucial occasion. We have an outright clarity of movement or gesture along with imponderable implications; and here the divine element inevitably blends with the human. When Achilles refrains from striking Agamemnon, does not Athena's influence reflect the swaying emotion of the hero himself? Here M. P. Nilsson sees the effect of a "precarious balance."[3]

This ambiguity is one with a baffling aspect of reality. At times even our thoughts come as a surprise; are they really our own or do they rise from some unknown depth? Seen in this light, the much-debated problem of human responsibility in Homer loses its edge. Where a god and a man are so merged in the same critical moment, how shall we assign to each their respective roles? Mortals, we may say, are not free agents, buffeted as they are by forces beyond their control; but, even more to the point, how can the gods govern human action, when they are themselves governed by the same emotions as men? Take the verse that expresses decision ἥδε δέ οἱ κατὰ θυμὸν ἀρίστη φαίνετο βουλή [this to him in his spirit appeared tbe best counsel], or the verse that expresses doubt μερμήριξε δ᾽ ἔπειτα κατὰ φρένα καὶ κατὰ θυμόν [he wavered then in his mind and spirit]: these, or their equivalents, apply to gods as well as men (cf. Il.2.2, 5; 14.159; 16.435, etc.). We are brought back to the moment of realization. The focus is on the act itself, not on the agent or agency. It is the act of thought that stands out in these verses, just as it is movement itself in a foot that steps out or a hand that seizes its object. There is, moreover, a tendency to sameness of form in verse and sentence. An ever recurring rhythm sways the movements of body and mind; and its effect is pervasive, subjecting gods as well as men to the ways of nature.

We are too conditioned to look at things in terms of cause and effect, analyzing and reducing to separate elements the encompassing actuality of an event. Arbitrary connections thus replace the integrity of a vital process. It is otherwise in poetry. Homer identifies cause and effect with an unfolding present. Wounded Hector rises up collecting his spirits, and yet it is Zeus who stirs him (cf. Il.15.240–2): the two things are part and parcel of the same occurrence. What we might analyze into separate factors is gathered into the same moment, it coheres, it takes tangible reality. A happening contains in itself its own logic and justification.

These reasonings may be applied on a larger scale. It has often been observed that the action of the poems could have the same course even without the gods or the so-called divine machinery. How is it then that the gods are so present at each step? The reason lies, again, in a reality that gives us pause. We are not struck by any exceptional feat, but we are made to wonder at the process itself, and the effect increases as we proceed. Especially the *Iliad* gives us the idea of a grand self-developing outline. It is as if we saw the rising and subsiding rhythm of any single verse arching over the whole poem. For the same flowing design transpires through much of the subject-matter—in the ebb-and-flow of the battle, in Hector's advances and retreats, and in Achilles' transformations from his initial wrath to his final peace. Things can hardly happen this way in realistic terms, and yet we keep within a natural sphere. Released from descriptive details, the moments of action are filled with an intrinsic energy and produce a swift, voluminous rhythm which only the presence of gods can sustain in its fullness.

Another consequence of Homer's focus concerns more directly human society and the relations of people with one another. Where the perception of a vital moment allows us to view hero and animal in the same light, it would be unthinkable that distinctions of class or race should play an important role. It is no wonder that, in such a context, Homer places Achaeans and Trojans on the same footing. It is no different if we look further afield. In the *Catalogue*, the Asian allies of the Trojans are given the same splendid setting, for example in Il.2.851 ff.: "the shaggy strong heart of Palaimenes led the Paphlagonians . . . who on the river Parthenios had their glorious abodes." When the gods are absent, they are pictured visiting the "flawless Aethiopians." In Il.13.3 ff., Zeus turns his eyes away from Troy and looks "over the horse-tending Thracians, the close-fighting Mysians, the bright-looking Hippemolgi drinkers of milk and the Abians, most just among mortals": we need not press the geographic or ethnic distinctions, the divine gaze gives each group its positive vital presence.

We find the same equality of treatment when it comes to persons of different classes or origins, as in "so spoke divine swift-footed Achilles" and "so spoke god-like Briseis." Image-making epithets of the same kind apply to man and woman, hero and slave. In each case a full-bodied shape is seen in an act or position that brings it to the fore. We are made conversant with a style that has a natural respect for form, whatever narrower judgment we might wish to apply. In Il.3.38, for instance, Menelaus, like a lion suddenly landed on his prey "rejoiced gazing on Alexander the god-like, he was sure to punish the sinner": in spite of any negative viewpoint, Paris enters the picture as a pure object of perception.

The Homeric epithets are symptomatic in this respect. Since they are not predicates or descriptive attributes, and they intimately cohere with a thing, it follows that they simply enhance a sense of form in the moment of representation, without any discursive connection with the general meaning of the passage. Through the epithets, we may therefore realize more fully how the Homeric moment appeals to our wider sympathies and not to any narrowness of attitude. Movement gives form its vibration, form gives movement its poise; and both concur in bringing out a common dignity of life. It is not without reason that the *Catalogue of Ships* presents us with people in movement—sailing, marching, advancing. Men thus caught in action cannot but be vividly present; and the epithets are here in place, arresting their presence for a moment, while they would be quite superfluous in a mere account of populations. Similarly any object or human and animal form finds its intrinsic pertinence in the act or state that brings it into focus.

Form here stands in contrast with status. It is not static. It is produced by action finding its center. It necessarily excludes any one-sided point of view. Hence comes a sympathetic objectivity. Regardless of precedents, an immediate spontaneous interest is stirred by anyone coming into view on the spur of the occasion. Thus Thersites—the commoner, the non-hero—is not put down on the strength of his background; he is taken at his face value as he rises giving vent to his undisciplined spirits. Class distinctions, when mentioned, are touched upon lightly. Odysseus, in Il.2.188 ff., does not discriminate, but he addresses both nobleman and commoner with the same appellative, approaching each for a moment and passing swiftly by. What stands out is the approach itself, the reproach meted out to both.

Slavery is an issue in point. We do not find in Homer the common Greek word for "slave" (δοῦλος), but we do find δούλιον ἦμαρ [day of slavery, Il.6.463; Od.14.340; 17.323], cf. ἐλεύθερον ἦμαρ ἀπούρας [robbing you of your day of freedom, Il.6.455, etc.]. It is typical of Homer to associate slavery with time and not to take it for granted as a social condition. The day of slavery can come upon each and all: "half the strength of a man does Zeus take away, when slavery's day falls upon him" (Od.17.522–3). Thus Homer does not mention a slave class, but highlights the occasion in which someone is driven into slavery (Il.6.454 ff.; 24.731 ff.). In Od.8.523 ff., a simile depicts a woman beaten into slavery as she cries over her husband slain in defending their city. By the same token, the freedom from bondage or the fact of being free-born is no inalienable right and privilege: the victor of today will be the vanquished of tomorrow, "impartial is Ares, he slays him who is about to slay" (Il.18.309).

Moralistic strictures are shunned in the same spirit. We have, rather, a moral sense that lets anyone share an impeccable moment of life. Thus, there are no outright villains, or idealized heroes; even the suitors of Penelope, for all their wrong-doing, are mostly presented as bright men in their prime, absorbed in the most winning of tasks. The present is what it is: neither diminished nor magnified by the thought of what is to come. "Such is the mind of man as the day that Zeus casts over him," says Odysseus to Amphinomus (Od.18.136–7). What we might call chance, fate or providence is the very ebb-and-flow of life.

Simone Weil[4] splendidly brought out this sense of relativity in the *Iliad*, on the strength of both the general action and particular scenes. But it is the verse itself that most contributes to this effect. For the very rhythm conveys climax and anticlimax, any act hovers in its transience; and the makeup of character is affected accordingly. In other words, the precarious situation of the Homeric heroes is made convincing by harking back to a verse that lets even the most forceful acts find their way through the fragile modulations of an unfolding moment. What the narrative tells us about a hero's or a people's fortune is first inscribed in the form of expression that, even unwittingly, always tunes us to a process of coming to be and passing away.

Homer's point of focus is not emphasis, arbitrary stress or exaggeration in any way. It simply singles out, touches off, and simply gives a thing its natural setting. Such a style precludes or discourages any gratuitous treatment of the characters, adventitious interpretation of motives, slighting innuendo or make-shift justification. The poet would rather use a simile than append any particular praise or blame. There is no point in partisanship where the focus is on the crucial moment that envelops both sides. The battle-scenes are essentially a fighting for dear life; and the bitterest feuds are a clash of positions, not matters of inveterate hatreds and age-old incompatibilities. The issue of right and wrong inevitably sinks into the background.

It is well known, on the other hand, how Homer was often regarded in antiquity as an educator—exemplifying, for instance, the prudence of Nestor or the prowess of Achilles as models for the young. Today we consider this point of view as little more than a curiosity. But the same tendency persists in our own times, except that the naive exaltation of certain virtues is replaced by historical intent to highlight the values of Homeric society. Thus Jaeger wrote about the *Iliad*: "Throughout the poem the brave man is the nobleman, the man of rank. Battle and victory are his highest distinction; they are the real meaning of his life. . . ."[5] More recently an anthropological trend has set in. We now have not so much a historical perspective as an effort to establish a whole system of traditional values of which Homer is the spokesman. Research has thus become more analytical. Keywords, phrases, and themes are isolated from their context and given a symbolic status. Such concepts as "glory," "honor," and "virtue" are pursued in their complex ramifications and presented as a mainspring of Homeric poetry. We have a prestigious currency that gives the epic its moral credibility.

What are we to think of these guidelines? A poet (like anyone else) must necessarily work on the available material provided by his age and country; and there is thus nothing wrong in using Homer to explore the culture of the pre-Homeric age. But the reverse direction is surely wrong: to explain Homeric poetry on the basis of these findings. Here we have a vicious circle. It is as if we were to appreciate an implement by looking first at its price tag, without considering its real value and function in actual experience.

Things ought not to be taken in such static terms. Homer lets nothing crystallize into an emblem. We find, rather, growing transparencies of thought, meanings that branch out from their material ground. Thus κλέος is "news," "hearsay" before it is "glory"; τιμή is "payment," "reward" before it is "honor"; ἀρετή is a body's vitality before it is "virtue." Similarly, what we call "soul" is first the vital function of an inner organ; what we call "body" is first the vigorous interplay of limbs and joints; and what we call "life" is first livelihood, subsistence.

It is "glory," κλέος, that concerns us most here, connected as it is with the idea of time. Never in Homer is glory abstracted into a transcendent ideal. The concrete etymological sense of "hearsay" is very much alive: τί δὴ κλέος ἔστ᾽ ἀνὰ ἄστυ; [what is the news in the city?], Telemachus asks Eumaeus (Od.16.461; cf. 23.137; Il.11.21, 227, etc.). Even where we get closest to the senses of fame or renown, there is always a strong connection with a specific deed or activity: "what κλέος did Orestes achieve by killing Aegysthus. . . ." says Athena (Od.1.298, cf. 3.204; Il.17.232; 5.3). At times, the "glory" is that of an inanimate object (Il.8.192; 7.451).

Consider in this respect the much-quoted passage, Il.7.87–91: Hector imagines people who, seeing the tomb of a mighty opponent slain by himself, will say one day: "here lies one whom Hector slew," and he adds:

ὥς ποτέ τις ἐρέει· τὸ δ᾽ ἐμὸν κλέος οὔ ποτ᾽ ὀλεῖται.

so shall one day someone say; and my *kleos* shall never die.

The boast sounds incongruous: Döderlein proposed ἑόν instead of ἐμὸν referring κλέος to the tomb rather than to Hector. But the verse is quite natural, if we bear in mind the concrete sense of κλέος: "thus shall someone say, and people will always hear." However we translate, the direct relation between the spoken words (ὥς ποτέ τις ἐρέει) and κλέος is evident. The very rhythm of the verse confirms this relativity: the initial rising movement of what is said (ὥς ποτέ τις ἐρέει) subsides into what is heard (τὸ δ᾽ ἐμὸν κλέος οὔποτ᾽ ὀλεῖται)—at one with the final cadence. Compare such verses as ὥς ἐπιμὶξ κτείνονται, αὐτὴ δ᾽ οὐρανὸν ἵκει [so pell-mell are they slain; and the cry reaches up to the sky, Il.14.60], or ἀνδρῶν πῖπτε κάρηνα, βοὴ δ᾽ ἄσβεστος ὀρώρει [down fell the heads of men, and unquelled rose the roar, 11.500]. Sequences of this kind are frequent in Homer: a sound and its echo, a light and its reflection, a blow and its impact. A process is caught in its immediacy: beginning, middle and end as parts of the same moment. Glory is no different. Its rhetoric is brought down to earth. It would be unthinkable here to have a digression, however short, on the values of glory. It would break the flow of the succeeding moments to introduce an abstract idea.

It is said that the Homeric heroes are preoccupied with the pursuit of glory. But who has ever pursued glory for its own sake? Least of all in Homer. There is no room for any long-range projection of personal glory, no interest in any state or city whose records might enshrine a hero's name, and no concern for a reward in after-life. There is, on the other hand, a present fullness—the impact of what happens there and then. What we call "glory" is the report of an event. It resides in the fact that a happening is seen, witnessed, and known as well as experienced. A moment is both itself and its repercussion.

Some readers might object: Is this all? Is there no further perspective, no message beyond the moment? We may answer that even the highest moral ideals are best appreciated in the moment of their perception and not when they are crystallized into principles. Homer brings us back to a creative source. Thus the sediments of tradition are set in a new key by the dramatic moments of the action. It is said, for instance, that κλέος ἄφθιτον [immortal glory, Il.9.413] goes back to a strong Indo-European theme; but, if so, it is all the more remarkable that the phrase should occur only here and as a verse-ending that is like a cry of infinite regret. Similarly, many ideas to which we attach the greatest moral or religious weight—like δίκη, θέμις, αἰδώς, σέβας [justice, law, awe, reverence]—are never hypostatized but presented in a moment that makes them immediately pertinent. "This is the δίκη of men when they die," says Anticlea (Od.11.18); "σέβας holds me as I look at you," says Odysseus to Nausicaa (Od.6.161); "The Achaeans stood firm by the ships, for αἰδώς possessed them" (Il.15.657). Principles extolled elsewhere, are here part and parcel of an act or state of being. It is as if the rhythm subjected them to the flux of existence. We are made to realize what life really is, not what should be its aims.

Poetry does not give us final answers; it gives us pause, makes us think and wonder. This thought-compelling quality is preeminent in Homer. The Homeric action is so removed from the historical or mythical links of cause and effect, and so suspended between gods and men that we may endlessly ponder upon its reason and purposes. We ask what motive was at work—was it chance or fate, or rather the force of converging eventualities; but each time we ask, we are inevitably thrown back to the action itself and its baffling dimensions. For what stands out is the winning actuality of what happens, not a series of narrative connections. Thus Achilles' wrath, Odysseus' return, and Hector's advances and retreats are things of no mythical or historical consequence, but have their roots in the nature of things; and the action proceeds apace developing its own momentum and sense of values. Even the battles of the *Iliad* have no semblance of a military campaign; they are not a matter of strategy or a show of prowess. Such a simile as that which compares the uncertain clash of heroes to the balance of the scales in a poor woman's hands (Il.12.433 ff.) tells us more about Homer than any precept we might find in the poems.

Homer's message is purely poetic. This is to say that he ultimately brings us back to essentials and does not expound any particular set of values. "Such as the generations of leaves are men's generations," says Glaucus (Il.6.462 ff.); "hapless mortals who now flare up in a vital glow

. . .and now come to nought," says Apollo (Il.21.462 ff.). And what about the course of history? "Many cities has Zeus brought down and he will evermore," says Agamemnon (Il.2.116; 9.24). Even the fall of Mycenae, Argos, Sparta is envisaged, like that of Troy (Il.4.51 ff.). On the other hand, the Homeric action stands out by itself in its full self-consistence. Circumscribed within its days, it embodies an excerpt of life: time in its human essence—not an era, a period of history explaining subsequent periods, or a glorifying biography. Homer's freedom from didacticism is one with an extraordinary sense of focus that highlights the general action no less than any single act or state of being.

ON COMPARISONS WITH OTHER EPICS

Homer's compression of the action into moments and days is a phenomenon *sui generis*. It is not characteristic of an early stage in composition: in this respect, Homer is as far removed from later epics as he is from much earlier ones such as *Gilgamesh*, the Babylonian poem of Tiamat and Marduk, and the Ugaritic *Keret*. Nor is this treatment of time due to the subject-matter. If Homer sang the wrath of Achilles rather than the Trojan war, or Odysseus' day of return rather than Odysseus' life, the reason lies not so much in a casual or deliberate choice as in a deeper poetic predisposition.

It is a question of perspective within the poetry itself. If we compare Homer and Virgil, there are obvious differences of age, environment, and subject-matter; but these differences take us outside the domain of poetry. Much more relevant here are distinctions of focus in verse and sentence—distinctions that come up even in the last detail. What stands out is a mode of thought, not given facts. Such an approach might bring out distinctions and affinities more directly than a comparative analysis of historical causes and consequences.

Consider, in *Aeneid* 1.34 ff., the point at which the action begins:

> Vix e conspectu Siculas telluris in altum
> vela dabant laeti et spumas salis aere ruebant
> cum Iuno. . .
> scarcely out of Sicily's sight towards the deep seas
> they spread their sails in joy, with brazen prow scattered the
> > foam,
> when Juno. . .

These verses are by themselves sufficient to convey the difference between Homer and Virgil, all the more in that the same moment of navigation is often mentioned in both. Whereas Homer highlights the actual sailing, Virgil suggests the challenging venture and direction to a vague but exciting destination. We have in Virgil the general gladness of the sailors: how different this is from Od.5.269, γηθόσυνος δ' οὔρῳ, πέτασ' ἱστία δῖος Ὀδυσσεύς where the gladness finds its immediate occasion in the favoring wind and in the spreading sails. Even the more concrete *spumas salis aere ruebant* [they scattered the sea-foam with brazen prow] conveys a mood: we are given the sense of a proud decisive thrust quite unlike, say, the cadence of πολιὴν ἅλα τύπτον ἐρετμοῖς [the white foam they beat with their oars, Od.4.580; 9.104, etc.]. Moreover, the ship itself is not mentioned in Virgil, absorbed as it is in the general drift and spirit of the story. Contrast Homer's ἡ δ' ἔθεεν κατὰ κῦμα διαπρήσσουσα κέλευθον [and she ran over the waves, passing over her path], a verse whose very rhythm renders the ship sliding through the water (Il.1.483; Od.2.429). It is no wonder that, in such a context, the voyage of Aeneas should be forthwith connected with a supernal design: *cum Iuno. . . .* Virgil's poetic focus lies elsewhere than in the concrete act. A visionary outlook informs the material. It lies at the source of the *Aeniad*; but it would have manifested itself even if the subject-matter had been a different one.

We shall not find anything like Homer's concrete moments in any epic that ranges over cycles of myth and history. We should, perhaps, turn to narrative in its purest form—narrative unencumbered by any transcendental design. There is, after all, the story-telling spirit that simply delights in itself. It scours above record and belief from incident to incident; and any one incident entirely absorbs our attention, even as we are carried forward to a beckoning conclusion. But, here again, Homer stands poles apart. No less than the high claims of a long-range epic, a story's casualness is inconsistent with the momentary fullness of the Homeric action. Take, for instance, Chaucer's *Knight's Tale* :

> Stories of old have made it known to us
> That there was once a Duke called Theseus
>
> He had subdued the Amazons by force
> And all their realm, once known as Scythia,
> But then called Femeny. Hippolyta,
> Their queen, he took to wife, and, says the story,
> He brought her home in solemn pomp and glory,
> Also her younger sister, Emily.
>
> This Duke I mentioned, ere alighting down,
> And on the very outskirts of the town
> In all felicity and height of pride
> Became aware, casting an eye aside,
> That kneeling by the highway, two by two,
> A company of ladies were in view

　　　　　All clothed in black. [6]
Here we have the immemorial "once-upon-a-time." No sooner does the
narrative open up than everything seems to take a vicarious and fanciful
kind of existence: far-fetched coincidences take place, dreams come
true, and seemingly unattainable goals are achieved. What appears to be
a casual detail bears decisive consequences ("also her younger sister
Emily"); a sudden detour points to unexpected consequences ("became
aware, casting an eye aside"). Description makes us curious, suspense
and surprise sustain our interest. Will a thing happen or not? How will it
be achieved or contrived? Its actual taking place, its breathing space and
moment hardly come into play. We are titillated, allured by details that
work up a pathetic or poignant effect; we do not find the inevitable
climax and anticlimax of sheer occurrence—as when Homer says: "they
looked; and wonder possessed them." We have an inherent brittleness
of description, not the gravity of things that materialize on their own
strength.
　　　　The subtlety of Homeric timing remains elusive. It either gets
dispersed in loose story-telling or it is spirited away by high epic
idealizations. It is as we might expect. Even at the lowest levels of discourse we discover the same sort of dichotomy: on one hand we find the
trivialities of hearsay and, on the other, the make-believe of peremptory
assertions. Flimsiness or empty rhetoric easily intervenes. The latter risk
is greatest where emphasis and celebration set in. Take, for instance,
Gloucester commemorating Henry V in Henry 1.1:
　　　　　England ne'er had a king until his time.
　　　　　Virtue he had, deserving to command;
　　　　　His brandished sword did blind men with his beams;
　　　　　His arms spread wider than a dragon's wings.
These lines solemnize but ring hollow because they entirely miss the
flow of action, have no narrative impact, only strive after effect. Thus an
epitaph crystallizes life into a record, an apologue exemplifies it, and a
prophecy or prayer projects it into an imaginary outcome. The focus is
on the outward importance of a thing, not the thing itself. The stateliness
of a monument or the definiteness of an aphorism is incompatible with
the immediacy of experience.
　　　　It is, however, a question of degree, not of hard and fast categories.
The notion of genre does not help us here. Different modes of perception
prevail, according to whether we recount, survey, evoke, or dramatize.
But, in each case, the sense of time is an underlying determining factor.
For the point at issue is to what extent a focal moment maintains its
ground or gives way to supervening interests. Homer's balance is a rare
one. We are usually drawn one way or the other. In a simple story we
move forward with its general drift, and no single moment stands out

except insofar as it has a direct bearing on the plot. But the opposite is true where mythical or fantastic elements prevail: we move here through a symbolic landscape, and the very imagery obstructs the narrative flow. Such is the case in the earliest epics. In *Gilgamesh*, for example, the succeeding points of focus stand out with lapidary effect:

> Gilgamesh
> who saw things secret, opened the places hidden,
> and carried back word of the time before the Flood —
> he travelled the road, exhausted, in pain,
> and cut his works into a stone tablet. [7]

Or further:

> Gilgamesh does not allow the son to go with his father;
> day and night he oppresses the weak. [8]

We have the effect of an inscription; each verse or sentence renders an attribute of the hero rather than a moment of action. Similarly, the various episodes (Enkidu and the animals, Enkidu and the Stalker, Enkidu and the Love-priestess, the fight of Enkidu and Gilgamesh) hardly develop like a Homeric scene. They reflect situations rather than actions. They seem to exist in their own sphere, quite apart from any particular spot or moment. They have a haunting, emblematic spell. As a result, the narrative connections are very slight: "He mounted the road; he set his face in the direction of Uruk" or "they mounted the road, went their journey."[9] The action does not flow; and the narrative strain tentatively finds its way, as if it could hardly cope with mysteries whose points of focus and connection lie elsewhere than in ordinary experience. Static situations are thus simply joined to one another. Though they each have a place in a mythical sequence, what absorbs us is their symbolism and not the way they come to be what they are. Here events are revelations rather than actual happenings. No wonder they are often preceded by a dream or a vision.

A closer analogy to Homer may be found in narrative parts of the Bible: for example 1 Samuel 16.21: "And David came to Saul, and stood before him; and he loved him greatly: and he became his armor-bearer"; ibid.18.1 "And it came to pass, when he had ceased speaking unto Saul, that the soul of Jonathan was knit with the soul of David, and Jonathan loved him as his own soul"; ibid. 23.18 "And they two made a covenant before the Lord; and David abode in the forest; and Jonathan went to his house."

This simple paratactic order is not unlike Homer's. Each act has a self-contained relief and yet comes in a natural sequence that thus acquires its own rhythm: the forthright presentation excludes any fastidious description of details; we have clarity and intrinsic solemnity. We miss, however, Homer's sensuous contours: any glance or physical touch at once absorbed into the passing act and letting the moment linger. Rather than stating "he stood," "he went" as irrevocable facts, Homer would convey more strongly the bodily presence and visual effect through epithet or simile. The biblical sentences have a different kind of high relief. The figures stand out in a bare, solitary self-relevance. The forceful impact is provided by their pertinent role, not by their immediate stance or movement. We are made to feel that any act or state is at once a decision, a choice, a destination. The focus is more conceptual than dramatic. If a character speaks, what matters is the weight of the message, not the utterance itself that forthwith blends with the immediate action. We thus do not have the thrust of act upon act, the process that engenders continuity of time. Here effects emerge at unspecified intervals. Hence comes the frequent phrase "and it came to pass that. . . ." Things take place for a reason that is shown later. There is an overriding cause. Episodes, even unintentionally, take the significance of a parable— as when David happens to look at Bathsheba taking her bath and incurs the wrath of God.

The originality of Homeric style lies in seizing the balance between momentary focus and contents, the narrative being continually gathered in a concrete instance of rest or movement. The story is one with the action, and the action is one with the cumulative acts that make it up. We have the impression that one great encompassing moment draws gods and men in its dynamic course.

Comparisons with Homer have been given a new direction by the theorists of oral composition. The whole body of popular, orally transmitted poetry has come into view. A. B. Lord's *Singer of Tales* is a book about Homer and yet it starts with an analysis of Yugoslavia's oral singers. "This book is about Homer," Lord writes in his Foreword:

He is our singer of Tales. Yet, in a larger sense, he represents all singers of tales from time immemorial and unrecorded to the present. Our book is about the other singers as well. Each of them, even the most mediocre, is as much part of the tradition of oral epic singing as is Homer, its most talented representative. Among the singers of modern times there is none to equal Homer, but he who approaches the master most closely in our experience is Avdo Mededovic of Bijelo Polje, Yugoslavia. He is our present-day Balkan Singer of Tales.

Here we have a radical differentiation between "oral" and "literary" poetry. The emphasis is on the oral tradition and how it works: compositional technique rather than style in its broadest sense, the complex of formulas and themes rather than poetry itself or the contents of any particular poem. The oral singer thus employs a step-by-step "adding" style because he is obliged to do so by the need of instant performance, while single phrases and larger narrative units are supplied by traditional patterns. As for the general subject-matter, what stands out is not so much any particular story as well-defined categories or thematic configurations, such as weddings, rescues, returns, and captures of cities. In some form or other, these all occur in epic oral song, including Homer.

These considerations concern culture and tradition rather than poetry itself. Let us turn, rather, to passages in which Lord deals with the poetic process. Two singers, Mumin and Avdo, sing a song with the same theme. Avdo is the greater one:

Avdo began and as he sang, the song lengthened, the ornamentation and richness accumulated, and the human touches of character, touches that distinguished Avdo from other singers, imparted a depth of feeling that had been missing from Mumin's version. . . . The main points of Mumin's account of the assembly are there, but by elaboration, by addition of similes, and of telling characterization, Avdo has not only lengthened the theme from 176 lines to 558, but has put on it the stamp of his own understanding of the heroic mind.[10]

Elsewhere Lord notes the almost Homeric touch in a scene that describes the caparisoning of a horse, italicizing "the lines which break the forward movement by providing ornamental descriptive details that add color and poetry to the actions themselves."[11] Or more generally: "The quality of an oral epic tradition depends in no small measure on the singer's skill in fashioning descriptions of heroes, horses, arms, and castles."[12]

Here ornamentation, expansion, elaboration, and description are the key words. We have the impression of a narrative scheme that gets filled with enriching details. A story would thus present itself in separate successive stages: contents and form, action and imagery, a central occurrence and its circumstances. It is as if things were first conceived and later sifted in varied detail. We have narrative theme on one hand and description on the other—the two abstracted from each other.

Homer does not fit into this picture. Whereas Lord's oral poet describes, Homer subjects description to movement: any detail becomes part and parcel of a passing act or state of being, we are carried forward from moment to moment. Consider such Homeric lines as "and around his shoulders he threw the sword silver-studded," "then the breast-plate he donned round his chest, variegated and starry," "and the fragrant robe she donned all around her," "under his glistening feet he bound the beautiful sandals." Here every act blends at once with the material that gives it tangible evidence, and the epithets do not so much describe as give the moment its necessary weight. Avdo, on the other hand, is burdened with description. In his "Song of Smailagic Meho" the hero is armed by his mother: "Then she gave him a cylindrical breastplate. It was not of silver but of pure gold and weighed full four stone . . . . Then she put upon him his silken breeches, of Damascus make, all embroidered with gold, with serpents depicted upon his thighs. . . ."[13] Every successive act is quite lost here in the curiosities of accumulating description. The Homeric sense of movement is quite lost.

Or take the theme of welcoming guests into a house. In Homer no sooner is any piece of furniture or implement mentioned than it is set in motion, used, handled—in Od.1.130 ff., for instance: "he led and seated her on a beautiful chair cunningly-wrought, spreading a cloth underneath . . . for himself he placed beside it a stool many-colored," and "hand-washing water did the handmaid bring and with a lovely golden jug she poured it over a basin of silver: at the side she laid out a well-polished table." The epithets again help evince each act in its fullness, without at all interrupting the forward flow and giving it, rather, a visual effect. Quite otherwise, Avdo steeps us in description: "That room was kept for such heroes as these. It was strewn with Venetian cloth, and around about were silk couches and fine pillows covered with white silk and embroidered in the center with gold. . . .In the middle of the room was a table spread with Venetian cloth and on it a metal platter. . . ."[14] We have here a show of wealth, not the vivid visual effect which Homer stirs up through a sense of action.

Lessing observed long ago the creative way in which Homer joins any material thing with the act that brings it to the fore.[15] Hence come energy and clarity of outline: the full presence of a thing asserts its claim, while the passing act precludes adventitious description. We are made aware of such a style right from the beginning of the *Iliad*. Nothing, nobody is mentioned except in immediate connection with its actual occasion: Apollo in that he sends the plague, Chryses in that Agamemnon wrongs him, the ships of the Achaeans in that Chryses reaches them, his fillets and scepter in that he carries them. Where we might most expect mere description, the same style prevails—in the palace and garden of Alcinous for instance (Od.7.84 ff.). We are not just told that a thing was there or what it was made of, or simply given a magnificent display: instead, each thing occupies its place and moment, therein finding its function: the walls are drawn one way and the other, the portals enclose the mansions, thrones rest against the parapet, columns stand up on the threshold, trees rise up or vegetate in fullness, their fruit ripens. Every detail covers its ground; it stands, rests, rises, touches, and the verse articulates modes of existence even while describing a scenery.

This exclusion of abstracted description is symptomatic; and it is also characteristic of Homer. Things cannot be detached from their actual presence, they cannot be abstracted from their taking place and affecting our experience. A certain spot, a certain moment are essential here. If anything is mentioned, it presents itself and takes position in the field of vision. There is always a perspective that opens up and extends along the narrative. Thus we have inevitable contiguities of time and space. It is as if things were juxtaposed by the order of existence. This is the reason why Homer's paratactic style finds no analogy in that of Lord's oral poets who simply add detail to detail. Take a passage quoted by Lord as an example of the "adding style" in oral composition:

> Wherever he went, he asked for Alija.
> They said he was in the city of Kajnida.
> When the messenger came to Kajnida.
> He passed along the main street
> then he approached the new shopkeeper,
> and he asked for Alija's court.
> The shopkeeper pointed out the court to him.
> When the messenger came to the gate,
> He beat with the knocker on the door.
> The knocker rang and the gate resounded. [16]

The only Homeric touch is in the last line: an act and its immediate repercussion. The loose realism of the rest is quite unhomeric. Indeed we have separate sentences, separate acts following one another, but they are incidental and not intrinsic to the action in itself. "Whenever he went . . . ," "they said. . . ," "he approached the new shopkeeper. . .": such details work up a suspense that might arbitrarily be shortened or prolonged. We are puzzled about the next step. In Homer there is no character hectically seeking another (Hector seeking Andromache in Il.6.371 ff. is obviously quite different). No, Homer would give us such straight inevitable sequence as "he saw. . .he came. . .he stood by him" or "he came. . .he arrived. . .he found" (cf., Il.4.199 ff.; 5.167 ff.; Od.4.1 ff.). He leaves out intervals that might be filled with all sorts of detail. Each sentence leans solemnly on the next in leading to a conclusion. Homer gives us action in the making where others narrate and describe.

This difference is a fundamental one. It rebounds in the composition as a whole. We may oppose to Homer's rectilinear action the complications and varied incidents in Lord's oral poets. The latter do not have Homer's compression of time, we lose track of time altogether drawn along as we are by the proliferation of episodes. Avdo's "Beciragic Meho," for instance, involves an indefinite lapse of time; the hero's reversals of fortune, the story of his love, his exile and return, a triumphal final battle, his wedding, and all the obstructions that retard these developments. In this respect at least, Avdo is more similar to Chaucer and Ariosto that he is to Homer.

To the theorists of oral composition, however, Homer is essentially a weaver of tales. They ignore the sense of time that subtends the plot. Lord sees in the Homeric poems a conflation of themes, not the developing action. This is how he explains the treatment of time in the *Iliad*: Achilles withdrawing from the army and later coming back represents the theme of a hero's absence and return—a theme that normally entails a long period of time but is cut short in Homer by the insertion of a similar subsidiary theme consisting in the loss of Patroclus (the "subsidiary") and his return in the shape of a ghost. Hence the traditional length of time is "telescoped" into a much shorter duration. As a result, the element of long duration remains "vestigial": that is to say, it is submerged in the idea of the ten-year Trojan war which is intimated in such scenes as the *Catalogue of Ships*, and the duel of Paris and Menelaus.[17]

Even if we admit these conflations and adaptations to be true, we should surely recognize this shortened time-span as the most distinctive Homeric trait. And we may argue that the brevity of the action finds its intrinsic reason in the poem itself—in the way Homer renders the immediacy of events and emotions: Achilles' wrath, his withdrawal, his grief for Patroclus; his revenge cannot but find immediate effect in Homer's style. Lord's traditional themes here are vanishing shadows, banished by the forward movement of the action that necessarily excludes narrative length. As in all great art, there is in the Homeric poems a motivating force that cannot be merely due to the desire of telling a story. The pulse of Homer's verse and sentence gives us a cue of what this force really is.

We have a mode of perception and realization. A quality of this kind is subtle, pervasive. It does not relate to the subject-matter or to any specific idea. Therefore it does not lend itself to being transmitted from generation to generation of singers nor is it an object of easy imitation. A certain theme can be isolated and traced in its various applications, a myth can be followed up in its successive versions, and a specific idea can be abstracted and its history written; but, in these cases, what stands out is necessarily an abstraction, a scheme, a pattern. Here our domain is entirely different: the mode of perception and not the thing perceived, the movement of thought and not the thought in its literal message.

NOTES

1. Significantly, we do find θάνε, ἔθανε in an independent clause, but in mythical passages outside the mainstream of the action: Il.2.642; Od.8.226.

2. *Matière et Mémoire*. Paris:1982: 234.

3.   M. P. Nilsson. *Götter und Psychologie bei Homer*, Archiv für Religionswissenschaft:1924: 361.

4. Simone Weil. *L' "Iliade" ou le poème de la force*, Marseille: 1947.

5. Werner Jaeger. *Paideia* . Trans. G. Highet, New York: 1945: Vol.1.18.

6.   Geoffrey Chaucer. *The Canterbury Tales* . Trans. Nevill Coghill. Penguin: Hammondsworth.1951: 42,43.

7. *Gilgamesh,* translated J. Gardner and J. Maier, New York: Knopf. 1985: 57.

8. Ibid. 67.

9. Ibid. 74.

10. A. B. Lord, *The Singer of Tales*. New York:1965: 78-9.

11. Ibid.55.

12. Ibid.86.

13. Ibid.87.

14. Ibid.108.

15. G. E. Lessing, *Laokoon* , ch.XVI.

16. A. B. Lord, *The Singer of Tales*, New York:1965: 54-5.

17. Ibid.186-7.

Chapter 6

Apollonius Rhodius

APOLLONIUS AND HOMER: SENSE OF THE COMPARISON

Distinctions show best against the foil of a common material: and the distinctive quality of Homeric verse may be made clearer through a comparison with Apollonius whose verse, though technically the same as Homer's, produces quite a different effect.

Any reader, even at first glance, may realize the difference. We sense in Apollonius a quality that makes him, say, more similar to Virgil than to Homer. But why does he so differ from Homer? The difference is as clear as it is hard to explain. For what we have is the *feeling* of a difference; and feelings are immediately convincing, but vague and elusive.

Can we account for such a feeling by pointing to certain characteristics in the verse itself? Can we do so quite objectively? We must look at Homer and Apollonius, taking either's verse at its own face value and reaching out for what qualities it might convey. We would get lost in a circular argument if we started invoking historical reasons—opposing, say, the Hellenistic to the Homeric age or, worse, differentiating between "literate" and "oral" poetry. Let us, rather, pretend that we are quite ignorant of history and social conditions. The thing itself, after all, is set before us for all it is worth. We must look at it directly with no other concern—as when, visiting a museum, we may better appreciate a work of art without finding out beforehand of what school or author it is.

INTRODUCTIONS TO SPEECHES

Consider, first, single details whose narrow focus may provide clearer evidence. Verses that introduce a speech come to mind. We have, in Homer the typical τοῖσι δ' ἀνιστάμενος μετέφη πόδας ὠκὺς Ἀχιλλεύς (1.58; 19.55). There is the sense of a definite spot and moment before the central caesura; then at the center, the act of speech; and at the end, the hero's name with its epithet. Give voice to this sequence: an initial rising movement finds its climax in the central verb and then subsides in the final image. The connections appear inevitable: the initial circumstance prefigures the following act and the act, in turn, prefigures its agent. By marking also the minor caesura, we may get attuned more closely: τοῖσι/ δ' ἀνιστάμενος ‖ μετέφη / πόδας ὠκὺς / Ἀχιλλεύς [and in their midst, standing up, so spoke swift-footed Achilles]. Here are modulations that make us realize the process in its delicate stages. It is as if the rising and subsiding movement of the verse corresponded to our sense of anticipation and fulfillment.

In Apollonius we find nothing of the kind. Where he has a single verse with the speaker's name, he usually lets the name come at the beginning of the verse, as in 1.331: τοῖσιν δ' Αἴσονος υἱὸς ἐυφρονέων μετέειπε [and to them Aeson's son kindly-thinking thus spoke, cf. 864; 2.885, 1134, 1140, 1178, 1276; 3.55, 491, 710; 4.1260]. Here we lack Homer's modulation; there is no rhythm of expectancy and fulfillment. The proper name, at the beginning of the verse, does not announce anything in particular; it might be followed by any predicate or complement. We have a smooth versification in which the caesuras simply articulate the narrative meaning of the sentence.

The strength of Apollonius lies in qualifying or characterizing the act of speech, as in 1.293–4:

αὐτὰρ ὁ τήνγε

μειλιχίοις ἐπέεσσι παρηγορέων προσέειπε

and to her

with sweet word in comfort he spoke.

(cf. 486, 792; 2.437; 3.24, 51, 463, 505, 687, 974, 1023, 1104, 1142; 4.394, 1740) What strikes us about this verse is a generalized mellowness of tone. As elsewhere, a sense of mood or emotion is essential to the verse: evenly distributed, it levels off the inner tension of the rhythm. Thus, in the present instance, "with sweet words," "consoling," suffuse the verse with softness. As a result, the act of speech loses its intrinsic contours; and the caesuras articulate separate descriptive details, but do not give us the natural pauses of the unfolding act. The phrase μειλιχίοις ἐπέεσσι is indeed Homeric, but not its position with a verb of kindred meaning ("comforting"). In Homer it either comes at the verse-end, prolonging the act of speech with a lengthening cadence (Od.9.363; 11.552) or, at the beginning, it picks up through enjambment an act intimated in the preceding verse (Il.11.137; 21.339; Od. 18.283, etc.). This style maintains the sense of movement.

Often, in Apollonius, a long qualifying word, after the central caesura, stretches over the whole of the third colon. It has an encompassing effect, affecting the tone of the whole verse—as in the verse-end 3.101, ἡ δ᾽ αὖτις ἀκηχεμένη προσέειπε [and again aggrieved she spoke, cf.1.1256; 2.443; 3.770]. Similarly, and most frequently, this also appears in verses that do not introduce a speech, such as 1.152, 262, 268. Homer, on the other hand, is much more sparing in this use of qualifying words. If he qualifies a speaker at all, he does so more lightly. Compare the way he integrates the quality with the initial movement of the verse, in such verse-beginnings as τὸν δὲ μέγ᾽ ὀχθήσας [and to him in anger . . . , Il.7.454, etc.], τὸν δ᾽ ἄρ᾽ ὑπόδρα ἰδών [and to him looking askance,1.148, etc.], and τὸν δ᾽ ἐπιμειδήσας [and to him with a smile, 4.356, etc.]. These phrases are like opening notes in the process of the verse. Anger, bitterness, and pleasure thus take their momentary position, as simply and lightly as any starting-point that touches off a certain climax. We might compare, in Homer, the initial εὐφρονέων [kindly thinking, Il.1.73, 253, etc.], whereas Apollonius has a final εὐφρονέων μετέειπε (1.331, cf. 2.437). The descriptive phrase "kindly said" blunts the verse at its edge.

Apollonius goes much further. At times the verb of saying is quite left out (3.10, 4.1013) or it seems lost in the midst of accompanying emotions and circumstances. A remarkable passage is 3.367–71 describing Aeetes' anger and suspicion when the Argonauts arrive. The phrase φῆ δ᾽ ἐπαλαστήσας [he spoke in anger, 369] finds itself embedded among others that render the king's behavior: his soaring spirits, his motivations, his flashing eyes. The moment of the utterance is thus driven to a corner by a sense of attending conditions. In the same way, anything mentioned as a detail contributes to a larger effect; and each verse finds its focus in driving a point further rather than in marking a necessary distinctive phase. Often Apollonius so blends emotion with circumstance, giving us modes of behavior and including the act of speech in a series of other acts (cf. 3.686–7, 734–7, 1063–8; 4.1096–7; 3.317).

Homer, on the other hand, gives any strong emotion its own independent place, as in Il.1.101–5: we see Agamemnon rising up, his midriff is filled with fury, his eyes flash like fire; and then the act of speech follows. There is a poetic logic in this sequence; and each act or state seems to have its inevitable position in the unfolding moment (cf.

199–201; 3.395–8; 16.5–6; 22.147–9, 475–6; Od 4.703–6; 5.116–7; 10.496–500; 19.471–3; 23.32–34).

Why does Homer maintain these distinctions of focus, much more than Apollonius? And why are these distinctions reflected in the distinction of verse from verse? The reason lies, again, in Homer's sense of the concrete. Even an emotion is something that takes place—an event rather than a psychological notion. In the passage just quoted, it fills Agamemnon's midriff, and flashes through his eyes. Here are movements that rise and pass away. They have their space in the verse no less than in actual experience; and their forceful distinction would be lost if they were paraphrased or charged with descriptive detail. In the same way, the moment of speaking out cannot be curtailed or put out of place.

The difference of Apollonius is due to a greater degree of abstraction. He blurs the act of speech (or any other), because his attention is turned to something else—to the idea of the situation as a whole. Aeetes is, like Agamemnon, a king who feels challenged; but in Apollonius we have the king's general state of mind; in Homer we have, rather, the moment of the challenge. Hence comes in the former a turmoil that impinges on details, in the latter an organic connection and expanding movement. The verse itself is naturally affected. We miss, in Apollonius, the upward and downward beat of the verse or the forcefulness of the enjambment. Thus in φῆ δ' ἐπαλαστήσας, μενέαινε δὲ παισί [and he said greatly angered, he was most vexed with the children, 3.369], a basic point of emotion is followed by explanation and not a necessary anticlimax. There is no sense, in other words, of heightening and subsiding tension. These are replaced by degrees of descriptive emphasis, as the poet first stresses the king's anger and then his motivations. A sort of narrative abstraction sets in. It is no wonder that words and phrases are abstracted from their natural concrete context. The Homeric midriff (φρένες), for instance, ceases to be the deep seat of emotions or thoughts and comes to signify "high-soaring spirit" (368).

SILENCE AFTER A SPEECH

Consider now, in the same light, a verse of Homer that often renders the silence of listeners after an impressive speech: ὣς ἔφατ᾽, οἱ δ᾽ ἄρα πάντες ἀκὴν ἐγένοντο σιωπῇ. We may translate, marking the caesuras and thus separating the "cola": so did he speak,/ and they all, || in stillness,/ fell into silence. (Il.3.95; 7.92,398; 8.28; 9.29, 430, 693; 10.218, 313; 23.676; Od.8.234; 11.333; 13.1; 16.393). First there is an echo of the preceding speech ("so did he speak"); next the presence of those who attend and feel the impact ("and they all"); then, after the main caesura, the first intimation of that impact ("in stillness"); and finally the sense of an encompassing silence in the closing cadence ("and they fell into silence"). The moment lingers and vanishes, as though the echo of speech passed into the ensuing silence. The same impression is amplified by an additional line rendering the Phaeacians who have just listened to Odysseus (Od.11.334; 13.2): κηληθμῷ δ' ἔσχοντο κατὰ μέγαρα σκιόεντα, which we may translate "and by a spell/ they were held ‖ in the halls/ full of shadows." Those halls with their shadows assuage the suspense; they afford a space upon which the silence lingers and comes to rest.

What Homer renders as an event exerting its sway is turned by Apollonius into a characterization of the listeners. Take Apollonius 3.503–4 (4.693,3.967):

δὴν δ' ἄνεῳ καὶ ἄναυδοι ἐς ἀλλήλους ὁρόωντο

ἄτῃ ἀμηχανίῃ τε κατηφέες.

or 3.422–3:

ὣς ἄρ' ἔφη· ὁ δὲ σῖγα ποδῶν πάρος ὄμματα πήξας,

ἧστ' αὔτως ἄφθογγος ἀμηχανέων κακότητι.

or, again, 2.408–10:

ὣς ἄρ' ἔφη· τοὺς δ' εἶθαρ ἕλεν δέος εἰσαΐοντας,

δὴν δ' ἔσαν ἀμφασίῃ βεβολημένοι· ὀψὲ δ' ἔειπε

ἥρως Αἴσονος υἱός, ἀμηχανέων κακότητι.

We could not read these verses in the same way as Homer's; the rhythmical effect is quite different. Let us try to translate, taking the caesuras into account:

for long/ in silence/ and speechless ‖ to one another/ they
looked,

by doom/and helplessness ‖ crushed.

and:

So he spoke: / and in silence ‖ upon his feet/ staring down
he sat just so/ without speech, ‖ helpless/ in his misfortune.

and:

So he spoke:/ upon them forthwith ‖ terror set on / as they
heard,

for long there they were/ without speech, ‖ struck dumb;/ and
at length did he speak

the hero,/ the son of Aison ‖ despairing/ before their woe.

Although the caesuras are metrically the same as Homer's, the cola which they enclose do not carry through the same kind of movement. These cola give us units of meaning rather than phases in the verse. They have a static quality. Here we find the image of a speechless desperate man, not the sense of an enervating tension that comes and passes. Apollonius defines and refines touch after touch, perfecting a mental image: where Apollonius has ἀμηχανέων κακότητι [helpless in his misfortune], at the verse-end, Homer would probably have ἀμηχανίη δ' ἔχε θυμόν [and helplessness held his spirit, Od.9.295], giving us the last phase of an active process and not a final qualification.

Apollonius' rhythm tunes us to a conflation of meanings in a certain key: as we repeat his verse, we may, for instance, see in our mind's eye a desperate man stranded on the shore or a love-lorn woman in her chamber. A finished figure is produced. What we gain in neatness of contour we lose in the forcefulness of movement or sheer presence. It is as though an embroidery replaced the underlying existential texture.

ORDER OF WORDS

More generally, this leveling of the verse into one uniform theme of description may be seen in the way Apollonius, unlike Homer, often has an initial adjective that agrees with a final noun, as in 2.570: λευκή καχλάζοντος ἀνέπτυε κύματος ἄχνη (cf. 1.9, 222, 337, 445, 521, 539, 917, 935, 1108, 1237). In these instances, again, a sense of quality smoothly informs the verse. Thus, in our example, "white" at the beginning and "foam" at the end at once frame the picture and coalesce with it; the whiteness of the foam blends with the splash of the wave. In order to render the impression, we might translate: "in the white splash of the wave surged the foam." An effect of color and sound blurs the movement of the wave. Contrast Il.11.307:

πολλὸν δὲ τρόφι κῦμα κυλίνδεται, ὑψόσε δ' ἄχνη
σκίδναται.

in fullness / the swollen wave ǁ rolls on:/ and up does the foam scatter.

(cf. 4.426; Od.5.403; 12.238) Homer has action rather than effect: a growing massive presence at the beginning; then (after the central caesura) its advance; and finally the rising foam. The enjambment makes us feel the wave's impact that cannot be contained within one spot. We might even forget the literal contents; the rhythm itself conveys the sense of a heaving mass that comes to its breaking point.

Apollonius' verse attains further preciousness when qualifications interpenetrate one another (ABAB or ABBA) as in 3.220: ἡμερίδες χλοεροῖσι καταστεφέες πετάλοισι (cf. 1.546; 2.600, 810; 3.1064, 1085, 1295; 4.128, 885. 1017). Here the adjectives are separated from their nouns by other intervening adjectives and nouns, the images crisscross one another; and the verse holds together a composite impression. The caesuras thus mark semantic relations, not fluid transitions of meaning.

The example just quoted gives us an effect of verdant fullness. Keeping more or less the same order of words, we might translate: "vines with verdure brimming on their leaves." Contrast Od.5.69:

ἡμερὶς ἡβώωσα, τεθήλει δὲ σταφυλῇσι.

a vine in its youth, and it bloomed with clusters of grapes.
Homer lets the moment of blossom intervene, breaking description. Even a plant is given inner tension. Hardly anything in Homer is presented as a still life. Around Calypso's cave (Od.5.63 ff.) the vegetation extends, blossoms, grows; the olive tree in Il.17.53–6 hardly exists as an object of description: the husbandman tends it, water flows around it, winds give it air, it blooms, it teems with blossoms. Hence the verse itself stirs with activity.

GENERAL EFFECT

Apollonius mostly keeps us to a leisurely pace, condensing or enlarging upon points of interest. The intrinsic rhythm of incidents escapes him. He generalizes, giving us the result of an incident rather than the incident itself. He has, for instance, in 1.655: καί ῥ' ὅτε δὴ μάλα πᾶσαι ὁμιλαδὸν ἡγερέθοντο [when all in one group they were gathered], a verse that merely reports a crowded gathering. Contrast Homer's οἱ δ' ἐπεὶ οὖν ἤγερθεν ὁμηγερέες τ' ἐγένοντο (Il.1.57; Od.2.9, etc.) which gives us a sense of the process: "they assembled/ and in one body were gathered." Compare other such generalizing verses in Apollonius: 1.234, 261, 394, 530, 877.

Anything striking must, however, have its due. In Apollonius, the striving for effect at times hits the mark. Consider, for instance, 3.71:

χείμαρροι καναχηδὰ κυλινδόμενοι φορέοντο

torrents roaringly rolling were rushing
(cf. 1.669, 1272; 2.600; 3.147, 655, 1251; 4.1158). In such instances, there is no distinctive point of focus, but an image encompasses the verse, and each word evenly contributes to the general meaning. Thus what stands out in the verse just quoted is a torrential vehemence. Accordingly the words blend in one continuous strain: the initial χείμαρροι suggests "winter-flowing"; καναχηδὰ, an adverb, expresses mode and not action; and κυλινδόμενοι φορέοντο gives us the effect of rolling water rather than the current itself. We are further distracted from the modulation of movement by the obvious alliteration as well as by the coincidence of each colon with a full heavy word. As a result, the verse has a sweep that overwhelms us; we are given no pause, no climax and anticlimax. Contrast Il.11.493: χειμάρρους κατ' ὄρεσφιν, ὀπαζόμενος Διὸς ὄμβρῳ [a torrent/ down from the mountains || forced on / by rain from the heavens, cf. 4.452; 16.389]. The caesuras here mark high points

of action and place: a flowing; a descent from the mountains; a swelling; rain from the sky. The rhythm itself spells out the focal points.

Elsewhere in Apollonius it is an emotion or mental condition that builds up with cumulative emphasis. Such is the case in 2.623: ἤμβροτον, ἀασάμην τε κακὴν καὶ ἀμήχανον ἄτην (cf. 2.229, 232, 346, 1202; 3.390, 695, 810; 4.445) "I failed, I am lost in wretched helpless delusion": we have here no development, but the burden of an encompassing stress. Contrast Il.19.137: ἀλλ' ἐπεὶ ἀασάμην καί μευ φρένας ἐξέλετο Ζεύς [but since I was deluded, and Zeus took away my wits]. Here is the sense of a process: the moment of delusion, the presence of mind quite lost—with the central caesura marking transition.

Apollonius achieves at times a purely aesthetic effect. In 2.933–5 he renders the even, swift flight of a hawk through the summer sky, describing the bird as εὐκήλοισιν ἐνευδιόων πτερύγεσσιν [resting in sunlight upon the ease of its wings]. The verse is hardly translatable, chiefly because of the long heavy word ἐνευδιόων blending with the other two. The outstretched wings, the sky, the very happiness of such a state constitute one encompassing impression. The very fact that the caesura is unimportant lets us enjoy the bird's unbroken flight. Contrast with this picture Il.2.462: ἔνθα καὶ ἔνθα ποτῶνται ἀγαλλόμενα πτερύγεσσι [Hither and thither/ they fly ‖ taking delight/ in their wings]: a nimble initial movement subsides into fullness of contour at the end of the verse. Homer has no room for the luxury of purely aesthetic impressions.

Apollonius outdoes himself on occasions. Especially in these last instances, he does not so much describe a fact as condense an impression. Mode, aspect, and condition replace the act itself. Abstraction thus gives rise to new perception. The hawk, though in swift motion, seems stilled in an idealized moment. Things lose their hard objective contours and dimensions are made elusive when we find the adjective εὔκηλος [glad, tranquil] applied to the bird's wings and even sunlight rendered as a state or quality of the bird itself by the word ἐνευδιόων.

ENJAMBMENT

A compression of meanings, however, is not necessarily poetic. In Apollonius we often find disparate things joined together for the sake of descriptive convenience, circumstances or moods casually modifying the action. Such is, for instance, the use of the genitive absolute as in 2.903: λαιφέων πεπταμένων τέμνον πλόον εὐδιόωντες [the sails being spread out, they cleaved their sea-path in joy, cf. 1.512, 688; 2.449, 494, 930, 961, 1112]. Homer would set in separate high relief a swelling sail or a ship cleaving the water (cf. Il.1.480; Od.2.426; 5.269). If any circumstance is striking enough to be mentioned, Homer treats it as a happening in its own right, either giving it a whole verse or letting it reach beyond, through enjambment. A circumstance thus ceases to be a mere circumstance. It has its own pulse and breathing space. The verse itself gives it body.

Since Apollonius' verse lacks focus, his enjambments are necessarily looser than they are in Homer. This looseness is shown most clearly by the frequency with which an adjective in the preceding verse agrees with its noun in the next one: 1.153–4, 182–3, 219–20, 239–40, 262–3, 325–6, 359–60, 417–8. In these instances a qualitative sense announces what comes later, obscuring the division between verse and verse. Take 2.551–2:

δινήεις ὑπένερθεν ἀνακλύζεσκεν ἰοῦσαν
νῆα ῥόος.

The meaning is plain: "a whirling current washed up against the ship as she moved along"; but it is so rendered that we have suspense first and the actual occurrence thereafter. The caesuras in the first verse do not mark points in a sequence, but concurring points of danger; only later is the situation made clear. To render the effect, we might translate: "a whirling, a stress from below, a flooding against the passage—/ such to the ship was the current." It is chiefly the separation between δινήεις and ῥόος in two different verses that works up the blurring atmosphere of danger. Such separation is very rare in Homer.

Just as the rhythmical distinctions of meaning within Apollonius' verse give way to a leveling trend, so do the divisions between succeeding verses lose their edge. Here we miss Homer's sharp shift of focus. Apollonius often lets sentences run over from verse to verse in a leisurely and casual sort of way. Consider, for instance, 2.155–7:

καὶ τότε μὲν μένον αὖθι διὰ κνέφας, ἕλκεά τ' ἀνδρῶν
οὐταμένων ἀκέοντο, καὶ ἀθανάτοισι θυηλὰς
ῥέξαντες μέγα δόρπον ἐφώπλισαν.

Then they stayed there through the night, and the wounds of
the men
who were injured they tended and with sacrifice to the gods
they made a great meal.

We have activities rather than acts, a situation rather than states of being. There is, therefore, no particular focus, no sense of flowing moments necessarily bound to one another. The passage has a discursive drift: versification rather than actual verse. Compare especially 1.910–44; 2.528–30, 22.1262–7, 3.253–9, 270–4; 4.78–82, 718–21, 1223–5. Cases in point are also those in which a conjunction starts the fresh verse—as in

1.1180-1: ἦια τὲ σφι/ μῆλά τε [provisions to them / and sheep, cf. 2.861–2; 3.389–90, 596–7]. The addition is weak, nerveless. We have, at best, a metrical treatment of the accumulating material.

Apollonius' enjambment differs form Homer's as we might expect. Where the rhythm does not contain and release the action, all sense of tension is lost; and the metre, left to itself, is more or less skillfully adapted to the narrative. It is a different case in particularly dramatic passages. Here the verse is given focus by the context; and the enjambment, if it occurs, takes a special significance. In 4.1032, for instance, ἐγώ. . .ἧς ἰότητι / ταύρους τ' ἐζεύξασθε [I. . .through whose will / you yoked the bulls], the enjambment highlights Medea's help. In 3.1129: οὐδ' ἄμμε διακρινέει φιλότητος / ἄλλο [nor from our love / shall anything else divide us. . .] the verse-end is a climax introducing the next thought (cf. 2.627–8; 3.681–2, 725–6, 741–2, 764–5, 1069–70, 1077–8; 4.355–9, 370–1). In these instances, a word takes increased significance from its position at the point of enjambment (whether at the end of the preceding verse or at the beginning of the following one). Such a word often denotes emotion. A change of tone sets in; and a heightening strain passes from verse to verse. The rhythm thus subserves a further motive. As compared with Homer, an arbitrary emphasis intervenes. Whereas in Homer the pathos is implicit in a mere shift of focus, Apollonius abstracts the pathos from the act itself and turns it into an independent theme. The undertone thus becomes the main thing; encompassing passions replace the shifting outline of actual happenings. See, for instance, Medea reproaching Jason in 4.356–9:   pride, forgetfulness, bitter constraint, and perjury are set in dominant position by the enjambment;   and verse after verse rehearses the theme of unrequited benefits.

DESCRIPTIVENESS

A single verse is often indicative of the whole poem;   the rhythm itself implies a certain mode of conceiving things or events. We may thus move away from isolated verses to a more general purview, looking at passages that bring out in broader terms the characteristics observed so far. What stands out is the contents. The way it is presented can be readily understood in translation. There will be no need to quote from the Greek. Comparing Homer to Apollonius along these lines, we may make it easier to understand the intrinsic quality of Homeric verse and poetry.

Take Apollonius' Medea contemplating suicide in a moment of repentance, 3.791–4:

But, even so, when I am dead, they will leer at me in future

with mocking taunts; each city far and wide shall decry
my doom; perchance bearing my name on their lips
hither and thither the Colchian women with base reproach shall
                                                        revile me.

Compare Homer's Helen in Il.3.410–12:

Thither I shall not go—a thing of shame it would be—
there to attend on his bed. The Trojan women in future,
all of them will reproach me; I have infinite pain in my heart.

Medea imagines a future that quite displaces the present occasion; Helen
is firmly rooted where she is: after letting the present branch out for a
moment, she returns to it forthwith ("I have infinite pain"). Medea
fantasizes; Helen realizes. Where Apollonius composes a possible
scenario, Homer brings back to its initial point of focus the opening
perspective. Thus Helen would hardly go into the details of a possible
suicide; she wishes at most that she had died at her birth (Il.6.345–7, cf.
3.173–5).

Homer thus portrays Odysseus and Nausicaa (Od.6.236–7):

He then sat away withdrawn upon the shore of the sea
in beauty and graces lit up; and the girl was gazing upon him.

Compare Apollonius' presentation of Jason and Medea in 3.443–5:

Wondrously did in their midst the son of Aeson stand out
in beauty and graces; with her eyes upon him the girl
askance gazed out, holding her veil on one side.

Whereas Homer isolates the images, Apollonius crowds them and adds
realistic detail. Hence the visual, non-narrative effect is much stronger in
Homer: all we have is a mutual presence, a meaningful gaze. It is as if
place and moment conspired to bring about the golden chance.

Where Homer has (Il.4.79):

Down she sprang in their midst, wonder possessed them
                                              in seeing.

Apollonius so renders a similar situation (2.681-2):

Them did irresistible wonder encompass; nor anyone dared
face to face to look out into the god's lovely eyes.

Again we have in Homer pure vision, bared of accessory details. The
epiphany and the wonder of the beholders are aspects of the same thing,
each taking its inevitable place through the very rhythm of the verse.

Or consider passages of a different kind in the same light.
Apollonius so renders a storm in 2.1098 ff.:

Zeus set astir the might of the North-wind to blow,
marking with rain the wet path of the Bear's constellation.
All day long in the mountains he was stirring the leaves
slightly with gentle breeze upon the uppermost sprays,
but at night he massively dashed on the sea, roused the waves

with roaring blasts; in dark fog were the heavens
shrouded, nowhere were stars to be seen shining out
from the clouds, black gloom pressed hard all around.
Contrast with this passage Homer's storm in Od.9.67–69, cf.12.323–5:
On the ships he stirred up the North-wind, Zeus-assembler-of-
clouds,
with wondrous blast, and with clouds he encompassed
both earth and sea; down from the sky emerged night.
In Apollonius, Zeus gets lost in the effects which he produces; in Homer
each phase is a stroke of his hand. The latter treatment does not
necessarily signify a greater belief in the god; instead, the god's acts
serve to articulate the storm's impact with clarity of outline. Homer's
storm is as powerful as Apollonius', and yet it is as simply rendered as a
hand that closes upon what it touches.

For the same reason we shall not find in Apollonius anything like
the sudden emergence of rose-fingered dawn, but (1280–2):
When from over the sky joyous dawn starts to glow,
as from the horizon it rises; translucent are all the paths
and the plains full of dew gleam in the brightness of light.
(cf. 1..519–21; 2.164–5; 3.823–4)
Nor again shall we find in Apollonius the striking moment of
nightfall as in the Odyssey (2.388,etc.), but instead (3.744 ff.):
Night over the world drew darkness; and out at sea
the sailors looked at the Bear and at the stars of Orion
up from their ships; and for sleep were they longing.
now, many a wayfarer or watchman. Mothers whose children
were dead
were lying covered up in deep numbing slumber.
No barking of dogs through the city, and no sound
of voices; silence was holding the blackening dark.
(cf. 1.450–2; 3.1191–4; 4.1058–60) In Apollonius, as in narrative
generally, the action runs through an indefinite lapse of time; and any
daybreak or nightfall can be singled out for special description. But in
Homer daybreak and nightfall are essential units of time as well as
phenomena. Hence they are rendered in their sudden wonder and yet
with the precision of light and shade upon a sundial.

This forceful immediacy is most remarkable in Homer's treatment
of character. The *Iliad* no sooner starts than Chryses makes his sudden
appeal or Achilles finds himself inspired to call the assembly. Chalcas
speaks, and rage fills Agamemnon's midriff; the latter utters his threat,
and grief encompasses Achilles. Passions rise and materialize like
natural phenomena. In Apollonius there is much more preparation or
elaboration: Pelias' malice or Alkimede's effusions at the beginning of

the poem are, in this respect, no less significant than is, later, the dark temper of Aeetes or Chalciope's solicitousness. Why then is Apollonius less forcible in his characters? We may, again, find the reason in Homer's sense of focus. Feeling or emotion is, in Homer, realized rather than described. It is something that actually takes place in response to an immediate event: "he heard, and feared in his heart," "he saw him fall and took pity," "he gazed and awe come upon him." The connection is always forceful. There is nothing arbitrary or contrived. The rhythm itself brings out climax and anticlimax, cause and consequence, action and reaction. It is as if poetic logic produced the characters through cumulative instances. The truth of character is one with the truth of the situation.

Apollonius is a master in the portraiture of love. Whereas Homer only gives us the central moment when love encompasses the mind (Il.3.442,446; 14.316,328), Apollonius highlights in his Medea the intensifying stages—from the initial shyness and awe to the crowning passion. Hesitations, fears, tentative steps, idealization, and resolution come into the picture. We have, for instance, in 3.286:

> the dart burnt up in the girl,
> deep under her heart like a flame; and ever before him,
> on Jason she cast sparkling looks; intensely up from her breast
> her toiling senses aspired, not anything else she had in her
> but this one thought, and flowing in sweet pain was her soul.

(cf. 3.444–7, 451–62, 645–64, 681–7, 724–7, 752–70, 806–16, 948–55, 1008–24, 1149–52, 1157–62, 4.16–19) Symptom blends with symptom, and emotion with emotion; Medea is no longer a dread enchantress, but a maiden growing into a full-fledged woman.

Does Homer give more than one or two verses to this crucial experience, describing it directly? No, the great scene in Il.3.383–447 approaches it dramatically. Here, Helen suddenly recognizes Aphrodite at her side:

> and when she perceived the beautiful neck of the goddess
> and her breasts full of desire and her dazzling eyes,
> she was astounded and spoke and called out.

Aphrodite is here the great goddess herself and yet also Helen's *alter ego*, embodying her fate, her life, her spirit. Helen thus asks her questions that have no answer, expresses intimations and resolutions that come to nothing. A divine presence is around her, above her. She has no choice but to submit. Like sculpture, it stills the intense moment. We find in it, on a larger scale, the effect of Homeric verse: a tension that rises and subsides.

It is significant that Homer has nothing to show like Apollonius' Medea or Virgil's Dido. The ambiguities of incipient love, the tentative advances, the progressive hold on the senses and on the mind, the fantasies and dreamy suggestions, and the crowning passion that at the end has its way—all these phases were too vague, too elusive for Homer's imagination. Like Shakespeare, he either gives us the instant effect or presents us with the *fait accompli*. Homer's Helen is love's votary—in this more similar to Cleopatra than to Medea or Dido. We have, in her case, a state or mode of being, not a fitful and catastrophic experience. Similarly, in Homer we find the stunning blow of grief and not a day-long sadness, intense anger and not brooding resentment, a sudden joy and not jollity, action and not behavior, wrenching doubt or resolution and not self-indulging temporizing. What appealed to Homer was, in other terms, a moment materializing in its full clarity, such as might be caught by the swaying rhythm of what actually takes its place and position.

In Homer no action is a mere characteristic trait, a mere fact to be observed and judged either in praise or blame. Even Thersites rises to the occasion before he gives up; even the career of the suitors must run its course: we get absorbed in its arching curve and do not hanker for the punishment of the villains. A final judgment or summing up is not uppermost in the poet's mind. What everywhere prevails is a rhythm that involves one and all, regardless of merits or demerits. Character springs from the vital friction of successive occasions. Hence, especially in the *Iliad*, there are no real villains or super-heroes; there are no characters crystallized in a mould—no cruel Aeetes, no murderous Medea, no invincible Jason. Far from being condemned as a sinner, Helen is a victim, or, rather, the butt of opposing forces, herself an unwilling force holding the others in sway.

In the same way we may look at anything that the epic brings into focus. Thus the *Odyssey*, like the *Argonautica*, touches upon distant places and adventures; but, as much as possible, it brings things within the pale of human experience. The various landings and stops and departures show a persistent rhythm—all attempts to find a refuge before the final return, to recover the ways of ordinary living in strange unknown places. Apollonius, on the other hand, gives us quite a different picture. Wherever they land, his Argonauts hardly seek refuge or livelihood, or linger in any familiar scenery; they are more like spectators of exotic uncanny things. The plot, like a dragnet, gathers any curious object that comes its way. A world of unnatural phenomena begs for recognition. Here is a host of mythical figments. It is as if a phantasmagoria brought them to view—Hypsipyle, Phineus and the Harpies, the birds of Ares, Prometheus, the Heliades, and the Hesperides. Apollonius works up the atmosphere of mystery.

Homer's hexameter thus became a narrative medium, losing its original intrinsic function and lending itself to all sorts of purposes. It was as we might expect. A mode of perception cannot be easily transmitted. Nevertheless the sense of focus which we find in Homer's verse remains a fundamental source of poetry.

Chapter 7

Conclusion

SITUATION OF HOMER

Focus, timing, modulation: can these elusive things be a matter of historical and comparative research? They certainly can. Though elusive, they are symptomatic of a mental climate. Thus a tune catches the public's ear, a word gains currency, a style expands. In all these cases, a mode of perception prevails on the strength of its inner truth, naturally influencing opinions and ideas. We have seen how Homer's focus on the action itself had the consequence of humanizing the subject-matter and abridging the mythical elements. Correspondingly, things generally were seen in a new light. We may suppose that all walks of life were affected, as old loyalties faded away and a more direct human awareness took their place.

The Ionia of the IX–VIII century provides the perfect setting for such developments and for the rise of Homeric poetry in particular. As G. Glotz puts it: "In the surroundings of the Maeander, the Cayster, the Hermos and the Caicus, upon the points at which converged the international trade routes and whence the ships set sail on their sea-paths, the Greeks had their first great cities. Their function was not only to be centers of commerce . . . but to produce new forms of art and of thought."[1] It is important to put Homeric poetry in relation to a certain time and place, to look at it at one with a vivid historical present. There was a period of heightened activity. Imagine the intense pursuit of form in those days; with what excitement the old materials were tapped and made to yield to the sense of immediate action. Things were moving at a quickened pace. The time required for the task must have been much shorter than it is commonly assumed; short enough not to let up the momentum—perhaps no longer than two or three generations. Here

Homer found his center. As it often happens, poetry was both a catalyst of the brooding present and a forerunner of things to come.

But we know hardly anything of IX–VIII century Ionia except through Homer. How then can we relate him more specifically to his place and age, without begging the question? We may do so by inference, retrospectively, through the suggestion of what happened later. The implications are many. Here is not the place to elaborate them and speculate at length. We may only point out a few signs. Consider, for instance, the natural philosophy of the Milesians: may we not find a presage of it in the feeling for nature in Homer's similes or in the very rhythm of his verse that so constantly gives us a sense of coming to be and passing away? Or consider the struggles of the city-states replacing the old kingships: may we not find a reflection in the quarrel of Achilles and Agamemnon, or in the feud of Odysseus and the suitors? And may we not see in the inquisitiveness of Odysseus the exploring quest of the early Ionian colonists or imagine their dreams realized in the miraculous ships of the Phaeacians?

The evidence of the arts may be more relevant—especially the sculpture of the *kouros* type whose earliest specimens come from Ionian Delos. Look at the *kouros* of Melos, for instance. We are reminded of Homer: his style in introducing any human or animal figure, not his presentation of any particular hero. We have the same absence of descriptive detail, the same vitality of pose and movement. The *kouros* stands before us, ready to advance: the hint of a step, the body's composure, the eager forward look—these render, in itself and by itself, an essential moment of life. Consider, in this light, such Homeric lines as Il.24.347–8:

βῆ δ' ἰέναι κούρῳ αἰσυμνητῆρι ἐοικώς,

πρῶτον ὑπηνήτῃ, τοῦ περ χαριστάτη ἥβη.

he stepped out to go forth—a majestic boy in his semblance,

with the first down on his chin, at its highest the grace of

youth.

or Od. 2.5:

βῆ δ' ἴμεν ἐκ θαλάμοιο, θεῷ ἐναλίγκιος ἄντην.

and he stepped out of his chamber, his front like that of a god.

(cf. Il.3.419; 5.778; 7.211) Forget for a while the narrative context; take any of these verses only insofar as it summons up an image. The epithets and attributes, essentially pertinent as they are, do not characterize or describe; they simply give volume and weight to the transient or incipient motion. As in a *kouros*, we have the emergence of shape, motion embodied and body set in motion. Here is a state of delicate suspense. We are placed beyond the realism of any characteristic trait.

For the rhythm itself draws the outline: by necessarily excluding description; it is sufficient to convey a sense of life taking form.

The early post-geometric vase paintings offer the same kind of suggestion. The way figures along a line create their own vivid space reminds us of Homer's forceful juxtapositions. "We find the meagre schematic forms swelling out and acquiring volume," writes J. D. Beazley.[2] For the figures are lifted above a merely decorative function, their increased substance implies action and mutual relationship, and a story is intimated through their taking position. The earlier geometric patterns are thus fleshed out; or, conversely, we might say that the ancient Minoan-Mycenaean exuberance is subjected to an inner measure. Compare such typically Homeric lines as Il.1.34:

βῆ δ’ ἀκέων παρὰ θῖνα πολυφλοίσβοιο θαλάσσης.

and in silence he went by the shore of the wide-roaring sea.
or ibid. 43:

ὣς ἔφατ’ εὐχόμενος, τοῦ δ’ ἔκλυε Φοῖβος Ἀπόλλων.

so did he speak in prayer, and him heard Phoebus Apollo.
What do we have essentially? A figure moving and vanishing in the distance, a voice tracing its course from speaker to listener; in both cases a brisk inception and dying fall. What might be treated as a descriptive detail takes a life of its own: it is an expanding moment, extending, and occupying its breathing space. We spontaneously realize a sense of place—not indeed a particular locality, but an integrating field of vision: an advancing step summons up the shoreline, a spoken word summons up two juxtaposed figures. The effect, of course, would not be the same if we were told in ordinary prose: "he walked by the sea," "he prayed, the god heard." The arching rhythm encloses a vivid tract of existence, letting it have its forward pulse. We apprehend, and empathize as well as understand. As when we first see a vase-painting, we are struck by the vivid composition, even before we learn the subject-matter.

Parallels to Homer are to be sought in art and poetry generally, not merely in an epic genre or tradition. For in Homer there is a continuous interplay of movement and form—a pulse that breaks through the narrative, over and above the finished epic product. Traditional themes, habits of thought, and compositional models give way and become a mere backdrop when the very process of perception and expression takes the upper hand, imposing its rhythm.

It required a newly won freedom to pierce through the traditional subject-matter—to bring out the natural dynamism of the action, let each fine point of focus have its turn, and realize the passage of form into movement and movement into form.

The infinite subtleties of Homeric verse are the inward side of the same Ionian spirit that outwardly was made manifest in the foundation of

cities and in the ways of practical life.   Sophocles brought out this
twofold aspect in one sentence, when he sang about man (*Ant.* 353 ff.):

καὶ φθέγμα καὶ ἀνεμόεν
φρόνημα καὶ ἀστυνόμους
ὀργὰς ἐδιδάξατο.
and speech and airy thought
and the city-moulding moods
he taught himself.

The passage is applicable to early Ionian civilization.   There was no
ivory tower, no self-enclosed school of singers.   The arts are inseparable
from the significance of general experience, inseparable from life and the
winds of change.   The Homeric touch, in particular, reached out far and
wide.   Homer's sense of focus was no less indicative of progress than the
Renaissance sense of perspective.   And yet G. S. Kirk writes:

Economic change, foreign contacts, colonizing and exploration, the growth of
the polis and the decline of kingship;   these and other factors must have
seriously disrupted a traditional way of life which had evidently persisted, even
in settlements overseas, for centuries. . . . Largely through the failure to develop
the technique of writing, traditional poetical methods survived into an age when
traditional restraints on the scope and form of oral verse had actually
disappeared.[3]

Quite the opposite is true.   Social change and poetic progress were two
sides of the same phenomenon. It will be objected that Homer is,
nevertheless, the representative of an epic or heroic tradition.   But this
common view is largely due to circumstances.   Homer's posthumous
fortune made it inevitable.   Once established as the metre of large-scale
epic composition, the Homeric hexameter became the standard heroic
verse and Homer was regarded the father of epic poetry.   As it is natural
in such cases, an external criterion prompted the canon.   Far deeper and
subtler was Homer's purely poetic influence.   Regardless of genre, all
Greek poetry from Archilochus to the Hellenistic age was profoundly
affected.   Quite Homeric, for instance, is the day-long compact action of
Greek tragedy with its immediate sense of place.   The same can be said
about the forms of expression.   Homer's use of the noun-epithet phrases
was, ultimately, the source of the high-wrought lyric imagery that gave a
momentary concrete life to abstract entities and ideas.   There is a
Homeric quality that reverberates beyond any given category.

AUTHORSHIP

The term "author" implies a distinctive sense of values: a
characterizing identity, an informing spirit.   Such is eminently the case of

Homer. We can only reach him through his poetry. We shall not find him in any particular subject-matter, but in the way this matter is transformed into poetry. The true Homer is one with the sense of focus I have been trying to elucidate. There is, at the core, a charge that expands, assimilating the subject-matter as much as possible. This intuited center is our starting point. It is not to be identified with a *motif* or factual element: it is a purely qualitative touch that penetrates the material in varying degrees. Homer is this inner thrust. We shall hardly get close to him on the basis of inert facts. Such concepts as adaptation or conflation do not apply. For they suggest a manipulation of static materials. What we have instead is a dynamic process—a keynote and its fluid range.

For the same reason we cannot rely on the narrative design. Was there first an *Achilleis*? Was a *Telemacheia* added later? Formulated as they are, such questions hardly concern us. Consider, rather, the way in which even the plot emerges from a mode of perception: no hero is portrayed in a narrative abstraction, in no place can the course of time be blanked out or paraphrased, and the days of Troy or Ithaca must be accounted for no less concretely than those of Achilles or Odysseus in their respective locations. This sense of time is intrinsic to the style. We might go as far as saying that narrative is subservient to style and not vice versa. The poet cannot ignore the contiguity of moments in the expanding action. As for the literal plot, it can be constructed and reconstructed: it is, in any case, a result and not a cause.

Where the subject-matter so melts into a mode of representation, the author's traces are more evident in the texture than in any general plan. The extensive use of similes is symptomatic. Homer looks at the subject-matter by way of pervasive analogies: Priam reflects Peleus as Hector does Patroclus; the battle scenes exemplify on a wider level what happens to the main heroes, just as the return of Odysseus exemplifies other returns. We have qualitative affinities and associations, parallel expansive moments whose compelling logic drives the story to its end.

The search for the original Homer is thus a search for Homer's originality. He is concealed in the genius of the language. Never did a style so encompass and transform an old material, giving it life and sense of truth. Homeric style is thus deeply original. For we shall not find originality in mere novelty: any doggerel might then be regarded as original. Nor shall we seek originality in any peculiarity or idiosyncracy: Hipponax would then be more original than, say, Simonides. We recognize Homer on the strength of a pervasive quality to which we so get attuned as to make it our own.

The originality of a great master, at a certain point, becomes almost impersonal. The art form is so true to itself as to seem unique, so

convincing as to be universally accessible. Shakespeare reverberates in
the Elizabethans, Petrarch in the love poetry of the early Renaissance.
We touch upon the delicate phase in which a style maintains its vitality
and has not yet declined into mannerism.

In the highest degree, Homer vanishes into his poetry. And yet he
must have been intensely alive as a person: his sense-perceptions are too
keen, his touch too discriminating for us to turn him into a figurehead.
But, at the same time, we can hardly conceive him as an ordinary author:
his remoteness, his silence about himself, and his encompassing
objectivity preclude any pertinent information.

We ought to look at Homeric authorship as a fluid condition and not
a literal fact. Imagine the concrete setting, and a poetic utterance whose
essence passes from one individual mind to another. A tune thus gathers
momentum, a word acquires resonance, and the final triumph is but a
proof of what universal validity was implied in the original. We are as
far removed from an author's ivory tower as from a particular poetic
idiom learned by rote.

There is enlightening common sense in saying that Homer was the
author of the *Iliad* and the *Odyssey*. This much is averred: an individual
poetic mind must have been primarily responsible; such poetry could not
come up automatically from a pre-existing tradition. We have, in fact, a
mode of perception (or style) which we call Homeric; but it was in its
nature to be universally applicable and to stir up analogies on the face of
nature. Hence we need not believe that Homer was *literally* the author or
both poems; we may even imagine many Homers as long as we
recognize in every instance the activity of a certain poetic mind.
Moments of perception can only be attributed to individuals, not to a
tradition or a school. No matter who came first, an original Homeric
impulse runs through the various modulations of an encompassing strain.

Or, in other words, the work itself takes on, as always, a life of its
own. There is no imitation where the same drift of thought is pursued by
another. Who shall tell at what points of the Parthenon frieze the work of
Phidias ceases and that of his followers begins? Or compare, in Homer,
Achilles embracing Patroclus' ghost with Odysseus embracing
Anticleia's: who could decide which passage was the model of the other?
The same touch is in both, though they may each be attributed to
different hands.

LANGUAGE

The same dynamic process that ran through the treatment of the
narrative material was naturally at work in the language itself. When we

speak of "Homeric Greek" or "Homeric grammar," we imply that poetry had a profound influence on the language.

The times were favorable: in this earliest phase of Greek civilization, things were in a fluid state, and so was language. Homer's text shows many signs of such linguistic fluctuation. We may mention a few: the treatment of the digamma, the non-contraction or contraction of vowels, long diphthongs and metathesis, the pronominal value of the article, the adverbial value of prepositions, no verb possessing as yet a complete conjugation, and coexistence of thematic and athematic forms. Here are alternatives of old and new, one system yielding to another, ambiguities and vacillations that are signs of a delicate organic growth. If, for instance, a vowel resists being contracted or a pronoun resists becoming an article, we have a similar state on two different levels: a loosening of self-contained concrete elements, and varying degrees of concreteness and abstraction. There is thus the resilience of individual words and, on the other hand, the tendency to gather around predominant types. Freedom and order are twin aspects of the same phenomenon.

What was an impersonal instinctive trend in the development of the language itself lit up with consciousness in the expression of the poets. Here the pace quickened. Linguistic change was intensified by the striving for expression and composition on a large scale. But it was rhythm that precipitated the process. Essential as it was to the modulation of rising and vanishing moments, it governed the articulation of thought in the unfolding sentences; and, in so doing, it imparted prevailing tunes to the language, widened the scope of analogy, prompted recurrences of sound and meaning, and persistently embodied thought in aesthetic form. The influence of rhythm on the vocabulary was no less profound. The choice of words was more often prompted by their sensuous fullness than by their literal exactitude. The noun-epithet phrases are an outstanding example. They give the verse its necessary weight, by bringing out the full presence of a thing in the transient moment. They realize rather than describe. Rhythm, latent in any word, came out into the open. A comprehensive harmony arose over the approximations of common usage, as when music establishes its realm rising up above the sounds of which nature or the human voice is capable.

Homer tapped the rhythmical potentialities of the language. He quickened their effect, he realized their natural range. We thus find no metrical constraint distorting common speech. W. Schulze[4] observes that the poet's analogical lengthenings are often prophetic of a natural development in the language, anticipating the times. Far from being strident, the anomalies offer further scope to the malleability of form and produce, in their turn, other analogies. Consider such a form as ἀκροκελαινιόων (Il.21.249) of swelling Scamander that is "dark on the surface" or ἐσχατόωσα (2.508) of a city that is "outermost" on the coast. The long participial ending gives the adjective a verbal force, and we are made to see the river's darkening surface or a distant city projecting on the sea. The anomaly enhances the word's poetic force without at all affecting the clarity of expression. The effect of movement and position is quite Homeric.

The admixture of dialects should be viewed in the same light wherever possible. Such a verse as ἐξ ἀκαλαρρείταο βαθυρρόου Ὠκεανοῖο [from Oceanus soft-running, deep-flowing Il.7.422; Od.19.434], admired by Tennyson[5], blends heterogeneous endings and word-formations into one sonorous image that has its own intrinsic clarity. The very volume of sound suggests fullness and breadth, as appears often elsewhere. Homer affects this richness of rhythm. Hence comes the frequency of metrical lengthenings, while we hardly find metrical shortenings.

The poetic momentum thus took full advantage of the fluid phase in the language. The poets adopted any linguistic element that was in unison with a native sense of form. Even obsolete epithets depicting obsolete objects were made transparent by their sound and position, displayed as they always were in a moment of pertinent focus.

A poetic language arose that naturally transcended any vernacular and, with its universal appeal, broke beyond the narrow boundaries of any tribe or social class. It is no wonder that the contiguous dialects of Ionia and Aeolia converged here; it is equally no wonder that the style does not lend itself to such social distinctions as "high" and "low," "noble" and "popular." In Homer we recognize the tendency of all poetry to universalize the modes of expression, removing us from what is too local, too provincial, too narrow and idiomatic.

We must never forget these broad implications. It is wrong, therefore, to emphasize the use of Aeolic where the Ionic equivalent does not fit the metre and thence regard the whole phraseology as a means of versification, only to conclude that we have an artificial language never spoken by man or woman. Such a view rests on a truism; for the words obviously fit the metre. Or it is, at best, a half-truth: a limited characteristic is elevated to an overriding poetic principle and we are ultimately led to believe that Homer's style is the result of adapting the diction to the hexameter. But how can language be so subordinate to metre? Surely a common element subtends both: rhythm as a catalyst of meaning, and rhythm as a formative principle both in the use of words and in the measure of the verse. If it were not so, there would be no limit to arbitrary alterations and adaptations.

As for the alleged artificiality, the problem cannot be easily resolved. What is artificial? What is natural? Where do art and nature part company? Are they not both present in language, and especially in any refinement and grace of speech? The ancient problem of νόμος [convention] or φύσις [nature] as the source of language should be raised again in this respect.

Nature and art conspired in the development of Homeric Greek. There is the force of nature in the rich organic growth of forms, and there is art in every poetic touch. These two aspects cannot be disentangled from each other. The diverging or anomalous case-endings, for instance, are drawn from collateral kindred formations within the language; they are not arbitrarily cut out and fitted to the versification. Hence comes variety within the encompassing unity. Any Homeric verse has its distinctive ring.

The Homeric language is language in the fullest sense. It stands its own ground, and has its own wide-ranging coherence and clarity. Its radiating center is a native sense of form and expression, not the idiom of a cultural capital or an obscure oral tradition.

THE SCHOLARLY DILEMMA

An open-minded approach to the problems of language, rhythm, and authorship leads us to a more intimate knowledge of Homer and his times. Scattered objects of study may thus be seen as elements of one process. What comes to the fore are not just facts brought together by external circumstances, but creative relations that are intrinsic to the phenomenon itself.

Scholarship, so far, has dealt mainly with the task of piecing together ascertained or alleged facts, without seeking an inner poetic reason for their integration. For this reason, the vast literature of the "Homeric Question" fills us, at the end, with a sense of perplexity and loss. The unitarians dwell on a single poet's work, but do not account for the encompassing style that transcends any individual effort; the analysts posit many different poets of different dates and places, but do not explain what distinctive poetic quality brought their contributions together; and the theorists of oral composition deal with the technique of formulas and themes, but have nothing to say about the merits of such an art-form. More generally, literary critics praise Homer's human contents, but ignore the language that gives it its forcefulness.

A common trait of these schools is their literal approach. The various aspects of Homer are presented as circumscribed static facts: there is a poet or poets; a plot that is either a premeditated design or a series of additions; a preexisting subject-matter; the hexameter as a means of composition; a diction that is the epic poet's stock-in-trade; and heroic characters and ideas. The rise of Homeric poetry can hardly be conjured up by piecing these elements into a more or less satisfactory reconstruction.

Things appear in a different light, if we concentrate above all on the poetic texture. What then stands out is the expressive material. In terms of its quality we ought to view the poet or poets, and not vice versa. We should, in other words, reach out for what we do not know through the evidence of what we intimately know rather than affect this vivid knowledge with the secondary notions of an epic convention. Suppose we are reading Homer for the first time, and are faced all at once with this luminous style: we would be led to intuit a whole mode of perception and representation, make it our own and imaginatively summon up the historical conditions. We would, in other terms, move from the center to the periphery.

Parry, indeed, may be said to have taken this path in that he turned his exclusive attention to style, whence he extracted his system of formulas and conceived his theory of oral composition, setting it in a pertinent environment. But the construction he formulated soon took the upper hand. What mattered most was the social oral milieu and the poetry itself came to be regarded as an epiphenomenon or an outcome of heterogeneous conditions.

Hence Parry's system functions in a matter-of-fact sort of way. The performer poet knows what the audience wishes to hear; the audience approves and confirms the poetic success; the tradition gains a new lease of life and epic poetry continues to prosper. We have a vicious circle here: a thing is good because it is traditional and popular; and it is traditional and popular because it is good.

Surely poetry and poetic expression have a much wider sphere and must break out of this automatic circuit. Let us look at the matter in more fundamental terms: a time and a place, a poet's utterance and its repercussions, the same occasion renewed again and again, a growing momentum and volume. Here was a fervent meeting of minds: imagine a situation in which poet and audience might exchange places. The Homeric effect must have been overwhelming—as if the popularity of a new song blended with the recognition of a lifelike truth in the very mode of expression. Listening was tantamount to knowing and memorizing at a time when language, rhythm and meaning were so integrated with one another.

Consider, therefore, this wider setting, the general climate or atmosphere; consider, above all, the expansive movement and the intensity at the core. We may try to recompose the situation in terms as concrete as possible: a recitation among friends, subsequent encounters, an ever-widening appeal beyond any particular circle, a sense of poetry penetrating outlying areas. The greatest artistic and intellectual achievements have often been prompted by a decisive impulse coming into the open—in a dwelling or in the street and marketplace. Such was the case in ancient Greece—witness early lyric poetry or the philosophy of Socrates. We should look at Homeric poetry in a wider context—as a wide-ranging poetic and intellectual process.

THE ORGANIC WHOLE

A principle of perception and expression runs through the Homeric poems. On its strength the various aspects of Homer outlined in these pages explain one another without any need of external reference points. I summarize here the chief features of this intimate interdependence:

1. Each verse represents a point of focus. In case of enjambment, there is a shift of focus in time and space.

2. The point of focus usually consists in a certain act or state of being.

3. Such act or state of being constitutes a self-contained moment.

4. It is in the nature of such a moment to come, linger and pass away; it is transient and yet highlighted in its own right.

5. The rhythm reflects this sense of coming to be and passing away.

6. The form of expression behaves accordingly. It must have fullness in that it highlights the essence of the moment; it must be brief, or else the moment of focus should be lost.

7. The narrative is thus made up of essential moments: moments that are typical or universally applicable. Occurrence becomes recurrence. Hence the use of the so-called formulas that condense meaning in fundamental instances.

8. These moments that follow one another explain Homer's continuous rectilinear narrative and account for the short duration of the action. Such a style would be impossible in covering an indefinite lapse of time.

9. Hence can be explained the subject-matter of the poems; Achilles' wrath, Odysseus' day of return. An account of the Trojan war or of Odysseus' life would have been incompatible with the sense of the moment and the ever-present succession of days and nights.

10. On the same grounds we may explain Homer's terseness and clarity. The Homeric moment is inconsistent with both punctilious descriptiveness and generic abstraction. It is concrete and typical at the same time.

11. In a similar way the language is neither realistic nor precious. We could hardly imagine the poems composed in a local dialect or in an esoteric style.

Here the power of rhythm in the form of expression is the most important element. It summons up the moments in their presence and transience; it imparts to the action the pulse of time. Poetry comes into its own. We have the sheer curve and shape of eventuality rather than any message. Deeds and exploits are depicted in their intensity; and yet they are made to appear like shadows of a more general flux through the verse that continually intimates the drama of coming to be and passing away.

NOTES

1. Gustave Glotz. *Histoire Grecque*, Vol.1, Paris: 1925: 260-1.

2. J. D. Beazley and B. Ashmole. *Greek Sculpture and Painting*. Cambridge: 1966: 7.

3. G.S. Kirk. *The Iliad: A Commentary*. Vol.1, Cambridge: 1895: 15-16.

4. W. Schulze. *Quaestiones Epicae* . Gutersloh: Bertelsmann.1892: 15-16.

5. *Alfred Lord Tennyson: A Memoir*, II, by his son. London: New York, MacMillan. 1897: 13.

Bibliographical Essay

No sharp distinction is usually drawn between metre and rhythm. Thus M. L. West ascribes to rhythm a more subtle measurement of quantities than that offered by the blunt metrical feet.[1] The difference is one of degree rather than substance. Almost indifferently we say, for instance, "dactylic metre" or "dactylic rhythm." The term "rhythm" delicately intimates what the term "metre" states objectively.

P. Maas writes: "The art of metric is the means by which a regular pattern is imposed upon the natural rhythm of language; so that a more correct name for it would be 'rhythmic'." And he adds in a note: "Metric implies measurement, and so might seem applicable only to quantitative patterns and not dynamic ones."[2]

Maas touches here upon a crucial point. We may oppose the dynamic quality of the verse-rhythm to the static measure of metrical feet. Rhythm is precisely this: an inner modulation that results from the interplay of word-endings and word-beginnings, punctuation and caesura, pauses and resumptions, incipient movements and their culminations. But Maas did not develop this passing insight. In his laconic way, he merely listed such rhythmical tendencies as had been discovered earlier, giving as concise and complete a picture as possible of ascertained facts.

Hermann Fränkel[3], followed by E. G. O'Neill[4] and H. N. Porter[5], marked a new departure. Fränkel's cola are especially important in this respect. For, whereas a foot is indifferent to meaning, a colon blends in itself both sound and meaning. It is a rhythmical unit of meaning. As a result, the mere metrical pattern could now be regarded as a means to an end, not an end in itself; and the very idea of verse was made to include a sense-producing element.

New possibilities of interpretation opened up. For whereas studies in metre usually ignore any necessary organic connection between verse-structure and meaning, these rhythmical cola appeared to highlight the unfolding phases of poetic thought within the verse. The distinction between metre and rhythm became inevitable.

Fränkel's approach, however, was checked. Milman Parry's theory of oral composition has been predominant. Scholarship centered on formulas.

The contrast between Fränkel and Parry is obvious: while in the former we have rhythmical phrases melting into one another, we have in the latter combinations of formulas. Though the two approaches might be artificially reconciled by identifying any colon with a formula, there is an incompatibility of intention. For what prevails in the one is a sense of movement, and in the other a relation of static positions: the formulas are juxtaposed in that they fit the metre and the idea of a mechanical procedure cannot be spirited away. But the Parryist approach enjoyed the widest popularity. It has the appeal of a specious rigor: arrays of formulas exactly correspond to certain feet of the hexameter. It is as if we had a recipe for epic composition. Fränkel's cola, on the other hand, are irregular; a longer or heavier word might displace them and reduce them in number—they hardly give us as even a picture as that of metrical feet. But it is this irregularity that is important. For it is symptomatic of a tendency; a quality that ever strives to manifest itself. We have a precarious stability rather than a rule.

Though difficult to define, the colon is rooted in language. Even in ordinary speech there are parenthetic phrases that stand out on their own strength. And yet the colon is no casual, arbitrary thing. It finds its place in artistic prose and poetry. In an important essay, Eduard Fraenkel[6] showed the sure signs of its occurrence, highlighting its syntactic and stylistic function.

We have a dilemma. The formulas, satisfying though they are in their precision, keep us deadlocked in an artificial self-enclosed system; on the other hand, the cola, vague though they are, open up to rhythm and language as a whole. The situation is well reflected in an essay of G. S. Kirk.[7] After reasserting the fundamental importance of the formulas, he points to the rhythmical structure of the verse in relation to the internal units of meaning and he writes: "A fuller understanding of these topics may well be a prerequisite for any serious advance in our knowledge of formular techniques; and it seems *a priori* probable that in many respects, though not all, rhythm and verse-structure conditioned formular practice rather than *vice versa*." He praises Fränkel at this point; but then he finds the cola too irregular and unreliable. He requires a greater coherence, tending to attribute word-end in certain positions to euphony, formular habit, or the mere availability of words. Later, in his commentary to the *Iliad* [8] he is more negative: "Much of Fränkel's and Porter's work was concerned with a search for detailed formalistic rules which are simply not inherent in the material, and it is perhaps the 'ideal' four-colon verse that is chiefly to blame."

As it is, scholarship appears satisfied with the exclusion of a dynamic *causa sui*: the Homeric hexameter is made up of formulas, and formulas owe their existence to the need of versification, preserving in this process a traditional poetic language. Hence came the extraordinary view that the Homeric language (and by extension Homeric poetry) was the product of the hexameter; an artificial amalgam of conventional heterogeneous forms. How did this view gain such credibility as to become a common assumption in textbooks and introductions to Homer? Many factors contributed: analysis unattended by synthesis, the didactic habit of separating contents from form, the tendency to juxtapose facts in an external relation of cause and effect and not see them as aspects of an encompassing wholeness.

An important step in this direction was the work of H. Düntzer[9] and K. Witte.[10] The former established the metrical values of the noun-epithet phrases; the latter saw in the same light the alternative ionic and aeolic forms as well as the general morphology. Their sweeping conclusions did not pass unchallenged. Criticizing Witte, P. Kretschmer wrote: "The statement that the language of the Homeric poems is the creation of epic verse needs rebuttal: too one-sidedly it subjects the whole Homeric language to metrical constriction. Language comes first and then the verse that developed out of the language."[11] Evaluating the Homeric language in this respect, K. Meister observed: "We have transformations rather than distortions, inflection or syntax seldom suffers, normal word-formation remains."[12] W. Schulze points to the influence of analogy beside that of metre.[13] On the other hand, it is strange to find so great a linguist as A. Meillet writing: "But this formulaic type whereby the Homeric poems differ from other literature is a fact of language; it is the mode of expression that is formulaic, not the thought itself. The characters have a fixed style, but each has a distinctive personality."[14] How can we reveal character through clichés? Is not language an expression of thought?

Contradictions and equivocations inevitably arise when trying to fit into categories such imponderable matters as language, poetry, and style. The difficulty is especially obvious in Homer. How then can we merge the apparent incompatibilities in a larger view? Interestingly enough, it is Parry himself who shows the way, when he writes:

The theory of Witte, even with the further work done on it by Meister, is unfinished; they have logically proved that the language of Homer is the work of the Homeric verse, but they have not at all shown how the verse in this case could have such *power* (italics mine). . .To say that the Homeric language was the work of the Homeric verse thus implies a poetry which is, at least to our way of thinking, of a very special kind, so that while the theory may be proved it cannot really be understood until we know just what this poetry was.[15]

Parry thus equates this poetry with a particular power. He does not elaborate on what this power really is; but the mere mention of it is highly suggestive.

This power lies in the pervasive rhythm of the Homeric poems. The particular metre is the medium of this rhythm, in the way syllables are the medium of words.

If this rhythm is so powerful, the reason lies in the way it touches off consecutive moments of action over a vast range. For, through the verse, it marks the beat of any single act or state, while, through its cumulative impact, it subtends the march of events. Hence a vital movement runs through Homer's continuity of time. There are no idle stretches, empty intervals, or dull descriptions; every detail participates in a moment that is enacted on the field of vision. We have an impression of time in the making.

Rhythm is naturally connected with time, timing. But it is not just a question of *tempo*. In Homer the connection is a concrete one. It relates the verse to the actual moment it embodies and, by extension, to the general duration of the action. Here rhythm is the pulse of time.

Time in Homer has often been discussed. T. Zielinski shows how Homer presents simultaneous actions as if they occurred one after the other, without subjecting them to a synthetizing narrative:[16] what this treatment implies is Homer's concreteness, for he only presents an event insofar as it actually takes place. H. Fränkel points out how, in Homer, the abstract idea of time pales, before the reality of night and day as vehicles of all eventuality.[17] H. and A. Thornton dwell on the appositional style that lets each incident take its place in turn, arresting it in a full positive present.[18] S. E. Bassett highlights the continuity of time in Homer—a perpetual flow that is made to appear as the sole reality and thus fosters the sense of an "Epic Illusion."[19] M. Lynn-George ponders on the significance of single moments and their transformation into an eternal present.[20]

We find elsewhere a more comparative approach. Often at the cost of hasty generalizations, Homer is opposed to other works of literature. E. Auerbach opposes the Homeric present devoid of background to the many-layered biblical narrative.[21] M. M. Bakhtin highlights the flexible treatment of time in the novel and sets it in contrast with the absolute past of the epic which is walled away from actual experience.[22] M. I. Finley points to Homer's mythical, non-historical character: Odysseus and Penelope have not changed one bit after twenty years, they are detached from their background, as timeless as the story itself.[23] We may oppose to these views E. Cassirer's remark that the suffering lives of the Homeric heroes disrupt any mythical or cyclical concept of time.[24]

None of these studies ever comes near to seeing an idea or sense of time in Homeric rhythm. An impediment lies in the fact that they usually take a narrative view of time. The pure concept of time yields to an account of situations and their temporal ramifications. In Bakhtin, for instance, the term "chronotope" involves the convergence of typical places, times or occasions; and the treatment of time comes down to an analysis of the subject-matter. Time is superseded by other interests. Such is also the case of works that deal generally with time in literature. Thus G. Poulet follows the progressive fragmentation of human experience from Montaigne to Proust;[25] H. Meyerhoff, facing similar problems, focuses on contemporary novelists;[26] and P. Ricoeur looks at the narrative as the mediating element between the inscrutability of time and the course of our own experience, as if the essence of time could only be apprehended narratively.[27] Time is thus overwhelmed by its associations. What takes the upper hand are such problems as self-identity and change, the conscious and the subconscious, chance and destiny, biography and historiography. The preeminence which these authors give to narrative is typical; for narrative presents us with a multitude of situations relating individuals to society. Here is a reason why structuralism deals with novels rather than poetry.

Quite different is the immediate experience of time—when we realize the suspense of a moment or the passage from moment to moment. We then have an essence of time. It cannot be defined. It can hardly be described for what it is in itself and by itself; but it passes into the mode of expression and we may glean it in unexpected ways. What comes to the fore is the syntax of the sentences—how it confers to mere factual juxtaposition a balancing realization in time and space. Such a trend is most notable in Homer who naturally gives position and breathing space to anything he mentions. Here we must be careful, to be neither too literal nor too abstract. Thus the work of G. C. Horrocks, though pointing in our direction, is far too narrow and schematic;[28] B. Hillweg, on the other hand, is too factual in mapping out the distribution of times and places: time is not merely a date nor space a location.[29] We should, in a sentence, somehow catch the movement that shoots through the separate static words and presents them in a new light. Take, for instance, the Homeric phrase "to go through the divine night" (Il.24.365

etc.). Is it an indication of space or time? Both are involved. But
Horrocks, in his classifications, misses this rich ambiguity. The sensuous
presence of night evaporates into a sense of duration, and the act of going
melts into its surroundings. The idea of time could not be more concrete.

We are not concerned, however, with parts of speech. A sense of
time and space runs through any sentence that puts occurrence into
rhythm: a pose, or a movement appear more important than the narrative
message. Such an effect is characteristic of Homer. Consider the whole
Homeric poems in this light: the narrative continually absorbed into
single acts that run into one another like the notes of a large composition.
We have at once stimulus and measure. A compelling forward pulse
gives life to the uninterrupted flow. What would otherwise be an inert
succession becomes a vital process. Time and rhythm coalesce in the
perspective.

Are we on firm theoretical grounds? Are we justified in applying to
the study of Homeric rhythm so difficult a concept as that of time? The
philosophy of H. Bergson comes to the rescue, and especially his idea of
durée "duration." Although he does not mention Homer, his sense of
time is most applicable to verse, and to Homer in particular.

For what is Bergson's *durée*? It is the transient fullness of a present
moment: fluid yet concrete, elusive and yet vividly experienced. Such a
moment can be realized but can hardly be described, for it is not identical
with a particular incident. Rather, it is a movement within the incident,
an inner vibration, a tension whose climax and anticlimax cannot be
reduced to any points of fact. We find it evinced everywhere in nature
and in art: in the effort of a gripping hand, the pace of footsteps, a
voice's tone, a painter's touch. The notion of "moment" thus passes into
that of a quality that comes to fruition. But how can we figure out the
emergence itself? It cannot be isolated as a mathematical point, for the
moment has concrete duration; it expands as it rises from the immediate
past and leans out to the future. We may think, rather, of a curve whose
arching movement has its hesitations and resumptions. Here beginning,
middle and end are not localized steps but phases whose contours
interpenetrate. Such, we may add, is the nature of verse. No division of
feet, no parsing of separate words and phrases can give us the essence: a
musical movement runs underneath—a movement that cannot be cut into
sections but only touched into subtle contiguities of light and shade.

In forcible and suggestive language, Bergson dwells on this aspect
of reality. I shall quote or paraphrase a few passages that, in different
connections, highlight the immediacy of time in contrast with
superimposed abstractions. For instance: "The present is not what now
exists but what is in the making. . .the pure present is the imponderable

progress of the past nibbling on the future."[30] Or, consider: "Through insensible gradations we pass from one state to another, in a continuity that is really lived but is decomposed for the convenience of current notions."[31] Again, concerning the interplay of perception and memory: "It is a succession of states, each announcing the following one and containing the one that precedes."[32]

Bergson often likens this effect to that of a melody, a note being a moment in itself and yet a prelude to the next one. Time and life are thus stirred by that sense of expectation and fulfillment which, as we have seen (see p. 76 ff) characterizes the nature of the verse. Bergson develops this insight into a general aesthetic principle:

We find a superior ease and grace in movements that let themselves be foreseen, in present attitudes that prefigure those to come. If jagged movements lack grace, it is because each of them is self-sufficient and does not announce those that follow. The perception of ease in the movement blends here with the pleasure of somehow seizing upon the march of time and holding the future in the present. . . .Rhythm and measure let us foresee the artist's movements and make us believe that we actually master them.[33]

These foldings and unfoldings, concealments and openings are like the articulations which the sense of time impresses upon the material. Meaning thereby becomes a developing thought, and thought a mode of perception; what was rigid is made supple. We somehow get into the texture of discourse, beyond the literal message or the external chain of cause and effect. Touching on education, Bergson writes:

It is well to discuss the work of a great writer . . .and yet the student must start by having a taste for it—that is to say, he must reinvent it, appropriate it, by fitting into the author's ways and movements. To read aloud is this very thing. . . Before intellection proper sets in, there is the perception of structure and movement; we have on the page we are reading punctuation and rhythm. To observe them, to realize the time relations between phrase and phrase, to follow the *crescendo* of feelings and thoughts up to their culmination—herein consists the art of diction. It is wrong to consider it mere décor. Rather than coming at the end of one's studies, it should come first and everywhere as an essential support. But we have the illusion of knowing a thing sufficiently when we can talk about it. In fact, we only understand what we can somehow reinvent. On the page it has chosen out or the world's great book, intuition would rediscover the movement and rhythm of the composition, relive the creative evolution by participating in it sympathetically.[34]

Compare: "However well chosen the words might be, they could hardly be effective, without. . .the whole choreography of discourse; incipient movements guide the reader to trace the curve of thought and of feeling."[35]

In no other way than through such a sense of time as suggested by Bergson can we account for the cumulative energy that, in Homer, runs from sentence to sentence, from verse to verse. Rhythm is the very vehicle of this energy, not an added element. The present draws strength from the immediate past and projects it into the immediate future. Continuity and contiguity conspire. In two juxtaposed sentences, their spatial relation becomes forthwith a temporal one. "So he spoke, and the old man feared," says Homer. We might dilute the meaning descriptively; but here the dramatic impact and development are all the stronger by being held tightly in place. Time presses on, driven by the concurrence of a certain moment and a certain spot.

What comes into question is Homer's parataxis (see. p. 86 ff.). It has been studied without regard for the animating force of rhythm. But, even so, J. Classen remarked long ago (1854) the stunning capacity of the language to trace the sinuosities of thought through the mere connections of words.[36] More particularly, he showed how Homer maintains the same level of exposure in independent sentences and yet lets an integrating trend arise from the way they are positioned in respect to one another (where we should use a parenthesis or a relative construction). The grammarians, on the other hand, naturally give us a purely syntactical appreciation. Most notably C. Hentze presents us with a laborious survey of juxtaposed sentences, classified according to what kind of relation binds them together—whether, for instance, a preceding fact leads to a judgment, command, threat, or wish.[37]

A bald historicism was soon associated with the term "parataxis" (opposed to "hypotaxis"), as if to designate an earlier stage of thought and expression. For what came to the fore was not only a parataxis of sentences, but of episodes, precepts, ideas, and beliefs. Significant in this respect is the work of B. A. van Groningen,[38] B. E. Perry,[39] and J.A. Notopoulos.[40] These scholars emphasize the juxtaposition and arrangement of parts at the expense of any organic unity or leading idea, invoking the mental habits of a pristine age or of an illiterate society. In doing so, they dwell on given attitudes and customs, highlighting what can only be explained in static descriptive terms; and the fluid rhythmic qualities of the style are necessarily left out. When van Groningen expounds the connecting devices that stitch up the composition like rings in a chain, he sets aside the compelling sense of continuity that is the very spirit of Homer's paratactic order. Or, when Notopoulos remarks that the oral poet is absorbed in the present moment because he is forced to do so by the needs of public performance, he ignores that this momentary focus has its own poetic reason and is central to Homeric poetry. Again, when Perry earmarks as "early Greek" those instances in which single elements stand out in contrast with their context, he forgets the countless cases in which, as in Rembrandt's *Nightwatch*, a solitary figure serves as foil to the whole composition.

"Organic unity" should be considered in the same way. It is not a historical fact, but a quality that appears in a greater or lesser degree in different ages and places. We should thus look at it in its emergence and development—as a process and not a compositional principle that, who knows how, came in vogue at a certain point. Seen in this light, organic unity was produced by the paratactic order itself: it is one with the powerful movement that, running from sentence to sentence, leads us into *medias res* and thus creates a self-sustaining sequence. What is organic gathers strength from internal growth. Notopoulos, on the other hand, dismisses Horace's *dictum* that Homer *ad eventum festinat,* "hastens to the event," and adduces Homer's "digressions." We may object that each alleged digression is filled with the same sense of immediacy. Notopoulos sees a literal reference to the plot in what really applies to a mode of perception. We have a reality of touch, not construction: the same impulse that touches off a simile also starts Chryses in his quest or Achilles in his wrath. The very rhythm of the verse draws us to the articulations of action.

There is, on the one hand, a vivid sense of what things are in their intrinsic qualities and, on the other, a static notion of their existence, a tendency to document them, describe them, define their status and explain them through external causes. These two attitudes are applicable to scholarship, and to Homeric scholarship in particular. They surface even in the minutest treatment of stylistic or rhythmical details.

Seen in this light, Fränkel's treatment of the verse-rhythm portended a more intimate knowledge of Homeric poetry: the verse could now appear as the expanding modulation of a floating moment, not a metrical construction determined by rules and restrictions. But Fränkel did not go beyond the analysis of single verses. We should extend the analysis with a similar criterion in mind. No stretch of experience can be made up of separate instances succeeding one another; no vivid story can consist in single end-stopped verses.

Enjambment is relevant here. Moments are naturally successive and places are naturally contiguous with one another; but, just as naturally, they overlap and interpenetrate in the fitful movements of action. It could be shown how, in such cases, enjambment is produced by the swerving movement that arises from within the verse, how it highlights a shift of focus in time or space and takes a concrete, poetic significance (see p. 39 ff.).

Here again, however, a crude ascertainment of facts has prevailed over any broader interpretation. We have, once more, a metrical rather than rhythmical interest. There is, on one hand, the sentence in its literal-grammatical aspect and, on the other, the way it is distributed between one verse and the other. What stands out are the various types of arrangement: classification rather than explanation. The effect is to present in static terms what, after all, is a dynamic process.

We thus find Parry's *unperiodic* and *necessary* enjambment,[41] Kirk's two additional types along with varieties of *cumulative* enjambment,[42] and C. Higbie's further modifications.[43] Parry presents the matter in broad outlines; Kirk is more analytical, concentrating on one book of the Iliad; and Higbie's wealth of details tends to obscure the exposition. What generally prevails is the statistical method. We are given, for instance, the relative frequency of each kind of enjambment, strong stops within the verse, or occurrences in narrative and direct speech respectively. Any phrase or sentence or passage becomes a specimen of its kind and a piece of evidence. We have crystallizations, not moments of expression. The task could be pursued indefinitely. What is the purpose? It is at times as if the classification were an end in itself, an attempt to map out what appears dimly significant one way or the other and yet remains essentially unexplained.

It might be objected that these statistics do tell us something about Homeric style. But what style? The conclusions do little more than repeat in different terms what is already assumed in the classification itself: a broken or enjambed verse denotes excitement, and an even or end-stopped verse denotes calm objectivity. Is this the result of so much labor? The statistical method here is more of a hindrance than a help. It certainly has a limiting effect. Kirk is handicapped by it, in spite of his sensitivity to style. He thus points to a moderate, leisurely style where enjambment is weak and, on the other hand, to a deliberately disordered and hurried style where integral enjambment prevails. "Rapid," "urgent," "interrupted," and "chaotic" are other qualifications used in a similar sense. It is as if style itself could be analyzed statistically.

We are faced with half-truths. The differentiation between, say, a "quiet" and a "violent" style is quite generic. It points to obvious characteristics. It scarcely touches on essential subtleties. It would be more rewarding to see a form in what seems to be chaotic, or movement in what seems to be still. Where we want a real answer we are presented with a truism. For it is, no doubt, true that there exists a correspondence between broken sentences and excitement, or between even sentences and cool objectivity. But this occurs anywhere in speech, it is not essentially Homeric.

We should look for other explanations. Take Achilles' passionate speech to Patroclus in Il.16.51–100. Here Kirk sees a very high proportion of periodically and integrally enjambed verses, as to be expected "in this kind of disordered utterance." But read the speech noting its references to time: the thought of Achilles continually turns from the present to the past and future. These shifts produce enjambment, as if the verse itself were pressed to turn in a different direction before coming to an end—for instance (60 ff.): "But let these things be past; it could not be/ for my mind to be ever enraged; indeed I thought/ never to let my wrath cease, except at the moment when/ the war and the battle-cry should reach my ships." Each enjambment is here the irruption of another moment, a note of a different pitch announcing a new sequence. Or take a battle scene in Il.16.373–5: Patroclus pursues Hector "with evil design on the Trojans; and they in uproar and flight/ filled all the paths as they scattered: high up did the dust-storm/ hover beneath the clouds." Here Kirk sees a disordered effect in the description of chaotic battle; but, in fact, we have the same presentation as 16.60 ff., with the enjambment marking now shifts in space rather than time. Patroclus, the Trojans, and the dust-storm are neither separate items of description nor nebulous aspects of a riotous scene; they are so presented that our eye passes from one to the other, integrating them into one picture. The enjambment gives us fresh focus at each turn, while the verse blends the separate parts. We have configuration, not confusion.

Scholars have paid no attention to these basic conditions of time and space. The reason is, perhaps, their excessive concern with formulas. They look at meaning in terms of a fixed phraseology, working out the ways in which blocks or molds of meaning are joined together, and missing the fugitive perspective. But formulas are to Homer what single words are to the modern poet—both inherited and yet both capable of fresh, indefinite projections.

Enjambment—especially *necessary* or *integral* enjambment—is a stumbling block for the formulary view. When a word group is divided between two verses, the identity of a single verse with its pertinent phraseology seems to break down, sentences overlap their limits or fall short; and the student is hard put to list the alterations or transpositions of formulas and thus carry out even further the work of classification. There is, on one hand, the free spontaneous flow of language and, on the other, the constraint of form: how can one codify into a system this ever shifting relation? The task is impossible. A shimmering, creative interplay is always at work. We should ponder on the idea of form itself rather than formulas. Parry himself show us the way; he had these perplexities in mind when he wrote:

Of course one would like to say that Homer's enjambement is better or worse than that of Apollonius or Virgil. But to do that, one must first be sure of the merits of the running and periodic styles as a whole, at least in as far as they suit certain lines of thought, and one will have to go into all the broader problem of the order of thought in the Homeric sentences. . . The subject is vast, for we shall have to know the word order in the Homeric sentence and within the verse, the use of the parts of speech, the length of sentences and clauses and the way they are grouped.[44]

So subtle a knowledge cannot be achieved through statistics. It is of a qualitative, not a quantitative nature.

Parry brought matters to a head. Sharply and clearly he gave an account of Homeric diction as he saw it; and, as for the poetry itself, he avoided aesthetics and relied upon a plain ingenuous appreciation of traditional style. Though a sense of Homer's greatness always transpires through his pages, he continually stresses at the same time Homer's lack of originality. He does not take sides. He shows no bias. His theory of oral composition is disarmingly matter-of-fact. And yet the very logic of his exposition had a tremendous effect on criticism and aesthetics. For by developing to its extreme consequences the old notion of a conventional epic language, and by doing so without using any double standards, he unwittingly exposed the inner contradictions of Homeric scholarship. In other terms, he made us implicitly face the question: is not Homeric poetry the essence of poetry, or is it primarily folklore? It might be no longer possible, henceforward, to regard Homer as the embodiment of poetic genius and, in the same breath, insist on his unoriginal formulaic character. One cannot have it both ways: either Homer is not a genius after all, or the formulaic style must be seen in a different light. In future the leading question might be: does not this imposing array of verse-making formulas conceal a universally poetic quality? And, as for originality, is it not a genuine sense of truth in the form of expression rather than any novelty, whether deliberate of casual? There is a need to turn inward; to study formulas and themes in their intrinsic poetic value—a value which, after all, must have been the primary factor of their success.

Such a need has been largely ignored. The usual practice is to keep the topic of style quite separate from that of contents. On the other hand, there have been many scholars who have dealt effectively with Homer's poetry (e.g., Bassett, Griffin, Schadewalt, Reinhardt): but they have little or nothing to say about language, style, and diction. Others take an apologetic tone, vindicating the poet in spite of his style. Kirk writes:

The prominence of repeated formulas, lines, passages and themes does not mean that Homer, the singer of the large-scale Iliad, is not original. His originality did not lie in the choice of specially appropriate epithets or phrases, but on the one hand in the whole conception and scale of the poem, on the other in the consistently fluid and adept handling of traditional phraseology—something not easy to achieve.[45]

Compare A. Severyns: "The singer's composition consists in metrical formulas and word-groups, not separate words as in the case of a modern poet. . .And yet this technique, strange though is might seem to us, does not check the freedom or originality of a poet who has learnt its recipes and subtleties."[46]

A more vital and vigorous vindication of Homer's style is to be found in the work of C. H. Whitman.[47] He writes: "It is the genius of the style itself, more than it is Homer's genius, which appears in the splendor and aptitude of individual phrases." He sees this genius in the symbolic and imagistic value of the formulas; in the way even a single epithet evokes the whole heroic world. Here words are both denotative and connotative, narrative and emblematic. We have at once a straightforward clarity of representation and a wider appeal that derives from associations embedded in the heroic tradition. The relative scarceness of metaphors in Homer is counterbalanced by this evocative range in the means of expression. Whitman thus describes the language: "It was a presentational, imagistic, and highly formalized language also, in which each unit had been turned on the lathe of generations of poetic artificers, into a perfect and inevitable device, satisfying both the functional and artistic needs of the poet." Homer thus gleans precious pieces from a treasure trove of diction accumulated through the ages. The combination and recombination of formulas are likened to "the falling of glass chips in a kaleidoscope," and the elements of composition are said to lie at the poet's disposal "like the chips of stone and gold before a mosaic is made."

Here is a beautified version of Parry. Although Whitman brilliantly describes the complex effect of the formulas, and points out how in Homer they transcend by far the compositional purpose that gave them birth, he still looks at the style as an artifice, a device, a means to an end. We are still within the tenets of oral composition. There is only a difference of emphasis. Whitman elaborates on the formulas, but without giving them a different general function. They remain what they are in Parry: magnificent pieces of diction designed to facilitate the work of composition and performance; but in Whitman they also become artifacts in their own right, and the whole style is filled with heroic suggestion. A rhetoric thus builds up—a kind of rhetoric which, for all its splendor, ends up being fragile and superficial in that it is not nurtured by the plain truth of what it is supposed to convey. We are thus led to a sweeping abstraction, when Whitman finally writes about Homer: "His whole world is a metaphor, an enormously articulated symbol of the heroic life. His apparent naturalness is the product of the extreme opposite, a highly contrived convention. But poetic truth is an artifice, and the more complete the artifice is, the more true is the poem." It would be hard to reconcile this statement with what Whitman asserts earlier in the same chapter: "Thus what might be called the 'first level' of the poems, the rational, factual level, has an intense beauty of its own, which partly explains Homer's appeal to children." Or, again: "The simplest statements of fact or action have a compact vitality and immediacy which put all naturalistic modes of realism to shame."

There are inconsistencies here. Whitman, like others, is thrown off balance by the differing claims of common sense, Parryism, and literary judgment. His aesthetics cannot bridge the differences. Such concepts as symbolism and imagism, if pressed hard, tend to cast on everything an allegorical veil; and we miss Homer's sense of reality, the actual moments embodied in verse, and the sustaining force of rhythm. No artifice could ever reproduce the encompassing and continuous movement of the Homeric action.

NOTES

1. M. L. West. *Greek Metre*. Oxford: Clarendon Press: 1982: 18 ff.
2. P. Maas. *Greek Metre*. Trans. H. Lloyd-Jones. Oxford: Clarendon Press: 1962: 1.
3. See Introduction, Note 3.
4. See Introduction, Note 6.
5. See Introduction, Note 7.
6. E. Fraenkel. "Kolon und Satz, Beobachtungen zur Gliederung des antiken Satzes." In *Göttinger Nachrichten,* I and II (1932, 33):197–213, 319–354.. Most notably, in II 319 ff., Fränkel ilustrates how applicable to cola is the basic rule that particles must have second or third place at the beginning of a sentence. Hence for example, the fact that the particle ἄν may occur in the middle of a longer sentence proves the existence of a colon.
7. G. S. Kirk. "The Structure of the Homeric Hexameter." *Yale Classical Studies* 20 (1966): New Haven, Connecticut: 76-104.
8. G. S. Kirk. *The Iliad: A Commentary,* vol. 1, Cambridge:New York, Cambridge Univbersity Press: 1985: 20.
9. H. Duntze. *Homerische Abhandlungen,* Leipzig: 1872.
10. K. Witte. *"Homer,* B) *Sprache."* In Pauly-Wissowa, XVI, 1913. Witte condenses here the purport of his other writings.
11. P. Kretschmer. *Glotta* 6 (1915): 281.
12. K. Meister. *Die Homerische Kunstsprache.* Leipzig 1921: 233-34.
13. W. Schulze. *Quaestiones Epicae,* Gutersloh: 1892: 15-40.
14. A. Meillet. *Aperçue d'une Histoire de la langue grecque,*. Paris: 1930: 177.
15. M. Parry. *The Making of Homeric Verse: The Collected Papers of Milman Parry.* Oxford: 1971: 328.
16. T. Zielinski. "Die Behandlung gleichzeitiger Ereignisse im antiken Epos," *Philologus, Supplementband* VIII (1901): 418-449.
17. H. Fränkel. "Die Zeitauffassung in der archaischen griechischen Literatur," *Beialgenheft zur Zeitschrift für Asthetik und allgemeine Kunstwissenschaft* 25 (1931): 97–118. Republished in *Wege und Formen früh-griechischen Denkens.* München: 1955: 1-22.
18. H. and A. Thornton.*Time and Style.* London: 1962. See especially 86-87.
19. S. E. Bassett.*The Poetry of Homer.* Berkeley: 1938: 33-56.
20. M. Lynn-George. *Epos: Word, Narrative and the Iliad.* Atlantic Highlands NJ: 1988: 270ff.
21. E. Auerbach. *Mimesis.* Translated by W. R. Trask. Princeton: 1953: 3 ff.
22. M. M. Bakhtin. *The Dialogic Imagination.* Trans.C. Emerson and ed. M. Holquist. Austin, Texas: 1981: 31 ff.
23. M. I. Finley. *The Use and Abuse of History.* London: 1975: 15.

24. E. Cassirer. *The Philosophy of Symbolic Forms* II. Trans. by R. Manheim. New Have: 1955: 196-7.

25. G. Poulet. *Etudes sur le temps humain.* Paris: 1950.

26. H. Meyerhoff. *Time in Literature.* Berkeley: 1955.

27. P. Ricoeur. *Le temps et le récit*, I - III. Paris: 1983-5.

28. G. C. Horrocks. *Space and Time in Homer: Prepositional and Adverbial Particles in the Greek Epic.* Salem, NH: 1981.

29. B. Hillweg. *Raum und Zeit im Homerischen Epos.* Hildesheim: 1964.

30. *Matière et Mémoire.* Paris: 1930: 152-3.

v31. Ibid. 207.

32. *La pensée et le mouvant.* Paris: 1938: 183.

33. *Essai sur les données immédiates de la conscience.* Paris: 1927: 9.

34. *La pensée et le mouvant.* Paris: 1938: 94-5.

35. *L'énergie spirituelle.* Paris: 1922: 49.

36. J. Classen. *Beobachtungen über den Homerischen Sprachgebrauch.* Frankfurt: 1879: 1-38. The book contains   papers of different dates.

37. C. Hentze. *Die Parataxis bei Homer*, I, II, III. Göttingen: 1888, 1889, 1891.

38. B. A. van Groningen. "Eléments inorganiques dans la composition de l'Iliade et de l'Odyssée," *Revue des Etudes homériques.* 1935: 3-24. *Paratactische Compositie in die oudste grieksche literatur.* Amsterdam: 1937. Summarized in English by J. Tate in *Classical Review* (1937): 174-5. *La Composition littéraire archaïque grecque.* Amsterdam: 1958: 30 ff.

39. B. E. Perry. "The Early Greek Capacity for Viewing Things Separately," *Transactions of the American Philological Association:* (1937): 403-427.

40. J. A. Notopoulos. "Parataxis in Homer: A New Approach to Homeric Literary Criticism", *Transaction of the American Philological Association*: (1949): 1-23.

41. M. Parry. *The Making of Homeric Verse: The Collected Papers of Milman Parry.* Oxford: 1971: 253 ff.

42. G. S. Kirk. "Verse-structure and Sentence-structure in Homer," *Yale Classical Studies* (1966): 105-51. This is a sequence to the article quoted earlier.

43. C. Higbie. *Measure and Music: Enjambment and Sentence Structure in the Iliad.* Oxford: 1990.

44. M. Parry. *The Making of Homeric Verse: The Collected Papers of Milman Parry.* Oxford: 1971: 265.

45. G. S. Kirk. *The Songs of Homer.* Cambridge: 1962: 82.

46. A. Severyns. *Homère, le poète et son oeuvre.* Bruxelles: 1946: 77.

47. C. H. Whitman. *Homer and the Heroic Tradition.* New York: 1965: 112. See here the whole chapter "Image, Symbol, and Formula," 102 ff.

Index

About the Author

PAOLO VIVANTE is Professor Emeritus of Classics at McGill University. He is the author of *The Homerica Imagination, Homer, The Epithets in Homer*, and *The Iliad: Action as Poetry*.

Recent Titles in
Contributions to the Study of World Literature

ISBN 0-313-30363-0

90000>

9 780313 303630

EAN

HARDCOVER BAR CODE